The Missionary's Role
in
Socio-Economic Betterment

Fordham-Rural Life Socio-economic Conference, Maryknoll Seminary, 1958.

THE MISSIONARY'S ROLE

IN

SOCIO-ECONOMIC BETTERMENT

EDITED BY JOHN J. CONSIDINE, M.M.

ublished under the sponsorship of the Fordham University Institute of Mission tudies and the International Rural Life Movement with the aid of the Bruno Benziger Fund of Maryknoll

EWMAN PRESS   1960

NIHIL OBSTAT:
Edward F. Malone, M.M., S.T.D.
Censor Deputatus

IMPRIMATUR:
✠ Francis Cardinal Spellman
Archbishop of New York

Library of Congress Catalog Card Number: 60–12058
Copyright, 1960, by
The Catholic Foreign Mission Society of America
Maryknoll, N.Y.
Printed in the United States of America
by H. Wolff, New York

Contents

INTRODUCTION

The *New York Times,* under dateline of April 8, 1958, carried an item from Ossining, New York, which stated that "forty Roman Catholic specialists in problems confronting the less-developed areas of the world opened a four-day conference here today at Maryknoll Seminary. They will seek ways to integrate religious and cultural efforts in those areas with action in the social and economic fields."

The four days of discussion referred to are the source of the material found in the pages which follow. This volume will represent one of the few publications in English which seek to survey socio-economic betterment from the viewpoint of Catholic workers in the less-developed countries of the globe.

The prime initiative for the Easter Week conference at Maryknoll came from Rev. Frederick A. McGuire, C.M., Executive Secretary of the Mission Secretariat of the Catholic Sending Societies, Washington, D. C., and Monsignor Luigi Ligutti, Director of the Catholic International Rural Life Movement. Monsignor Ligutti secured from a foundation the grant which met the financial requirements of the gathering. The organization meeting for the conference took place August 12, 1957, at the Fordham Institute of Mission Studies, whose Director is Rev. J. Franklin Ewing, S.J. It was decided that the two sponsoring organizations for the conference were the Catholic International Rural Life Movement and the Fordham Institute of Mission Studies. The title for the venture was established as the Fordham-Rural Life Socio-Economic Conference.

The conference sessions, occupying Tuesday through Friday of Easter Week, 1958, totalled seventeen. The first day was devoted to general considerations, beginning with an overview of the Catholic approach to world socio-economic problems. The role of the missionary as normally that of catalyst and by exception as that of technical specialist was enunciated. Community development, the modern technique for the over-all approach to socio-economic action at the community level, was reviewed. Emphasis was placed on knowledge of the people through social anthropology, particularly through the study of culture change.

The remaining three days were devoted to twelve topical divisions of the socio-economic program as follows: 1) community planning and housing; 2) socio-economic improvement of the family; 3) public health and nutrition; 4) agricultural betterment; 5) rural problems; 6) urban problems; 7) employment of leisure for socio-economic betterment; 8) credit unions and co-operatives; 9) community small industries; 10) rights of the worker; 11) women and minors in industry; 12) population problems.

The participants in the sessions consisted of twelve lay specialists, thirteen non-missionary clerical specialists and sixteen field missionaries chosen for their experience in the matter under consideration. The list of the participants follows:

Arceneaux, Doctor T. J., Dean, College of Agriculture, Southwestern Louisiana Institute, Lafayette, Louisiana.

Bauer (M.M.), Rev. Thomas J., South China, Editorial Director, Maryknoll Publications.

Berna (S.J.), Rev. James J., Economist, India.

Blomjous (W.F.), Most Rev. Joseph, Bishop of Mwanza, Tanganyika.

Clark, M.D., Duncan W., Professor of Public Health and Environmental Medicine and Nutrition, New York University, WHO travelling fellow.

Coleman (M.M.), Rev. William J., Chile, Professor of Mission History, Maryknoll Seminary.

Collins (M.M.), Rev. William J., Tanganyika, Assistant General, Maryknoll Council.

Comber (M.M.), Most Rev. John W., Manchuria and Chile, Superior General of Maryknoll.

Considine (M.M.), Rev. John J., Professor of Contemporary World Missions and Director of Maryknoll Publications.

De Reeper (M.H.), Right Rev. John, Kenya, Assistant General of Mill Hill Fathers, London; in early 1960 named Prefect Apostolic of Ngong, Kenya.

Dijkstra (S.J.), Rev. John J., Industrial Relations, Indonesia.

Dumpson, James R., Sociologist, Pakistan, Commissioner of the Department of Social Welfare, New York City.

Fitzpatrick (S.J.), Rev. Joseph, Puerto Rico, Dean of School of Sociology, Fordham University.

Ganey (S.J.), Rev. Marion, Specialist in Cooperatives, British Honduras, Fiji Islands.

Gibbons (S.J.), Rev. William J., World Population Specialist, New York.

Gladwin, Doctor Thomas, Social Anthropologist, Pacific Islands, National Institute of Mental Health, Bethesda, Maryland.

Goncalves de Souza, Doctor Joao, Brazil, Social Economist, Executive Director, Technical Cooperation Program, Organization of American States, Washington, D. C.

Groeschel, M.D., August, Director of New York Hospital, Associate Professor of Public Health and Preventive Medicine, Cornell University Medical School.

Higgins (M.M.), Rev. Eugene, Bolivia, Director Maryknoll Extension Service.

Higgins, Very Rev. Msgr. George G., Director Department of Social Action, NCWC, Washington, D. C.

Hoffman (O.F.M.Conv.), Rev. Ronan, Doctor of Missiology, Catholic University, Washington, D. C.

Illich, Very Rev. Msgr. Ivan, Vice-Rector Santa Maria University, Ponce, Puerto Rico, Sociologist.

Lang, Doctor Gottfried, Applied Anthropology, Catholic University, Washington, D. C.

Lawlor (S.J.), Rev. Richard, Japan, Doctor of Missiology, Jesuit House of Studies, Weston, Massachusetts.

Ligutti, Rt. Rev. Msgr. Luigi, Founder International Rural Life Movement.

McCarthy (M.M.), Rev. Charles F., South America, General Communications.

McGlade (S.S.C.), Rev. Joseph, St. Columban's, Dalgan Park, Dublin, Ireland, Missiologist.

McGuire (C.M.), Rev. Frederick A., China, Executive Secretary, Mission Secretariat, Washington, D. C.

Malone (M.M.), Rev. Edward F., Professor of Dogmatic Theology, Maryknoll Seminary.

Meyer (M.M.), Rev. Bernard F., China, Missionary Sociology.

Miniclier, Louis, Chief, Community Development Division, International Cooperation Administration, Washington, D. C.

Mora-Rubio, Doctor Rafael, Community Housing Specialist, UNESCO, United Nations.

Murphy (S.J.), Rev. Edward L., Philippines, Jamaica, Doctor of Missiology, Jesuit Missions House, New York.

O'Dea, Doctor Thomas, Sociologist, University of Utah, Salt Lake City.

O'Doherty (S.S.C.), Rev. Kevin, Professor of Dogmatic Theology, St. Columban's Seminary.

Schiffer (S.J.), Rev. Hubert, Economist, Catholic University of Tokyo, Japan.

Shelly (S.V.D.), Rev. Otto, Agricultural Specialist.

Topshee, Rev. George, Socio-Economics Specialist, St. John's University, Antigonish, Nova Scotia.

Vizzard (S.J.), Rev. James L., Rural Social Economics, Vice-President, International Rural Life Movement.

Weinberg, Jules, AFL-CIO Labor Research, Pakistan.

Zeegers, Doctor George H. L., Religious Sociologist, Founder International Catholic Institute for Social Research, Geneva, Switzerland.

The Fordham-Rural Life Socio-Economic Conference was pronounced not only profitable by the participants but quite definitely pleasurable. It proved one of those rare occasions when the chance assembly of dedicated people from widely scattered geographic locations and sharply differing fields of action brought together a group of men who quickly found themselves in tune with each other. Caught almost inexplicably by an excitement for their common purpose, enthusiasm ran high throughout the four days, wits remained sharp and a gracious camaraderie made the sessions a delightful and exhilarating experience.

"I am finally back home," wrote Monsignor Ligutti, "recalling with pleasure the wonderful week at Maryknoll. I met several of our participants along the way, and they all feel that it was one of the most outstanding meetings they ever attended. It is my hope and my prayer that from the findings of our sessions our missionaries will be able to carry on, at least in a small way, a better program in the fulfillment of the mandatum of Christ."

"A brief word of sincere thanks," wrote Father Fitzpatrick of Fordham, "to all who enabled me to participate in the most wonderful conference I have ever been through. I certainly derived from it endless information and inspiration which will be helpful to me. I never realized so clearly how important to the missionary and to mission specialists is the support of social scientists in our universities."

It is the earnest hope of the participants that the pages which follow will contribute in some modest fashion to the guidance of young missionaries faced with organizing socio-economic programs in the less-developed lands of the earth.

The Missionary's Role
in
Socio-Economic Betterment

CHAPTER 1

The Socio-Economic in Our People's Lives

The Betterment of Our People. Monsignor Jose Salcedo, the originator of the very successful Popular Education Movement of Colombia, which through radio schools has improved the lives of so many thousands of mountaineers in the Cordillera Central, speaks feelingly of his struggle to get started.

As a young pastor with 8,000 people in his parish, he used to look out among the mighty peaks and across the deep valleys dotted with innumerable peasant huts. His parishioners were basically honest and loyal but they suffered from the handicaps of people deprived of training and of any hope or incentive for bettering their lot.

"No wonder they turn to drink and give themselves to violence," he would remark to himself. "These mountains serve as prison walls to cage in men's minds and hearts from growth and better living. If only we could stir these folk with a plan that would lift them out of their misery, they would be better men and better Christians."

The Importance of a Plan. Monsignor Salcedo discovered

the plan that suited his needs and executed it brilliantly. His very mention of a plan revealed his recognition of this basic requisite for accomplishment. Half-way, hit-or-miss, measures for helping his people would almost surely fail. Back in 1602 when a body of Jesuit missionaries gathered at Salta in what is now Argentina to prepare a mission program, one of their meaningful conclusions read, "The zeal of the apostle is, like the individual bravery of soldiers, to be subordinated to tactics." This has been a good missionary principle in every century since Christ and on every continent of the globe.

A Realization Program.   Determining the betterment plan that fits is not easy. Plans should be built on principles, but often among educated men there is too much contemplation of principles and of theory and too little of practice. Thus the tendency to spend precious time in indecisiveness.

Professor George Zeegers, a leading spirit at our Easter Conference at Maryknoll, issued a warning on this point at the outset. "On one occasion, in 1952," explained this very able authority from Holland, "Pope Pius XII made the observation that the time is long past for repeating principles over and over, for searching out new goals. The goals are long since well known. Only one thing is wanting, said His Holiness: the realization of these goals."

Doctor Zeegers made a plea for a realization program. "Our aim," he said, "should be to determine how the missionary in his parish wherever it may be, all over the world, can make better employment of the world socio-economic program as developed in our day. More specifically, we should seek to indicate the service which the social and economic sciences can render to the needs of the missionary Church."

The Parish the Basic Unit.   Practically speaking, the basic unit for application of such a program is the parish or the individual communities within a parish. The greatest number of workers in any field of endeavor operates at the local level and such workers have need of guidance at the local level. This applies to the missionary task as well as to many others. The missionary like Monsignor Salcedo lost in the mighty peaks of the Andes, the apostolic pastor in India or Formosa or Japan, the pioneer in the heart of Africa, can best apply a technique if it is delineated not merely in terms of a great national or regional program but if it is reduced to its day-to-day operation in the grassroots country.

The World Frame. Nevertheless our first concern in approaching our subject must be to see it in its world frame. We are witnessing today the beginnings of a new concept of socio-economic effort, which sees the task not in terms of our own individual nation alone or of a multiplicity of disparate nations but as a joint enterprise of the entire human race acting as a single whole.

Since 1945 some 750,000,000 non-Western people, or approximately 30 percent of the inhabitants of the globe, have obtained self-government. In this same period over 50 countries have either adopted constitutions for the first time, or voted new constitutions, or introduced substantial changes in their existing documents.

Practically all of these constitutions highlight human betterment for the mass population:

1 larger goals in education, aiming usually at universal literacy;
2 advanced systems of public health institutions and services;
3 improved provisions in labor laws and workers' welfare;
4 social security provisions;
5 improved agricultural policies which include:
   i *land reform,*
   ii *land settlement and resettlement,*
   iii *assistance to farmers,*
   iv *protection of small family-sized farms and medium holdings,*
   v *farmers' welfare services;*
6 state encouragement of cooperatives.

Higher Concepts of Human Rights. Current world thinking indicates higher concepts of human rights:

1   The right of the individual to some kind of an education is recognized in nearly every country of the world, even though in at least portions of some countries it remains a principle respected in the breach.

2   In the field of health, the right to individual medical care as a public service is recognized in a fashion analogous to that of individual education.

3   In the field of labor, provisions include:
  i   *the right to organize and bargain collectively;*
  ii *the right to a minimum wage by local standards of adequacy;*
  iii *the right to weekly rest and annual vacation with pay;*
  iv *protection against accident and occupational disease.*

4   As to the problem of poverty, the poor are no longer conceived as a special class in a permanently fixed status; rather, they are seen as in great measure victims of circumstances over which society can and should exercise control through preventive, protective and remedial measures.

Huge Lag between Plans and Performance.   But the builders of the new nations have made two important discoveries. First of all, they have found that a truly adequate socio-economic program for their country would require large sums of money far beyond the capacity of the present economies of all but the richest countries of the globe. Secondly, they have come to realize that this adequate socio-economic program calls for a body of leaders and technicians with know-how that is all but non-existent in great areas of the globe, at least if they are to bring substantial benefits to living generations.

A great deal of research and planning on a world scale must be supplied by the more advanced segments of the human race through the United Nations and national organizations, voluntary as well as governmental, before the world's socio-economic dreams may be realized. The socio-economic millennium is not very near at hand.

The Vastness of World Want.   Even men actively engaged in alleviating want are often unaware of its vastness. The first concern of society is for schools, which do not enter directly into this socio-economic study, but even the world's needs in schools are colossal. A recent UNESCO survey notes that there are over 250 million school-age children on the globe, from five to fourteen years old, who have access to no school of any kind, while an even larger number are possessed of school facilities but of very poor and inadequate character. The two-thirds of the world's 2.7 billion people who live in rural areas are the major sufferers.

Thailand graduates 2,500 elementary teachers a year and needs four times this number. In Cambodia farmers have built several hundred schools in the hope that the government would supply teachers for them, but their hopes have proven vain. Bolivia, with a large Indian population almost wholly illiterate, has but 234 elementary teachers for each hundred thousand of its population. Peru, a relatively advanced nation, has 24,000 elementary teachers but less than half of them have any kind of diploma.

To supply the socio-economic field, Latin America turns out only 1,300 graduates in agriculture each year for its population of 180 million, 70 percent of whom are farmers. The graduates in home economics, who should guide the tens of millions of farmers' wives, total only 4,000 a year.

The Papacy and the Human Race. In the field of human welfare, the only institution with planetary goals possessing the geographic scope of the United Nations is the Papacy. The object of concern of the Vicar of Christ is the human race. It was interesting at our Easter Conference to hear Doctor Zeegers, a hard-headed scientist but a warm-hearted son of Holy Mother Church, establish the profound practical importance of the Sovereign Pontiff as our guide in determining our socio-economic responsibilities toward the human race.

"In my opinion," stated Doctor Zeegers, "the most social of the papal encyclicals is the encyclical on the Mystical Body. Some seem to misunderstand it; for them it is the encyclical on the Mysterious Body. For me this encyclical represents an appeal to employ all the powers of my head and heart to comprehend the spiritual richness of that host of human beings that comprises the universe of immortal souls who reach toward God.

"The encyclical on the Mystical Body is an invitation to us to comprehend the grandeur of the Church of God, the Church Triumphant, the Church Suffering, the Church Militant, the immense sweep of all the races of man who dwell within the geographic divisions of the globe, in Europe, Asia, Africa, the Americas, and who in some fashion acceptable to God aspire to eternal salvation.

"Do most of us keep a sufficiently vivid picture before us of the vast realm of human creatures who represent the object of the work of the Church? I think not. I think this should be our first step as we undertake to understand the socio-economic program necessary to meet the full potential in building Christian society over the globe."

We find the fundamentum for Doctor Zeegers' words in Pius XII's lines on the Mystical Body. "The love of the Divine Spouse is so vast," wrote His Holiness, "that it embraces the whole human race without exception in His Spouse the Church. Men may be separated by nationality and race, but our Savior poured out His Blood to reconcile all men to God through the cross, and to bid them all to unite in one Body. Genuine love of the Church, therefore, is not satisfied with our being within this Body members one of another, mutually careful one for another, rejoicing with him who glories, suffering with him who suffers. We must also recognize all those others who have not yet joined us in the Body of the Church as brothers of Christ according to the flesh, destined together with us to eternal salvation."

The Papacy and Social Economics.   Our recent Popes have expressed quite clearly their views on the socio-economic program.

"In the sphere of social economics," explained Pius XI in his encyclical on Communism, "although the Church has never proposed a definite technical system, since this is not her field, she has nevertheless clearly outlined the guiding principles which, while susceptible to varied concrete applications according to the diversified conditions of times and places and peoples, indicate the safe way of securing the happy progress of society."

"Only on the principles of Christianity and in accordance with its spirit," said Pius XII in 1948, "can social reforms . . . be carried out. . . . Wherefore we turn to the Catholics of the world, exhorting them not to be satisfied with good intentions and fine projects, but to proceed courageously to put them into practice.

"Neither should they hesitate to join forces with those who, remaining outside the ranks, are nonetheless in agreement with the social teaching of the Catholic Church and are disposed to follow the road she has marked out, which is not the road of violent revolution but of experience that has stood the test of energetic resolution."

Genuinely global socio-economic effort must be based upon a genuinely universal philosophy of the human race. Such a philosophy, the Catholic recognizes, must be built upon the sanction of a theology, upon divine teaching which makes it clear that it is not merely "nicer" to grant equal social status, equal human dignity, to all other men but that it is morally requisite to do so. Global socio-economic activity must be based on a global application of sound principles of social change.

Technology for Global Socio-Economic Activity. For the development of global socio-economic activity, specialists with experience in the world field recommend a sound body of supporting knowledge for the effort:

1   the development for world application of the principles of social change;
2   the further development of the science of social anthropology as a means of increased understanding of the principles of social change.

A second division of requisite ordered knowledge calls for:

1 a science of comparative socio-economic techniques whereby successful methods in one world culture may be satisfactorily adapted to other world cultures;
2 a technology of planning that will remove much of the vague floundering and unending experimentation from socio-economic activities.

For global socio-economic activities technical centers are needed where the elements for research and planning will be assembled. Social service schools have already introduced courses for careers overseas. From research and planning, training centers for social welfare will deepen and strengthen their facilities for preparing ever more effective socio-economic Catholic leadership to serve the human race.

Catholic Socio-Economic Weakness. A major factor in considering the socio-economic program, Doctor Zeegers noted, is the relatively small role that the Catholic millions generally have played thus far in the world in promoting this program.

"The world strategy and world initiative for the promotion of the socio-economic betterment of mankind have not been to any great degree in the hands of Catholics. We are said to number some 480 million, 18 percent of the world's population. Thus almost one in five of the entire human race is Catholic. The total Christian family exceeds 900 million, about 35 percent of mankind, one in three of the human beings on earth. Yet we must admit frankly that world socio-economic leadership does not come from Catholics. What is the reason for this?

"First, Catholics despite their number hold generally a secondary position in world society. Almost 90 percent of the earth's Catholics are in the Western world with 5 percent in Africa and 7 percent in Asia and Oceania. Catholicism in Latin America must be regarded as a deficit body, requiring more help from outside the continent than this continent contributes to the world at large. Catholicism in the United States is vigorous but has not yet reached strong development in public achievement. I estimate that Catholicism in Western Europe represents two-thirds of the population of the continent but possesses not more than a quarter of the continental income.

"Catholicism in Europe has high records in the bad categories—poverty, illiteracy, mortality rates, and the like. The regions of indigence include peoples who are predominantly Catholic. We are very frequently the poor in this world, the have-not peoples, the receivers. We have the problems."

The Temptation to Be Timid.   Thus Doctor Zeegers established his first point—that Catholics have the problems. But having the problems, certainly we should step forward manfully to solve our problems. Unfortunately, asserted Doctor Zeegers, this is not the case.

"My first point, then," he stated, "is that we are poor. Next, I regret to say that, on the whole, European Catholics are timid and indecisive in their poverty. 'We have lost the initiative,' they seem to say, 'and we shall never regain it; the situation is hopeless.' This passive attitude toward socio-economic problems is our greatest single source of weakness.

"My third point, then, must be the failure of many European Catholics to recognize the need of a practical, down-to-earth socio-economic program, so conceived that every parish and community that finds itself in need can roll up its sleeves and go to work on solving its problems.

"An important obstacle to better living conditions among Catholic Europeans is the improper employment of the Social Encyclicals of the Popes. The Social Encyclicals should be accepted for what they are, normative sociology. The Social Encyclicals are not a solution to problems; they are meant only as a beginning, a program. They require teams of specialists to translate them into action. There is too much of a tendency on the part of priests and lay leaders to give magnificent platform performances expatiating on the beauty of the Social Encyclicals. Everything is said, and yet nothing is said, because everybody goes away without having a practical program that can be put into effect.

"Let us beware lest in the mission world as well our good
Catholics will spend their days admiring the Social Encyclicals
but failing to bend their backs to the solid spade work of applying the encyclicals to local programs of community betterment."

America and Socio-Economic Awareness. Doctor Thomas
O'Dea, the sociologist from Fordham, now at the University
of Utah, quickly followed up Doctor Zeegers' words regarding
European weakness.

"Doctor Zeegers' remarks may well be enlarged to apply to
America," observed Doctor O'Dea. "In our Catholic universities, Catholic colleges and Catholic seminaries there is a tremendous amount of residual unawareness. There is an unawareness of what Doctor Zeegers calls being in second place.
Catholics in America, I think, suffer very much from being in
second place. They have almost no awareness of what they are
suffering from and what it does to them, and until they acquire
this awareness they cannot apply a remedy. The remedy undoubtedly must take the form of some resolute self-help program at the community level which will aim to destroy the
bugaboo that they are forever destined to stay in second place."

Doctor Thomas Gladwin, social anthropologist presently on
the staff of the National Institute of Mental Health in Washington, D. C., sought to explain the weakness of Catholics in
the social science field.

"I think," he said "that behind the Catholic's unawareness
and resistance to the full utilization of social science techniques
lies the fact that social science as it has developed is entirely,
or almost entirely, deterministic, a child of the philosophy of
Auguste Comte. It is referred to as behavioral science. The determinist operates on the premise that unless you can demonstrate something you don't utilize it. Our religious are taught
to understand the nature of man and the relevance of grace
and the spiritual effects in man's behavior, something that you
cannot demonstrate to the determinist.

"There is very small representation of Catholics in the social science field. There is evidently a tendency to stay away from the field itself that is the object of this determinist philosophy. It is necessary, I feel, for missionary specialists to be realistic in utilizing social science and knowledge and research approaches and techniques. These are the tools. God's grace will guide them to use their intelligence to find the answers."

Accent on a Program. "In the early centuries," noted Doctor Zeegers, "the Church knew how to employ social and economic betterment as a vehicle for her religion. Nowadays Communism has captured the imagination of great portions of society by pretending to have the answers to the problems of human need. Let us appeal to our fellow churchmen to present the Church once again in its true light as possessing both the religious vitality and ideals and the philosophy of life to give the fullest force to the social and economic techniques that should be applied to the problems of human needs.

"I see three steps as required in our program.

"First, we should increase and improve our Catholic specialists in such fashion that we can make a substantial contribution to the world-wide research apparatus for socio-economic achievement.

"Secondly, we should aim to coordinate more clearly into the Church's program for meeting the world's human needs these activities in the socio-economic field. We should become known and respected for our technical excellence in these fields. Governments and inter-governmental organizations should come to recognize that our representatives possess this technical excellence. Bishop Fulton Sheen explained to the Congressional Committee in Washington that the Church has large numbers of men at the grassroots level in the backward areas of the world, a manpower that has great knowledge of the people at the grassroots level. To this we should be able to add an assurance of proper appreciation of the technical requirements needed, in order that men among our Catholic lay leaders may be entrusted with government-supported programs to better our peoples.

"Thirdly, we must aid the individual missionary pastor and his assistants to arrive at a practical socio-economic program for his missionary parish. As I see it, the individual missionary in the field, if he has the vision of the possibilities and is passably well trained to promote a program, can work miracles. If he does not possess the vision, all the global programs in the world, all the international Catholic scientific projects imaginable, will be in vain."

The Role of Social Economics in the Parish. Doctor Zeegers and the other participants at the Maryknoll Conference understood clearly what must now be made very clear to our readers, namely, that mention of a socio-economic program in the missionary parish presupposes a much more comprehensive and, of course, much more important over-all program of apostolic action into which this socio-economic program should fit as a complementary factor.

"Our message to the non-Christian world cannot be a mere technique," observed Doctor Zeegers. "We shall be as bad as the Communists if we bring only a technique. If we say to men, 'You are suffering from grave human needs; we'll cure your grave human needs,' we shall be betraying them. We must say as our religion intends, 'You are suffering from grave spiritual and material needs; we'll help you with the material while caring for the vastly more important, the spiritual.' "

If we examine the schema of parish activities in the more vital parishes of the homeland as well as of the mission field, we find that they may quite properly be divided into two general categories: first, the spiritual and formative activities; secondly, the activities that concern themselves with human need. In these general categories, we may list the following:

1   *Spiritual activities*
    a   Christian worship and life:
       i   *the direct acts of religion, primarily the Mass and Eucharistic life, the sacraments and sacramentals, morning and evening prayers, the rosary and other formal devotions;*

      ii   *the doctrinal and devotional practices woven into general Christian living.*

  b The direct apostolate:

      i   *the winning of souls (in which, it is true, many activities that represent the indirect apostolate enter as well);*

      ii   *the instruction and formation of converts;*

      iii   *the guidance of the neophytes.*

2   *Educational and cultural activities*

  a Catholic schools.

  b Christian literature and conferences, the arts, life's embellishments which are comprised in our ideal of building Christian civilization into the life of the new Church in mission lands.

The Program to Meet Human Need. "God is charity," the Scriptures tell us; the cornerstone of Christian living is love of neighbor. A modern term for much that is embraced by the ancient ideal is the meeting of human need. On examination, problems of human need cover a vast area. They may be divided primarily between the economic and the non-economic.

Contrary to popular belief, the non-economic field of human need in turn covers a far greater area than the ordinary onlooker realizes. The rich man in many respects suffers as much from human need as does the pauper. His money cannot save him from cares, from human failures, from mental illnesses, from acts of God that bring suffering and consequent human need.

For Catholics and all who recognize the spiritual in life, the problems of human need fall into two general categories, the religio-social and the socio-economic.

The religio-social field may be described as concerned with:

1 The non-economic problems of human need. In secular circles the term for this area of action is social work or social welfare. Among Catholics we may rightly employ the term religio-social activities since the religious worker is concerned

with the whole person, the soul as well as the body. Remedies for man's social ills include the spiritual as well as the
material.

2   The alleviation of economic human need by material assistance. The secular world terms this relief work; traditionally
the Church calls it Christian charity.

The field of socio-economic activities represents the combination of preventive, protective and remedial measures taken
by society to improve man's economic life, not exclusively for
economic ends as such but for the improvement of human
society. The Catholic includes in this concept the spiritual as
well as the material betterment of man's life on earth.

A Glance at Religio-Social Activities.   Antecedent to a consideration of the socio-economic field, to which this book is
devoted, we should secure a clear picture in our minds of the
religio-social activities which we hope to study in another
volume and which therefore are excluded from this volume.
We list here the religio-social activities as it is customary to
consider them.

    I.   Religio-social activities for the individual
     A   Social case work:
        1   care of the child deprived of normal home life;
        2   care of the aged;
        3   care of the physically handicapped;
        4   care of the mentally ill;
        5   guidance of delinquents, prison work;
        6   special categories, unmarried mothers, etc.
     B   Maintaining health, fighting disease:
        1   public health work, sanitation, nutrition;
        2   medical care;
        3   hospitals and clinics;
        4   medical social work, institutional and home nursing.
   II.   Religio-social activities for the family
        1   family case work;
        2   training in Christian family practices.

III. *Religio-social activities for the community*
  1 social group work;
  2 intercultural relations;
  3 leisure program work;
  4 youth work;
  5 immigrants and migrants;
  6 special urban problems;
  7 special rural problems.

IV. *Religio-social relief work*
  1 alleviation of economic need at the individual, family and community levels by dispensing food, clothing, shelter, medicine, etc.;
  2 St. Vincent de Paul work.

Note: Health and medicine get major and general consideration here (*I*, B). In the outline of socio-economic activities, which follows, *Section III, Health and economic betterment,* is concerned only with the relation of health to earning a living.

Outline of Socio-Economic Activities. The greatest service that can be rendered the majority of men over the earth who experience human need of an economic nature is guidance to solve their problems by their own efforts. This is the basic principle behind the activities embraced in the following outline of social economics.

I. *Programming and other preparatory considerations*
  1 analysis of community development techniques;
  2 knowledge of one's people;
  3 consideration of population and migration problems;
  4 community planning.

II. *The home and the family*
  1 housing and building;
  2 social effects of problems in family economy;
  3 economic problems affecting women and minors.

III. *Health and economic betterment*
  1 relation of medicine and public health to economic life;
  2 sanitation;
  3 nutrition.

IV. *Agricultural betterment*
   1 improvement of agricultural production;
   2 more effective marketing;
   3 improved farm family life;
   4 problems of land tenure.
 V. *Institutions for economic strengthening*
   1 cooperatives and credit unions;
   2 community small industries.
VI. *Socio-economic problems of various communities*
   1 urban problems;
   2 rural problems;
   3 problems of mining, fishing and forest extraction communities;
   4 economic betterment through leisure programs.
VII. *Organized labor*

The Harmonious Balance of Man. The pastor of souls occupies himself with the socio-economic program to guide men wisely in solving their problems of human need. Pius XII in an address to Italian workers June 7, 1957, explains this.

"We are well aware of the difficulty and complexity of this problem," said His Holiness, "which presents itself under various aspects, sometimes as a promise, sometimes as a threat. It is fitting that you should approach this uncharted terrain not merely as scientists and technicians, but also as sociologists and Christians, since a mistaken approach to the question might well have dangerous repercussions both in the material sphere and in the moral and spiritual. As you know, these spheres are inseparable in the life of the individual."

For recommended reading, see Bibliography No. 1, page 260.

THE MISSIONARY A CATALYST IN THE SOCIO-ECONOMIC PROGRAM

The Practical Approach. The young missionary, contemplating the very substantial proportions of the field of socio-economic action as we have reviewed it in the previous chapter, asks himself how directly in line it is with essential parish work. In the seminary his manual of pastoral theology ran to hundreds of pages but gave little place to these activities.

With this in mind it is well for us to turn to Rome's directives. A generation ago Cardinal Pizzardo, Pius XI's protagonist of Catholic Action, commissioned Monsignor Luigi Civardi to prepare what, practically speaking, was an official manual of Catholic Action. In this manual the Monsignor devotes a chapter to socio-economic activities.

"Social-Economic Action, if Christian-wise inspired," states Monsignor Civardi,[1] "wishes to realize a level of social justice that is conformable to the principles of the Gospel. True, the Gospels neither teach nor prescribe any determinate social system. None the less, not every system can be called consistent with the principles of justice and charity contained in the

Gospel. Catholics aim at precisely this: that in economic and social relationships these very principles may be realized, so that each may receive what is his due; and that the conditions of those who have less may be continuously bettered."

Monsignor Civardi proceeds to specify for Catholic Action a program of cooperation with this field of activity. "Let us note," he says,[2] "that what helps Catholic Action can and should provide for social-economic works. The principal ones are as follows:

"(a) The promotion of such social-economic works where they do not exist but where they would be useful for the aims of Catholic Action;

"(b) Assistance to the laity lest in the formation of their social-economic programme or in the fervor of their activities they deviate from the principles of the faith and the rules of morality;

"(c) Study, formulate and defend the principles of Christian doctrine which regulate Catholic activity, in the social terrain and from which social-economic works must constantly draw their inspiration;

"(d) Care for the religious, moral and cultural preparation of their directors, on whom as a rule the upshot of the whole movement depends;

"(e) Collaborate in the religious and moral assistance of the members, so that their material improvement be never dissociated from their spiritual advancement."

These five directives serve as a practical approach for every parish priest to the socio-economic program. Circumstances may lead many priests to deeper involvement in the technical or administrative phases.

The Missionary a Catalyst. Individual missionaries and members of the homeland clergy around the world have demonstrated outstanding capacity in the socio-economic field not only as leaders but as technicians. However, the normal role envisaged for the parish priest in promoting the socio-economic program is that of the catalyst, the stimulator, and under ordinary circumstances lay leaders and technicians should be assigned the major tasks in the program.

This was made clear at the Maryknoll Conference on several occasions. Mr. James Dumpson, Commissioner of Welfare in New York City, made the point quite directly.

"I would like to emphasize," he said, "that we make a mistake if we refer to a situation which involves the missionary *versus* the technician. More correctly we should speak of the missionary *and* the technician.

"The missionary has a very important role to play even when he is not a technician. He can be what we call in social work a catalytic agent. He can be a stimulator if he has under his belt certain broad principles of the way programs should move. He can stimulate action among his parishioners, among the villagers in general and of course make use of what technicians are available.

"I recall that during my assignment in Pakistan the missionaries there made great use of the international experts who were in the vicinity of Karachi. As missionaries they knew what was wanted but they didn't have the techniques and the skills for putting their ideas in motion. Establishing relationship with the technicians is I think a terribly important responsibility of the missionary."

"May I ask you, Mr. Dumpson," inquired Father John Dijkstra, the labor priest from Indonesia, "how you feel we should prepare our priests to be catalyzers, stimulators?"

"I think there are two suggestions that I would make," Mr. Dumpson replied. "One is that the missionary be equipped with the skills of community organization. He should know how to work with groups, how to bring to bear his influence, how to identify indigenous leadership, how to establish relationship with that leadership.[3]

"Secondly, I think the missionary often has an important duty to perform in reconstructing the community's image of him as a member of the community. Certainly the communities that I know in Pakistan and in the Middle East think of the missionary as concerned only with the Christian religion. They do not see the missionary as interested in their welfare as people. As Moslems they believe that the missionary feels indifferent toward them, valuing them only if they will join the Christian group.

"In point of fact this is not true. The Catholic population in Karachi is quite sizable but the Fathers work not only for the Catholics. They work for those in need wherever they find them, but evidently they have not as yet succeeded in conveying this all-important fact of their devotion to all to the population at large. In the two years that I worked with the Karachi Community Council of social agencies not once did we have a priest representing the diocese at the planning table. I think that if missionaries would acquire skill in knowing how to work with groups of different ways of thinking, how to carry on effectively as a minority in a majority, both the Church and the local people would gain through this more sympathetic image of the missionary thus created."

The Missionary an Agent of Liaison. As well as being a spark to achievement, the missionary may also serve as a line of communication between his people and their needed sources of knowledge. Doctor T. J. Arceneaux, Dean of the College of Agriculture at Southwestern Louisiana Institute, placed great emphasis on this.

"The missionary priest in agricultural areas," noted Doctor Arceneaux, "is often the sole contact between the people he is serving and the whole field of scientific advance in agriculture. The agricultural officials are generally eager to improve conditions in the area they are serving. To perform this very vital service of liaison the priest need not be a highly trained agriculturist but he should have enough knowledge to recognize problems. Persuading the people who have problems to be solved to accept the guidance of the research centers should be, in my opinion, the main agricultural task of the rural missionary priest. It offers tremendous possibilities for the fruitfulness of his ministry."

Doctor Joao Goncalves de Souza of Brazil, Executive Director of the Technical Cooperation Program for the Organization of American States in Washington, D. C., seconded Doctor Arceneaux's opinion.

"To my mind, Doctor Arceneaux puts his finger on the major factor in the role of the missionary in rural areas. Often among backward peoples the priest cannot start immediately speaking of God or religion. He must begin at the bottom; he must talk of food, of the cold; he must open the road to confidence by his concern for the farmer as a man. He has a big role to play in applying the social justice of the Church to millions of farmers all over the world. His great role, I think, is to link the farmers with technicians and technical institutions that can help them, to bring in ideas and experiences from outside through pamphlets, through conferences, through person to person conversations, through any kind of contact. This is something that a zealous priest can do admirably and with great results for the Church."

Education to Preventive Charity. As an economist, Father James J. Berna, S.J., has studied the role of the missionary in relieving the destitution of the villagers of South India.

"It is not the missionary's direct problem to promote the industrialization of India," noted Father Berna, "but he gets into this problem through the dire poverty that he encounters among his people.

"I have in mind the case of a village of 600 Catholics in Kerala, a small state where economic woes had much to do with a recent victory of the Communists. Two-thirds of the people are landless agricultural workers. The men are paid a rupee a day (20 cents) for eight to ten hours work in the rice fields. The women receive half a rupee. When the rains are heavy no one can work and no one gets paid. Often these wretched people are reduced to one meal in two days with existence on rice water in the interval.

"Unbelievable though it may seem, these people suffer in silence or cry out in anguish but remain completely baffled in their predicament. The idea of getting some additional source of income, as might occur immediately to us, is beyond their imagination. The priest in this village has been their educator; he has gone from hut to hut and has taught each family with patience and persuasion how a community small industry, in this case hand-loom weaving, can provide the difference between destitution and at least a bare sufficiency."

We shall discuss the practical details of such projects as this later on, in the chapter on community small industries. Basic to our whole problem, however, is this recognition by the pastor of souls that he should regard it as part of his responsibility to educate or at least to seek an educator for his people when, through ignorance, their economic misery remains unrelieved.

It is worthy of our attention that the village in Kerala to which Father Berna referred is a community of old Catholics probably served by zealous priests for generations. Why is it that it is only in this present generation that the problem of seeking a supplementary source of subsistence for the wretched people is getting attention? Possibly one reason lies in the limited concept of aid from which priests at times suffer, through failure to grasp the positive and constructive philosophy embraced in the Church's social mission of charity.

In this Kerala village it may well be that the priests have begged food, generation after generation, for these peasant families in their hour of critical hunger. This is remedial charity, the relief of dire want after its appearance. Behind the reasons for a socio-economic program as a phase in the Christian apostolate of our people lies still another concept, that of preventive charity. Here the goal of the pastor is the elimination of basic causes of suffering in the lives of his people, through a program of social economics that seeks to anticipate the crises of life insofar as this is reasonably possible. Which is better, to bring food to the people in a valley who are starving from hunger, or to build a dam in the valley to insure water

so that there will be no famine? Both forms of charity have
their place.

It goes without saying that this doctrine of preventive charity
should prompt the pastor to interest himself in the good of
society far beyond the current needs of his villagers. He concerns himself, according as he is able, with altering a general
situation in society that permits the unjust grinding down of
peasant workers. However, in addition to this general concern
for the solution of social problems in a region or nation, the
missionary should seek to set up an aid plan in the here and
now to meet the specific socio-economic needs of the parish
in which he labors.

A Vision of the Role of Economics. Father George E.
Topshee of St. Francis Xavier University, Antigonish, made a
powerful plea to the missionary to understand the influence of
economic life on man's religion.

"If the missionary is to do any effective and enduring work
in this field," stated Father Topshee, "he must have a strong
conviction of the great importance of the role of the economic
side of life in the establishment and *in the maintenance* of
Christianity. Without this conviction the missionary will be
regarded with a certain amount of suspicion by his people. They
will readily sense any lack of conviction and dismiss his efforts
as superficial dabbling.

"Faith is a free gift of God and no one will say that faith
is linked as cause and effect with the economic order. Nevertheless we have witnessed the defection from the Faith of
whole nations for economic and political reasons. The maladjusted economic society is at least the occasion, the excuse,
for leaving the Church and joining the screaming revolution-
aries who claim that they have the answers for the masses of
the people.

"The day is coming, I believe, when the Pope will make it
mandatory for Church leaders to take a more realistic view of
the role of economics in the establishment and maintenance of
Christianity."

An Asian Program for the Priest.   Father John Dijkstra has Java in his bloodstream; his work there and his people color all his thinking. Therefore, despite the fact that he was born in Europe, he talks as an Asian. As an Asian by adoption, a member of the Church in Asia that counts but some 30 million Catholics in a human mass that totals one and a third billion souls, he has no illusions about the need to create ruggedly strong Catholics if they are to survive. Hence his insistence that we give great attention to the socio-economic field.

"Our Catholics in Asia," he said, "must be educated to a stronger and livelier consciousness of socio-economic problems. This is a giant task because so many of our priests and religious do not possess this social consciousness. The priest has a key position in this socio-economic work. He is able to fulfill his role, however, only if he understands that the basic material needs of society—food, raiment, shelter—must be provided before the average family in a society can live according to Christian principles. A priest cannot say that these problems are not his field, not his work. They *are* his field and his work because most important basic moral principles are involved in these socio-economic problems.

"The papal encyclicals must be recognized as assigning a task to all Catholics at every level, from the Pope himself to the humblest layman. The hierarchy is not permitted to let the laity fight their socio-economic battles alone. For this struggle our Catholics must sanctify themselves. We priests must not underestimate how great are the sacrifices that the laity must make. As priests we cannot and must not try to assume the role of the laity. We must establish clearly our position: to win them God's grace and give them guidance, to serve as mediator for the people."

Don't Leave the Field to the Reds.   Father Dijkstra, who witnesses at close range the giant Communist effort to capture control of Indonesia, pointed out the importance the Reds give to the socio-economic program.

"The Communists in Indonesia," he noted, "have chosen

the socio-economic way to get their totalitarian dictatorship. What an easy plan they have! They corrupt and undermine every democracy, and would corrupt the Church itself if that were possible.

"With this the case, should it be precisely in this field that we do nothing? If we Catholics of Asia will avoid being destroyed by Communism we must begin to employ all our apparatus of organizations, institutions and physical plants for effective achievement in the socio-economic field."

Exhortation Is Not Enough. To fulfill his role as catalyst the priest understands that merely to exhort is not enough. Monsignor George Higgins, Director of the Department of Social Action of the MCWC, sought to make this clear.

"A rather narrow and somewhat artificial dichotomy seems to some of us to dictate separate roles for the priest and the technician," he warned. "By technician we mean the public health man, the economist, the sociologist. With all due respect to all the groups that make up these professions—and we need far more of them—I don't think that the major social problems in Asia, any more than in the United States, are going to be solved by men who would insist on being exclusively technicians. We have technicians in the labor unions but their role, though important, is a relatively minor one. They are not the ones who solve the economic and social problems in the United States.

"It is men with the gift of leadership, with the capacity for inspiration and organization, who are primarily needed. Some technicians can fill this role; certainly the priest should contribute leadership in friendly cooperation with the technician."

This positive factor of leadership in the priest was emphasized by others. Doctor O'Dea described the priest's role as that of "diligent amateur." Doctor Zeegers explained that the priest must have genuine knowledge of the socio-economic problems but not necessarily of the techniques for solving them.

"It is not my intention to make a socio-economic expert of

every missionary," he stated. "He is an expert in the care of souls; for the socio-economic program he should be backed by experts. Nevertheless the missionary should have an intelligent understanding of the key problems and their solutions. He must get a feeling for the strategy necessary in his mission to solve the local problems."

As basis for the missionary's work, Father Dijkstra called upon the parish priest to supply socio-economic education in his parish. "Our schools, our hospitals, our press, our organizations, must not be mere walled ghettos protecting our flock from evil," he explained. "We must provide our lay people with sufficient guidance to live their faith as apostles in the socio-economic field."

The Priest Specialist in the Socio-Economic Field.   Every priest, it has been explained, must be a catalyst to inspire and guide in socio-economic activities while directing the general program of his parish. But to have a certain few priest specialists, who can assist both pastors and technicians as well as people in an area or a nation, is recognized as advisable even if not always an absolute necessity.

Father Berna, drawing on his experience in India, called for such a specialist. "I think that each mission territory," he proposed, "should have a priest properly trained in this whole field who can journey about and advise his fellow missionaries."

Father Dijkstra was of the same mind. "We do not see the need of many priest specialists in the socio-economic field," he observed. "One or two for every vicariate is sufficient. But these few can prove a wonderful power to help the movement.

"These priests as representatives of their Bishops should aid and instruct their fellow priests. In spirit they should not be too far removed from parish life. They should live and work close to the people, demonstrating socio-economic work, building it into the parishes. They must avoid in any way becoming the sole social priest of the vicariate who isolates himself from the other clergy and tends to do everything by himself. In this latter case the parish priests won't participate. They'll throw

every socio-economic problem to the priest specialist who will
end by being ineffective, attaining little of importance.

"In addition to this priest specialist, however, we feel in
Indonesia that our socio-economic program must possess the
full-time services of capable lay organizers, each receiving a
high enough salary properly to support his family. In each
vicariate there is something like a Social Information Service
Bureau in which the cooperative association, the union and
labor movements have their headquarters. It is impossible to
get a hold on the mass of the people and provide for the economic progress of the poor without zealous and capable Catholics giving time to this work.

"But who will pay their salaries? The Bishops of Indonesia
after reading the recommendations of the social committee of
August, 1957, decided to provide the money to set up a decent
headquarters in Jakarta. In every vicariate that can at all afford
it, a central office and one organizer was voted, the funds for
three years to be supplied by the Bishop and after that by
the worker and farmer movement itself."

The Missionary Extension Service.   In addition to trained
missionary specialists, important aid for the parish priest can
be provided by organized information centers found in some
mission territories, a number of which are prepared to assist
the missionaries in their socio-economic programs. An example near at hand to those at the Maryknoll Easter Conference was the Missionary Extension Service Bureau operated
under the direction of Father Eugene Higgins at the Maryknoll
Motherhouse.

The Pastor Should Not Fight Alone.   In this book we are
concentrating on the parish program and we seek to establish
the fact that no pastor should feel justified in saying that, because there is no diocesan socio-economic program, he cannot give thought to the material welfare of the needy among
his people. Nevertheless it is true that the pastor who is required to fight his battles alone is carrying an unwisely heavy
load. As we have already indicated, there should be an organi-

zation above and beyond the parish. There should be a socio-economic program and sources of guidance for the parish missionary. Indeed, the parish missionary should be able to coordinate his efforts into a program that represents the thinking of the Church and of the state at the regional, national and even international level.

Today continuing guidance in socio-economic activities can be expected from Church sources, beginning with the Vatican and certain of the Roman Congregations. It takes its origin sometimes at the continental level, as in the way of conferences of the episcopacy of Asia or of Latin America. In many individual nations the hierarchy has studied socio-economic problems and given directives. Finally, then, it becomes more and more the practice for the individual diocese, whether in the missions or in the homeland, to formulate a socio-economic program fashioned to meet local needs.

Pioneer missionary groups in areas where the Church is very young frequently avoid establishing at the diocesan level a common organization or platform for social activity. Each missionary pastor does what he sees fit in the way of setting up institutions of charity or relief, one pastor emphasizing certain phases of activity, another choosing different projects. However, there is a heightened interest today among peoples everywhere in meeting problems of human need, and there is a recognition by missionaries that leftist forces are challenging the forces of religion as regards genuine concern for the rights of men as men. The social program today has strong apologetic value for the Church in facing the world outside its ranks.

In homeland countries the common program that this involves often centers in a diocesan bureau of charities or a social welfare center. There would seem to be good reasons for a unification of the various efforts to meet local problems, whether economic or non-economic, and for the early proclamation in a mission territory of the Church's interest in all forms of human need, even if in these new areas only a small portion of the Church's program can be acted upon in practical fashion.

Very important also is the publicly recognized participation of the local body of lay Catholics in this social program, however inchoate may be their Catholic life. If the program of charity and economic guidance is seen as exclusively the activity of the foreign missionaries, the non-Catholic populace will merely label it as an importation from abroad, which, however commendable in itself, will not redound sufficiently to the credit of the newly created segment of local Catholics.

The Indonesian Plan. Father Dijkstra explained to us the view on this matter held by the missionary Church in Indonesia, intelligently directed by Bishops and priests from the Netherlands.

"In Indonesia," he explained, "a social committee composed of priests and laymen was created by the Bishops. This social committee meets annually and makes recommendations to the Bishops. These recommendations are accepted by the Bishops as representing the findings of the specialists, and in turn they are presented by each Bishop to his Catholics as his own decisions for socio-economic action in his vicariate. In this way the Bishops of the country call on their lay people to do their duty.

"However, if this call is stated in general terms only, the people will do nothing. It is important to be specific. The key problem of the moment must be pointed out, the lever must be indicated that will efficiently help the people through socioeconomic action. The economic needs of farmers, workers and the huge mass of unemployed must be met—by cooperatives for the farmers, unions for workers and work for the unemployed."

Coordinating with Government Programs. In addition to carrying out Church programs, many Catholic missionaries around the world have coordinated their efforts with international programs, such as launched by UNESCO and UNICEF, or with programs promoted by the International Cooperation Agency (the ICA) of the United States Department of State. A socio-economic program that has encountered notable success is Operation Bootstrap, initiated by Governor Munoz Marin of Puerto Rico. Some social phases of the program, such as advocacy of birth control, have unfortunately marred the popularity of the program among Catholics.

"Operation Bootstrap is a huge enterprise," explained Monsignor John Illich, Vice-President of the Catholic University of Ponce, Puerto Rico. "It achieves its program through a Planning Board which currently has 2,000 employees in its central office and a considerable number as well in the 84 communes of the island. Ten years ago when Operation Bootstrap was started, its program was based on the assumption that Puerto Rico's principal commodity was its surplus supply of labor. Thanks to remarkable accomplishments in stepping up the economic life at both urban and village levels, labor today in Puerto Rico is described as in short supply."

In Indonesia we find an organized movement among Catholics to advocate making common cause with all elements in the community that are not openly hostile, in order to solve their nation's socio-economic problems. Father Dijkstra explained this to us.

"It is of first importance," he said, "that the members of the neutral worker and farmer movement, inspired by Catholics, aim to make their own movement strong. But this does not mean that our movement does not need the cooperation of other movements in the country. We must ramify into and grow with Indonesia society.

"To face problems which exceed the strength of our union, our leaders must use the help provided both by our national government and the international agencies. For instance, the Indonesia Government has a Department of Cooperatives. Our worker and farmer movement must be aware of this and know how to use its facilities. The government also has a Community Education Department and a department for the development of agriculture. Our leaders must be adequately informed of the ways and means to use all available government aid. At the same time our members must be stimulated to help themselves. Helping the people to help themselves must be the main objective of our movement, with outside aid regarded as subsidiary."

Catholic Concern for the Total Community. "Does the Catholic missionary always plan his socio-economic program in terms of the total community?" asked Father Fred McGuire, C.M., executive secretary of the Mission Secretariat. "From my experience in the Far East I would say not. Generally speaking, when projects came up along the lines of socio-economic development, a good number of the missionaries thought in terms of serving only the Catholics. They did not think of bringing in the other people. It seems to me that in addition to being defeatist, their attitude represented a lost opportunity to demonstrate their desire to do good."

"I was shocked by an experience I had on this point in a country of Asia where I was working," commented Mr. Louis Miniclier, Director of the Community Development Division of the I.C.A. "I visited a cluster of three villages. Village A was a Catholic community, Village B was Buddhist, Village C was Catholic. Villages A and C were profiting nicely from a Catholic community action program, but Village B because it was Buddhist was left out of the picture entirely so far as help was concerned. Evidently a parish does not always embrace the total community. In some areas in the United States I have a feeling that it does, as in Carlinville, Illinois, where the priest services the whole community."

"Not only in mission lands but in the homeland the local pastor has an obligation to all the souls within the limits of his parish," noted Father Richard Lawlor, S.J., the missiologist. "Canon Law lays this down and current missionary thinking emphasizes it. Missionary method calls for serving the common good through cooperation with groups of all kinds, whether they be Catholic or not. The Church is to be looked upon not as an alien, isolated, ghetto group but as one which serves the whole community."

Father Lawlor's reference to Canon Law concerned Canon 1350 of the Code which reads, "Let local ordinaries and parish priests regard those non-Catholics within their diocese and parishes as committed to their care in the Lord." The modern missionary, as did the monks of the West when Europe was receiving the Faith, must build up not only the life of worship but the entire fabric of a Christian society among the entire body of souls committed to his care.

All Things to All Men. Monsignor Luigi Ligutti, the apostolic leader of the National Catholic Rural Life Movement, concluded our consideration of the missionary's role with some categoric directives.

"The missionary must be all things to all men—to humanity, to the Christians, to a pagan world, to a materialistic world. I must be all things to the Communists, I must be all things to the anti-Christians, I must be all things to the Moslems, I must be all things to all men.

"And the meaning of all things is extremely important, lest we should be narrow in our view. If I am narrow I cannot be another Christ because Christ redeemed all men, preached to all men, ceaselessly served all men.

"The missionary lives by Pius X's motto, to restore all things in Christ. Any kind of a program—a housing program, an agricultural program, a soil conservation program, an industrial program, an urbanization program—must be guided by the right Christian principles. Does the Christian layman always understand? Sometimes he does not understand; I'll give you an example:

"I shall never forget driving out one day to a Chilean *fundo*. The owner, with his poor people in the most abject poverty and misery, living in unChristianly miserable huts, showed me a beautiful chapel he had just built and that the Bishop had consecrated for him.

" 'It would be far better,' I said to the owner, 'if this church were not here and the houses were better—Christian houses in place of this house of God which merely tickles your pride and vanity.'

"Of course I hurt him. He did not invite me to his *fundo* again."

For recommended reading, see Bibliography No. 2, page 262.

EMPLOYMENT OF COMMUNITY
DEVELOPMENT TECHNIQUES

The Sense of Community. Parishes throughout the Catholic world total approximately 150,000. The *Annuario Pontificio* for 1959 lists 2,104 dioceses and mission territories, each of which counts from 20 to 500 parishes.

A substantial proportion of these parishes embraces a single civil community of some thousands of souls. Others, then, in urban areas will represent a segment of a large city, but even in this contingency the parish often consists of a single neighborhood area and thus qualifies as a social community.

Some densely populated urban parishes, however, will possess fifty neighborhoods; in parts of New York City every block is a distinct neighborhood. Hence such parishes are multi-community in nature. In thousands of other instances the parish embraces a considerable number of villages and extensive rural areas and thus is likewise multi-community in composition. In mission lands this is almost always the case; a single parish may possess a hundred thousand souls and two or three score civil communities.

Even in mission lands where the Catholic flock is small and scattered and seemingly lost in an ocean of non-Christians, the shepherd of souls sees as his fundamental task the establishment of the Christian community. "One of the things we should insist upon with our missionaries," declared Bishop Blomjous at the Maryknoll Conference, "is that they recognize as the real aim of missionary work not alone the making of converts but the establishment of the Church, and the Church as a Christian community. This is one of the fundamental ideas of missionary work. Once we have understood it, all that we are saying here about socio-economic betterment follows quite logically. In Africa we train our people to understand the nature of Christian society by paralleling it to their tribal society that embraces all phases of living.

The Church and Development of the Community. Is the Church interested in the development of the civil community as such? A striking piece of evidence that it is, comes to us in the way of a quite unusual letter of praise addressed by Pope John XXIII under date of February 12, 1959, to Monsignor John O'Grady, Secretary of the National Conference of Catholic Charities in Washington, D. C., in his capacity of Vice-President of the International Conference of Catholic Charities which has headquarters in the shadow of the Vatican in Rome.

The International Conference of Catholic Charities is a federation of some forty nation-wide organizations of Catholic charities existing throughout the Catholic world. It was organized on the initiative of the Holy See in 1951 and took over, as one of the sponsored projects of its international headquarters in Rome, the cooperation of the Catholic Church with the government-operated community development program in the then British territory of the Gold Coast in West Africa. This program began as a mass education effort but today represents community development work in the new and specific meaning of this term.

Of interest to us at the moment is the fact that Catholic cooperation with this government community development program in the now independent nation of Ghana has so pleased the Holy Father that he addressed to its principal promoter, Monsignor O'Grady, a document of strong approbation from which we quote.

"It has been a source of much comfort for Us," the Pope's letter reads, "to learn of the meritorious work which the International Conference of Catholic Charities is accomplishing in Ghana under your wise and zealous direction, beloved son; and Our satisfaction was made all the greater by the knowledge that this historic portion of the great continent of Africa is benefiting, during these early years of self-government, by your efforts to put into practice the evangelical precept of fraternal love.

"In accordance with the Church's teaching concerning the universal brotherhood of men, the Conference has endeavored to foster a spirit of neighborliness and to promote the real welfare of the people; and it has succeeded in a measure which indeed provides well-founded hopes for the future.

"We are well aware that if the work of the Conference was able to achieve such noteworthy results during these early and vital years, it was due in no small measure to the valuable cooperation given by the civil authorities and to the sympathetic relationship which exists between them and the Church.

"And We would add that We derived great consolation from the fact that not only the hierarchy and the clergy but also the Catholic laity are playing their part in these community efforts, thus utilizing this opportunity to exercise a greater influence for good by their example and by their work for their neighbor.

"What is being accomplished in Ghana by the International Conference of Catholic Charities might well serve as an example for other countries both in Africa and elsewhere which would also derive considerable benefits from this practical application of the virtue of Christian charity. And it is Our confident hope that everywhere the heralds of the Gospel and the civil authorities will be willing to render every assistance toward the promotion of such praiseworthy aims."

Community Development a Christian Enterprise. Bitter enemies of the Church undoubtedly are found among the promoters of community development around the world. It is Monsignor O'Grady's contribution, now approved by the Holy See, to note that regardless of these hostile bedfellows whom we may encounter in the course of engaging in this activity, the basic goals in the service of the common good are such that we should look upon it as a Christian enterprise.

"On the basis of my eight long treks in Ghana," stated Monsignor O'Grady, "and my contact with community development in many other countries, I have come to the conclusion that there is more life and more participation on the part of the people of Ghana in their program than I found in any other country. . . . One of the wholesome things about Ghana is that one can see new life steadily coming up from the bottom. I see this as part of the contribution that the Church has to make to community development if it is going to remain as a vital Church. However, in order that the Church may be able to make its most effective contribution, it must join hands with other religious denominations. In other words, all the religious denominations must put all their force and all their enthusiasm into the movement.

"One can very well regard sharing in community development as the true expression of the Mystical Body of Christ. Wherever we find a group of Christians gathered together in the promotion of common objectives, there we find Christ, and we find all His graces; there we find the finest fruits of the Redemption. From a Christian standpoint, therefore, community development can be regarded as a true expression of Christ's Redemption. It really makes every Christian an active participant in Christ's Mystical Body."

The Scope of Community Development. Community development may be regarded as an umbrella instrument for socio-economic action. All community effort cannot be lumped under the term but it has become a major division. Community development processes are educational and organizational. As *educational,* they aim 1) to change such attitudes and practices as are obstacles to social and economic improvement; 2) to engender particular attitudes which are conducive to these improvements; 3) to promote a greater receptivity to change. As *organizational,* they aim to create or increase community action, principally through local leaders who will not only themselves participate but urge the community as a whole to participate.

"Community development can no longer be considered merely an art phrase or a fad," explained Mr. Miniclier who, it will be recalled, is the Community Development Director of the State Department's International Cooperation Administration. "It is a reality in many parts of the world. The I.C.A. is assisting 23 countries in furthering community development self-help efforts. In these lands we have not imposed our programs on the people since this is a kind of program that must develop from the roots up. The United Nations is helping approximately an equal number of countries in this same field."

India is an outstanding example of how extensive a program can be. In the first five years of India's activity, the program affected the lives of more than 80 million rural people in its population of almost 400 million. Stimulation of self-help and cooperation in the villages resulted in the establishment of 12,000 new schools and 30,000 adult education centers, the building of 28,000 miles of new roads, the reclamation of 895,000 acres of land and the irrigation of an additional one and a half million acres.

Community development today includes some of the movements also known as Village Development, Community Action, Community Education, Rural Development, Village Agricultural and Industrial Development.

The loose way in which the now popular term "community development" is used has created a great deal of confusion. Many types of undertaking can contribute to the improvement of the productive capacities and living conditions of the hundreds of millions of people who live in the hundreds of thousands of local villages in underdeveloped countries. It is doubtful, however, whether it is either conceptually or administratively helpful to call all of these types of undertaking "community development." Community development is used more correctly only to describe the methods by which the people who live in local villages or communities become involved in helping to improve their own economic or social conditions.

Definition of Community Development. The U. S. Government's International Cooperation Administration defines the term as "a process of social action in which the people of a community: 1) organize themselves for planning and action; 2) define their common and individual needs and problems; 3) make group and individual plans to meet their needs and solve their problems; 4) execute these plans with a maximum reliance upon community resources; and 5) supplement these resources when necessary with services and materials from governmental and non-governmental agencies outside the community."

"The U. N. definition of community development," observed Mr. Miniclier, "was developed at the same time as the U. S. definition but completely independently of us. It was with fear and trepidation that I heard a U. N. representative say in my office one morning, 'It is about time the U. S. tries to describe this movement.' 'We have,' I replied. It took nine and a half months before we could get the various subject matter specialists of both groups to agree but now our two definitions run parallel."

The Missionary's Role in Community Development. As missionaries we have reason to be strongly interested in community development. Even though many of us are as yet unfamiliar with the application of its principles and its techniques, we are assured that it represents opportunities for building better people—better individuals, better families and better communities.

"It is my thesis," observed Doctor Zeegers, "that community development begins with the development of the missionary as the prime instigator among the people of the principle of self-help. Through this procedure we can make a switch in our attitude toward mission activities, community development included. Catholics all over the world think in terms of building the missions through alms from the homeland. Too many still think that the main problem is to give every African a pair of trousers.

"A great deal of aid from the homeland is needed. But, more important, we must switch from considering missions as a consumptive investment to seeing them as a productive investment. We must conceive our program as representing a relatively small investment from the homeland for various pilot projects in each mission field, and then through our socio-economic program advance the local growth of our new Catholic society in the field into a self-maintaining Church.

"I see our procedure as follows: first, a certain amount of socio-economic research in each new area; secondly, a supply of socio-economic technical assistance from the homeland or from elsewhere for each such area; thirdly, careful instruction of missionaries and local laity on how to tackle their socio-economic problems; fourthly, a well-coordinated plan to accelerate the emancipation process of the indigenous hierarchy and laity toward a self-maintaining Christian society through this socio-economic program."

Thus Doctor Zeegers emphasized again the role of the missionary as a catalytic agent. In missionary circles we should call for a few of the priests, Brothers, Sisters or foreign lay apostles to be skilled in the duties of the higher command. Nevertheless our principal path to achievement in this field stems from our advantage of proximity to the village world and the character of our religious work which provides us with a great potential in zealous local volunteers.

"I think we've got to create greater conviction in the missionaries," noted Father Ronan Hoffman of the Franciscan Conventuals, Professor of Missiology at the Catholic University, "They must possess a conviction of the relevance of all these socio-economic problems to their missionary work."

The Example of the Church in Ghana. Very important for the socio-economic program in mission lands is the investigation by qualified missionaries of the possible assistance available locally through the national programs supplemented by international agencies whether governmental (as provided by United Nations agencies) or non-governmental (as provided by voluntary social welfare agencies).

Monsignor O'Grady had an interesting comment on this in relation to his work in Ghana. He said, "When I first discussed the possibility of active participation by the Catholic Church in community development in Ghana with Robert Gardiner, a Ghanaian and then Director of the Department of Social Welfare and Community Development, I noted that this truly great man immediately waxed eloquent. 'We need the participation of the Church,' he said. 'We want it immediately. We want it for the development of our people. You should not wait until all the churches are willing to join in a common effort. Begin with your own groups. Make a beginning in the villages here and there; you will find that the program will grow. It will not take long before its finest fruits will begin to appear. Eventually all the churches will join you. It is inevitable.'

"I was inspired by these words of Robert Gardiner as I have been by my contact with him through the years. He has been the basic inspiration of this program from the beginning."

When Monsignor O'Grady first spoke to the missionaries of this, some demurred, saying, "We're afraid the government people will accuse us of interfering in their program; they'll merely give us the brush-off."

The Ghana Catholic Program. This hesitancy was overcome and in December, 1956, the then Director of Community Development and Mass Education in Ghana, Mr. Peter du Sautoy, and representatives of all the dioceses in Ghana met under Archbishop Porter in Cape Coast Castle. This vital new nation in West Africa, with a population of 5,000,000, spends some 600,000 pounds a year to operate a very vital community development organization, employing a community development staff of a thousand, of whom 400 are so-called Mass Education Assistants at the village level. Notable are its eight mechanized field units, each headed by a foreman and possessing technicians and construction equipment that includes a bulldozer.

Three fields for mutual cooperation were determined upon between the government and the Catholic parochial groups at the village level as follows:

First, Du Sautoy proposed that wherever the villagers showed the necessary initiative, joint efforts should be made to provide school buildings, meeting halls, hospitals and clinics for the back country. The local groups would provide voluntary labor and raw material while the government through its mechanized field units would provide: a) the planning of the buildings, b) skilled mechanics, c) building tools as needed.

Secondly, government and parish groups got together in the literacy campaign. The government trained the literacy teams while parish leaders guided the teams in rural areas where the government could not hope to supply personnel.

Thirdly, a rural betterment program was worked out. A great problem in Ghana is the future of the 24,000 sixteen-year-olds leaving middle schools each year. Only about 4,000 of these are finding jobs. The entire social complexion of the rural areas must be altered to persuade these new family folk to stay away from the big cities. By local self-help programs these younger people were to be prompted to build up satisfying careers as modern farmers or rural enterprisers.

A certain number of foreign missionaries and native-born priests were selected for special training as sectional leaders in this program. Goodly numbers of promising villagers were trained for community development and adult education work at the local level.

The Missionary as Catalyst.   In Ghana teachers and catechists and other village leaders carry the main burden of the community development program at the local level. The missionary for the most part keeps the spirit glowing. So in similar efforts elsewhere in the world.

"During my ten years in British Honduras," explained Father Marion Ganey, S.J., the specialist in cooperatives, "experience taught me, if nothing else, the great fact that I should not try to dominate the movement. This applies as well to my years of action in the Fiji Islands. It is a difficult lesson to learn and I learned by many mistakes. We hurt the people and the movement if we figure too positively in the program."

"One of the factors involved in the introduction of change in mission lands," noted Doctor Thomas O'Dea, Fordham sociology professor, "is the kind of help we render to develop an indigenous leadership. The outside agent, who is the missionary, cannot be the day-to-day field leader and he should not really try to fill this role. He should seek to guide and inspire so that local indigenous leaders are produced."

It was pointed out at the Maryknoll Conference that this role of catalytic agent which the missionary should play is by no means a negative one. He should not picture himself as merely standing on the side with bated breath, not daring to utter a word lest he break the magic spell. The missionary as catalyst must possess a great capacity to draw out from inside plain men's minds the aspirations toward better things that lie within them, to encourage their expression, to persuade, to convince men to determine to act toward their realization. His immediate goal may be to open the door to the technician.

In longer terms, the missionary fills the tremendous role of the monks of the West during the early Middle Ages who slowly, gently, ceaselessly through generations and centuries built Christian society in Northern Europe. Many of the monks were technicians as this term is used today, but the major contribution of this missionary body was, as a normal application of the Gospel teachings, the vision and inspiration to more abundant daily living, a daily living that prompts the father of every family to provide adequate food, clothing and shelter for earthly careers directed toward enduring Christian cultural pursuits.

Analyzing the Parish Community. Not every body of missionaries will find, in the country where they work, a government that appreciates the value of direct action with the Church on social matters, as has been the case in Ghana. There will be instances when the missionary pastor can help his people by serving merely as a consultor in community matters. In other situations, governments place little importance on voluntary agencies and he may be ignored. In still other areas, the government will be so handicapped by circumstances that no local socio-economic program is in operation. In this last case the community development idea may be employed at least partially by the missionary to aid his people through direct initiative on his part.

Half the battle in considering a use of the community development idea is to make a satisfactory analysis of the community. Are there areas of weakness in your parish beyond the realm of faith and morals that will represent, if you ignore them, a default in Christian humanitarian obligations? A number of criteria provided by Carl Taylor and others will serve as a measure to find out.

The Criteria:
1 marked physical and cultural isolation of the community or communities in the parish. This factor in itself would indicate that the parish would need to be rural and in point of fact most community development effort is rural. But many experts contend that such techniques as the self-help principle, the "greatest felt need" principle, the local leadership principle, can serve as well in backward areas of large cities;
2 substantial illiteracy, often to the degree of 65 to 95 percent;
3 poverty on the part of the people and their government;
4 the absence of adequate activated local technical assistance personnel;
5 ill-functioning channels of communication between the local community and political, social or economic forces outside;

6 a high degree of cultural and educational stagnation locally;
7 a marked degree of poor conditions as regards health and community welfare;
8 a low productivity in the provision of livelihood, unsatisfactory marketing conditions, a general evidence of lack of know-how.

The Approach Important. It is a mistake for a missionary on arriving in a village to tell the people that they are uncivilized or uncultured. Indeed, it is a mistake on arrival to say anything that indicates a judgment of any sort. Few peoples on the earth welcome a stranger; backward peoples are wary and suspicious, even in already Christian areas where the image of the missionary is established as one who is genuinely devoted to them for the simple reason that they are people.

Padre Protase, a German Franciscan who is a legend in an area north of the Amazon River because of his ability to visit forest Indians who are hostile to the white, explained this point which has application to people much more tractable than the wild tribes of the globe. "The first requisite," he noted, "is to win their confidence. The first hour has great importance in this respect. The Indians must be convinced that the missionary has come for *their* sakes, not his own. I gather a great deal of information and make many plans to help the people, but this is all secondary to my effort to prove to the Indians that *they themselves* are the primary object of my regard."

Stimulating village people to change must be done by someone whom they know and trust. Even then, the changes proposed must represent, at least in the beginning, things they easily recognize as desirable.

Prompting the Villager to Self-Help. In the new world in which the missionary finds himself, he has less need for fear than had his predecessors to propose new ways of doing things. "It is a traditional commonplace among specialists," commented Mr. Miniclier, "to mention the fact that people are slow to change. To me, it is frightening to see how rapidly the leaders of countries want to change, and to note the response of some of the little people who want to move much faster than the outside planner believes they should."

A basic prerequisite for the young missionary is the knowledge that illiterate villagers, no matter how isolated physically and culturally, have self-recognized needs and desire to satisfy these needs. If these villagers are seemingly lethargic and not interested in change, it is chiefly, if not solely, because they have never been permitted to participate, much less to lead, in programs for improving their own lot in life. They have always been told by others what their needs were. Traditionally the government officer has come to them as the policeman, the inspector, the tax-collector.

Hence the truly revolutionary nature of the community development principle of stirring the people to self-help. "We are completely reversing the direction of things," states a community development officer in India. "We have always tried to develop communities from the top down. Now we are going to develop our nation from the bottom up. That is what community development is."

"The essence of the community development philosophy now begins to emerge," stated Mr. Miniclier. "Underlying it all is the concept of the worth of the individual and faith in the potential of the people to help themselves. The idea of the worth of the individual is a recent discovery in many parts of the world. Community development seeks to capitalize on human imagination and initiative. It seeks to involve people in decision-making, in expressing their own needs in terms of what they can do for themselves, in taking action with the minimum of outside assistance, and having met with success in one project to move on to other projects.

"Community development requires understanding of each cultural situation. Education in its broadest sense and community organization are the two major keystones if lasting change is to come from the bottom up rather than be imposed, benevolently or otherwise, from the top down. This latter is the antithesis of the social action that we seek in community development."

The Grow-More-Food Committee of India's Community Projects Department seconds Mr. Miniclier's statement: "No plan can have any chance of success in India unless the millions of small farmers in the country accept its objectives, share in its making, regard it as their own and are prepared to make sacrifices necessary for implementing it."

Professor T. R. Batten, Senior Lecturer in community development at the University of London, decries the use of the so-called directive approach and the manipulated approach. "Agencies are learning," he says, "that people cooperate more willingly when they feel that they have a real share in deciding what should be done and how it should be done, as well as in doing it." [1]

Most agencies direct too much—a statement which applies to government staffs, business organizations and missionary groups. It is a tradition in Asia, Africa and Latin America for the Westerner to be paternalistic. The community development techniques are time-consuming and patience and skill are required in prompting people to self-help. It is easier and quicker for an agency that has a sum of money to pay people to construct a given project. But such methods, observes Professor Batten, "encourage a type of community mendicancy—an undue dependence on material help from outside."

Launching a Program. Carl C. Taylor is a standard source [2] for the missionary as well as for government officers in launching a program. The elements of a simple program may be summed up as follows:

1 The program catalyst: This in our present consideration would be the missionary himself who will stimulate the villagers toward growth in outlook, prompt them to mobilize for action and to determine their material resources, who will find them technical assistance and possibly additional material aid from outside, who will arrange with govern-

ment or other sources for the training of village level
workers.

2 *Change in village practices:* The principal fields are production (chiefly agriculture), health, sanitation, education, leisure, development of such socio-economic aids as cooperatives.

3 *Technical direction:* Technicians from government and other
sources and leadership specialists may be brought in from
outside.

Taylor [3] has broken down the process of instituting a community development program into a series of four progressive
steps:

First step: "Systematic discussion among members of the
community of their common felt needs. It is only when discussions are systematic, even though among a relatively few
representative persons or families, that analysis of important
commonly felt needs is accomplished."

Second step: "Systematic planning to carry out the first
self-help undertaking that has been selected by the community.
Systematic planning for aided self-help community undertak-
ings leads to selection of the type of first project which, because it is practically feasible, will mobilize the local manpower
and ingenuity of those living in the community."

Third step: "The almost complete mobilization and harnessing of the physical, economic and social potentialities of
the local community-groups. Once a goodly sized organized
local group starts working on a project which if completed will
yield obvious and early benefits to the whole community, members of the community who have thus far been only mildly
interested or even skeptical start contributing to its successful
completion."

Fourth step: "The creation of groups or community aspirations and the determination to undertake additional community
improvement projects. Until this step is taken the universal
problem of how to get local villages and villagers to desire and
initiate improvements is not yet solved."

Program Points. Experienced workers warn that the villagers should be urged to choose with special care their first community development project. It may be a village well, a new road, a schoolhouse, a community center, but it must not be the missionary's greatest felt need; it must answer the greatest felt need of a large portion of the populace. It should have these characteristics:

1 it should suit the needs of the average person in the community;
2 it should render an immediate and tangible service;
3 it should not conflict at least openly with local ways and traditions;
4 it should appeal to the rank and file as not too costly in the light of what was spent in time, energy and materials;
5 it should point toward a broader outlook in the village;
6 it should be of a nature to win the village a bit of prestige among its neighbors.

Leaders constantly emphasize that the way to do the community development job is to attack situations and conditions as a whole in a given village by getting organized village groups to work not exclusively to solve, say, the problem of literacy or the economic problem but to work for what will be spiritually, culturally, materially, a better village.

"In contrast with the specialist line of approach," declared Mr. Miniclier, "community development is, for want of a better phrase, the comprehensive community approach that helps introduce change from where the people are, based on what they, the people, want."

While the missionary should hold back discreetly on pushing his own views, he should nevertheless study continuously the thoughts of his people, and often he will uncover what might be called the "unfelt felt need," more exactly, the unexpressed solution for one or many needs which people seem to desire to satisfy but do not know how.

Such a need might be a community center. People say they want sports, want more folk dances, want certain educational services. The missionary might do well to propose to the villagers that they consider a community center which would serve many purposes:

1 recreational activities;
2 cultural activities: adult education, art, drama, handicrafts, library, discussion groups, photo clubs, sewing and knitting classes, housewifery, films, demonstration center for farm and home aids;
3 assembly hall for village societies, youth clubs, church sodalities;
4 welfare services: maternity and child welfare clinic, dispensary, family welfare center;
5 information center;
6 private social activities such as wedding parties.

Training the Helpers. The missionary will need a community leader and auxiliary workers for each village in which he launches a program. He will need to uncover a number of technicians for whatever projects his people undertake that require technical guidance. If his program embraces a number of villages he will need to provide a district community leader. It is best that the leaders and their auxiliaries be local people who from the first have the sense of belonging. The missionary should consider carefully whether they can be safely chosen by the villagers or whether, at least at the start, he should appoint them.

It goes without saying that, particularly as regards his technicians, if he is alone in a region the missionary will be handicapped in his community development efforts. Should his Bishop see the value of a territory-wide effort in which all the parishes participate, staff problems can be solved jointly. In some countries the government will be operating training schools to which staff candidates may be sent. For information on training, the United Nations Department of Economic and

Social Affairs (UNESCO) has considerable literature. A source for course outlines is the UNESCO Kit.[4]

The huge national programs of India and other countries possess a necessarily complex personnel chart. The relatively simple organization for British African countries lists a battery of ten officials for each administrative district within each country: 1) District Officer, 2) Assistant District Officer, 3) Education Officer, 4) Headmaster of Area Training Center, 5) Agricultural Supervisor, 6) Livestock Officer, 7) Health Inspector, 8) Building Foreman, 9) Inspector of Cooperatives, 10) Local Assistant.

There is a Local Assistant, naturally, for every community and his duties run somewhat as follows: 1) to explain the meaning of community development (self-help, village improvement, etc.); 2) to direct the Laubach method for teaching illiterates; 3) to employ propaganda techniques for demonstration purposes (films, posters, etc.); 4) to conduct informal adult education; 5) to direct recreation and dramatics; 6) to organize folk singing and dancing; 7) to provide elementary first aid; 8) to conduct simple village surveys of community development progress, keep a journal and other simple records; 9) to teach certain practical skills such as how to mix concrete, how to make and lay mud bricks, how to make simple provisions for a water supply.

Mr. Miniclier displayed practical realism in facing the problems of small-scale community development efforts in more isolated areas. "I am wondering," he said, "if problem-oriented, in-service training courses of four to six weeks on a regional basis out in the back country are not the partial answer in the mission field. The practitioner so often cannot come in to a training school, and an academic setting with the lecture approach is not too helpful. Key missionaries engaged in community development, 20 or 30 of them, might meet in a region like South Asia and review their problems with specialists."

Mr. Miniclier's proposals presuppose our making a distinction between community leaders and technicians. The technician usually comes exclusively to provide technical knowledge and at times is not instructed in or sympathetic to the philosophy of self-help. A statement by the World Social Welfare Assembly when it met some years ago in Madras indicates the lack of adjustment of many technicians. "Much of the technical assistance rendered by various agencies over the last few years has proven at least ineffective and often positively harmful," the statement reads, "because they were operated by 'experts' more familiar with techniques than sensitive to situations. . . . Experts who knew the answers before they got overseas were no use at all."

In short, technicians sympathetic to the local culture and to the self-help program need to be found or educated.

Whatever compromises are to be made to provide a viable program for smaller voluntary projects, the general principle holds that thoroughly trained specialists should be recognized as necessary in community development as in every other field. Words of Doctor O'Dea are worth recording on this point: "The need must be recognized to have *some* people in the organization who are experts in these matters and can be utilized by people in the field as resource persons. Ongoing research to build up a fund of experience and knowledge and to train individuals by participation is important in this respect, and larger mission organizations should give such matters serious thought."

Uncovering the Leaders. Community development represents among other things an instrument for uncovering, for discovering, leaders. How is this done?

"I think that our basic problem is, we don't know what a leader is," stated Doctor Gladwin, a thoughtful and experienced student of this subject. "He is defined only as the guide who leads, but what does it take? I am not aware of any systematic theory or practice that is necessarily the answer to the majority of situations.

"There are essentially two philosophies, I think. One is particularly characteristic of our own culture, which is to try to create them, to sort of hothouse them out of group dynamics sessions, in some cases the feeling being that you are bringing out latent qualities which never would otherwise have appeared. The other is based on the recognition that at least in times of crisis—very clear in many studies done systematically of disasters—there are always leaders who will rise to the occasion.

"There is a school of thought which says that if you want to develop leadership, the leadership inherent in the community, you sit around and watch and see what happens and who takes the leadership. This can be very misleading in some communities and very effective in others. If you have a certain traditional, perhaps hereditary, prescription of leadership functions with respect to given activities, you will find that people are leading the activities simply because they are the ones who are supposed to do so. There might be others in the community better suited to the task."

"I hear people use the phrase 'leadership training,' " stated Jules Weinberg, experienced with leadership problems in the labor field, "and it always makes me shudder because to my mind there is no earthly way to *train* leaders. You don't train them. You sharpen them up a bit, you give them some of the knowledge, the know-how, the savvy they need, but you don't really train them. What you do with a good educational program is, you *activate* the leaders.

"I think there are some observations which were taught to me by experienced organizers that might be helpful.

"For instance, in a tough organizing situation we were taught to be wary of the first group that answered a call for volunteers. This first group includes the cranks, the people who are not certain of their jobs and therefore are not stable types; it includes the hotheads. Hence, in spite of the fact that many may be excellent people, many sincere, we were taught to be wary of the easy volunteers for the odd balls among them.

"Secondly, instead of looking for the popular concept of a leader, the dynamic personality you think you see on the soap box, we were taught to look for stability. Look for a stable character, a man with a good solid family life. Despite what you think might catch the fancy of a community of workers chatting in the barroom, these men have an instinctive respect for the man who has stable relations with his family.

"Thirdly, look for the man of religious convictions. This for two reasons. One is you can talk to him about matters of principle as well as of just economic interest. The other is that, no matter what the morals may be in a community, the person with some religious background commands a degree of respect.

"We begin with a serious formation program that calls for sacrifice with the conviction that what we are doing is activating leadership. We educate but principally we challenge, we stir. In Pakistan a labor leader in the Punjab reluctantly sent us six good young men and I met him later at a trade union function. 'You know,' he said, 'I am very happy that I sent my men.' 'Why?' I asked. 'Well, I don't know if you taught them anything but they work now; they are eager.' As we see it, this is our aim, to *activate* leaders."

Doctrine and Methods for Leaders. Father Edward Malone, Professor of Dogma in Maryknoll Seminary, called for indoctrination. "The trouble in France in the last few years," he explained, "seems to have been caused by a failure in proper indoctrination. These leaders had worthy aspirations but these were not solidified by indoctrination, not only on religious lines but as regards concrete goals for their work. Lay leaders in our Catholic projects seem often to lack that nice feeling of belonging to the main stream of a movement; they are not sure enough how exactly they are to proceed to reach their goals.

"I think that certainly the concepts of group dynamics should be presented to local leadership candidates by the missioner. Group dynamics are a practical summary of principles of social psychology and cultural anthropology, and our work both in mass communications and in face-to-face contacts suffers for want of it."

Father Bernard Meyer, veteran of a life-time of village work in East Asia, corroborated this call for group dynamics. "I think our people need to know this technique in order to sell our socio-economic program. When we go out into the villages we need this technique to encourage the local leaders to push these socio-economic ideas that can mean so much to them."

Standing out prominently in the maze of detail concerning community development appears one factor which seems important above all else, namely, a dedication to the millions of faceless folk of the back country who stand to profit from the effort. An Indian official in his country's community development service sums it up well: "The first and foremost prerequisite is a band of people who are prepared to work for and with the poor peasants, with humility and a spirit of service and sacrifice. Especially those who serve at the village level must possess a complete knowledge of the village life and be in a position to appreciate the problems of the peasants. Above all, village workers must like village people."

The missionary will appreciate this sentiment. By his calling he spends much of his life with the folk who live at the grassroots level in the back country of the world.

For recommended reading, see Bibliography No. 3, page 263. For Group Leadership Techniques see Bibliography No. 13, page 281.

How Well Do We Know
Our Local Culture?

Our Attitude toward Change. A basic weakness in many a program for betterment in the so-called underdeveloped countries of the globe is the tendency of the outsider (and among outsiders we must include many of the educated elite from the capitals of these countries themselves) to engage in careless criticisms of local customs.

Such careless criticisms are often born of two factors, first, an attitude of impatient disdain toward the local people and, secondly, an ignorance of the true nature of the thought patterns and of the values that the local people place on the details of life. Outsiders may live for years among a people and never really know the people; they presume that they know by measuring everything according to standards which they as strangers bring in from outside. This may happen in the United States of America in the case of a city man living in a rural area, even though in the United States differences among the various social groups have been reduced to a minimum.

In New York City recently, a safety campaign employed the

slogan "Careless driving is kid stuff." We may apply this idea to a knowledge of people: "Careless criticism of social or racial groups is kid stuff." Serious men had best face this problem of the knowledge of their fellow men by feeling ashamed of themselves if they fail to take the necessary elementary precautions in obtaining a knowledge of any social group with whom they have not had previous experience.

Respect for Local Ways. Not only should the missionary give careful scrutiny to the local ways and ascertain the reasons behind them, but he should follow the advice of the Holy See which will guide him in establishing his attitude toward his people. Basic to this attitude is the recommendation of respect toward local cultures and their ideals. Everything of enduring value in the findings of twentieth-century scholars in anthropology, sociology and psychology bears out this same principle.

The modern Popes in their instructions to all who have a role in the global expansion of Christianity have consistently emphasized this recommendation. It may be said that Pope Pius XII, beginning with his first encyclical *Summi Pontificatus,* made the respect of all cultures the guiding star of all his teaching.

Most remarkable, however, is the consistent emphasis on this theme that has marked the instructions issued by the Holy See to its missionaries down through the centuries. An outstanding statement of Church policy on this subject is a document almost exactly 300 years old, published under date of November 10, 1659. Georges Goyau, the historian, characterized it as "a document which commands the future."

Rome's Word on Local Customs. A passage from the three-centuries-old Instruction of the Propaganda [1] states the case succinctly: "Do not make any effort or offer any argument to convince these people to change their rites, their manners, or their customs, unless they are obviously contrary to religion and morality. What could be more absurd than to transport France or Spain or Italy or some other country of Europe to China? Do not bring them our countries, but the faith, that faith which neither rejects nor offends against the rites or usages of any people, provided these practices are not completely objectionable. Quite to the contrary our faith insists that local usages be maintained and protected.

"It is inscribed, so to speak, in the nature of every man to esteem, to love, to uphold his country and its traditions above everything in the world. And there is no more powerful cause of hatred and antipathy than the introduction of changes in local customs, especially those that have been in use longer than the oldest inhabitants can remember. What good will come of it if you try to abolish such practices and replace them by introducing the customs of your own country?

"Avoid, then, the habit of contrasting the usages of your new country with those of Europe. On the contrary, strive zealously to become accustomed to the local way of doing things. Admire and praise whatever deserves praise. And if something does not deserve it, there is no need to engage in blatant criticism of it. Have the prudence not to pass open judgment on it, or, in any case, not to condemn thoughtlessly or excessively.

"As to usages which are patently evil, they should be dislodged rather by silence and kindly indirection, seizing upon every occasion to uproot them imperceptibly, once souls are disposed to embrace the truth."

Knowing Our People as a Means to Constructive Change. With this admirable admonition to the missionary to respect all cultures, we tackle the matter of meeting socio-economic betterment today, in the spirit not of destruction but of fulfillment. We intend to leave to the peoples who possess them their varying cultures. We intend to serve as catalysts in stirring needy societies to better their positions in meeting their problems of life. We have every intention that they should retain their identity, their cultural legacy.

To this end we need an intelligent knowledge of the peoples we would aid and we begin by recognizing the far-reaching effects of cultural diversity. Peoples, while basically the same as persons, live under widely varying physical conditions, widely differing historical backgrounds, social ways, economic practices. Today certain universal cultural elements prevail over the globe and complicate rather than simplify our problem. The growing prevalence of trousers, of movies, of automobiles, tends to deceive us into believing that all peoples think and feel pretty much alike. In this we can be deceived.

Doctor Gottfried Lang of Catholic University presented for the missionary a concrete plan for studying the ways of a new people whom he desires to help better itself.

*A Plan for the Study of a People Prior to Launching
a Local Program of Socio-Economic Betterment*

Studying One's Community.   A study of a local group prior to a development program could be undertaken in the traditional manner of the anthropologist or occasional missionary by consulting handbooks like *Notes and Queries*.[2] or the *Outline of Cultural Materials*.[3] The difficulty with such aids lies in the fact that the categories are too many, too specific, and do not focus on relationships. A more general framework is needed which will aid in asking the kind of questions that will lead to an understanding of the structure, as well as the functioning, of a given society.

Basic to this understanding is the concept of culture. If this concept is properly understood it can provide an organizing frame for encompassing the details that make up the life of a community, and will facilitate an understanding by the specialist of the perceptions of the people he has to deal with. The concept was defined long ago (1871) by Tylor [4] as "That complex whole which includes knowledge, belief, art, law, morals, custom, and any other capabilities and habits acquired by man as a member of society." There are many definitions of the concept, including such notions as "conventional understandings" [5] or "designs for living" by which individuals orient themselves in a given culture and which provides the norms that help people adjust one to another.[6]

The implication of this notion then is that human behavior, though highly variable from group to group, is not random, but patterned. These patterns derive in part from certain biological conditions of man: the dependence upon a mother for physical nourishment and emotional support until the young adult becomes capable of self-support; the different functions performed by the two sexes in the reproductive cycle; and finally, death which requires adjustments in old age and certain behavior adjustments by others.

The Basic Functions of a Community.   Aside from these gross patterns, there are many recurring bodies of behavior which are unique and characteristic for certain groups: regions, communities, neighborhoods or smaller aggregates of people within each of these groups. These unique patterns that are characteristic of a society we label a culture. When we go below the level of superficial observation we discover recurring elements in every culture. The missionary who will go beyond the common sense and acquire an unusual sense for observation and analysis will discover the following list of basic qualities which the society that constitutes his parish must possess:

1   *Provision for adaptation to the physical environment.* This would involve an analysis of the physiological relationships of the people to the natural setting, including: getting food, providing for warmth, shelter, sexual recruitment of new members, and so forth.

2   *Provision for full differentiation of responsibilities and role assignment.* This would involve a knowledge of the ways for assigning the roles—the division of labor in accomplishing the task with which the society is faced. All societies have at least a division of labor by sex and most have a much more elaborate system of specialization of function.

3   *A system of communication.* This would involve an analysis of the channels of communication—usually a language or, where diverse linguistic groups exist, a *lingua franca*. The social analyst must understand not only the media of communication (languages, slang), but also the social barriers to

communication—the patterns of flow of various types of communication, etc. No society can exist in the total absence of communication among its members. Most societies have very complex patterns of selective communication by subject matter, status of various members and the like.

4 *A shared set of basic definitions.* This means that when its members use a certain term, they can do so with some assurance that the other members will understand the same meaning in the term (e.g., a system of weights and measures, a system of keeping time, of defining situations calling for action, etc.). While any society of great complexity can contain many differences of definition without serious disintegrating effects, they must have certain basic definitions in common in order to function as a social unit. These should be determined by the social analyst since they are the core of concepts which hold together the social system.

5 *A shared articulated set of goals.* This would involve the discovery of values, aims and dispositions characteristic of a society. Again, while sub-groups in a complex population may have many areas of difference in their goals (e.g., the difference between religious groups in our own society), they must have some basic, common goals to avoid the tendency to disruption and ultimately "war of all against all," e.g., a shared value of democratic procedures in electing the power organs of our society.

6 *Regulation of the means to the goals mentioned above.* The question here is, how does society regulate the choice of means for arriving at these goals? A system of social sanctions will always exist according to which some means will be designated as appropriate for achieving the valued goals and other means designated as not appropriate (e.g., in our own society the goal of wealth; the means of stockmarket speculation is considered legitimate and acceptable, but the means of armed hold-ups is not acceptable). The definition of the range of acceptability is made by society in its various areas of life, and the kinds of sanctions for deviating from this path show various degrees of harshness according to the culture.

7 *A system to regulate effective expression.* Certain expressions of feeling are designated as appropriate under some cir-

cumstances and not under others—no society can allow un-regulated expression of all feelings on the parts of its members, or disruptive consequences would be inevitable.

8 *Effective control of disruptive behavior.* This implies that, if a member of society chooses to adopt non-acceptable means of arriving at the goals he accepts, the society must bring to bear certain sanctions (e.g., jail, the electric chair, etc.). The social analyst must be aware of these as being of possible relevance to the changes his program might entail as introducing new means, or even new goals.

9 *Adequate institutionalization.* This implies that there must be adequate means provided for the realization of the society's own goals. There must be adequate ways for socializing its members, both children and adults. This is of particular importance and relevance to the missionary. If the missionary is able to appraise correctly any particular in the social system as lacking adequate institutionalization in precisely the areas of his new program, he has a persuasive argument in favor of his program. These may be gotten at sometimes through asking members of a society what their felt needs are. But more often it can be obtained through a careful analysis of a particular, given society.[7]

If these nine basic characteristics have any validity, and the discipline of anthropology seems to support them, then every community will organize itself in one way or another in relation to its physical environment, in relation to its members and to the larger society of which it may be a part or with which it may have contacts and, finally, in relation to its system of values. The questions which we shall have to ask ourselves in studying a community may then be divided roughly into three categories: 1) how people in a community make a living; 2) the groups into which people in a community form; 3) the cultural values found in a community.

How People Make a Living. The questions which we have to ask under the heading of man-nature relationship would include, first of all, an assessment as to what people do to make a living. How do people organize themselves to insure a food-supply, shelter, clothing and transportation? We find, for instance, that in small isolated societies the family in its various forms functions as the social unit which is primarily responsible for the satisfaction of these material needs. With the increase in technology comes a more complicated property system, greater occupational specialization, marked division of labor and special social arrangements for production and for distribution.

Thus, any attempt to change methods of production, for instance, or to equalize distribution, or to alter consumer demands, must take into account the existing patterns for solving these problems, no matter how inadequate these patterns may appear to the missionary. For instance, an attempt to introduce a new technology may be frustrated because a particular community has not yet entered the cash economy, or the introduction of a new food may be refused because it is taboo. In addition, one must ask what are the social arrangements which govern these economic activities. Some of the economic activities typical of our society are dependent upon a high degree of individualism and competition. Such activities may seem not only inconceivable in another community, but may be positively forbidden.

Influence of Physical Environment. The seasons of the year tend to produce certain cycles of activity. These activities are dependent upon the kind of technology a people has, and the climatic variations that are typical of an area. These factors may conspire to make aggregations of people possible only at certain seasons of abundance, and at no other time. It may also determine the rhythm of work, the availability of leisure time, and the patterns of geographic mobility and of residence. A migratory people certainly poses a different problem from a sedentary group in regard to an innovation such as formal education.

Furthermore, not all elements in the physical environment are equally important to a people, and hence they do not bother to make distinctions in certain matters. For instance, we are content with one word for snow while the Eskimo has many terms, all related to their way of life, and suggesting the tremendous importance of kinds of snow in making a living in a harsh environment. Similarly, the Zulu have different color discriminations and put blue and green together, but make careful differentiations in shades of brown in keeping with a strong cultural interest in cattle and their color variation.

The exploration of the man-nature relationship is a useful first step to understanding the culture of a community. Such a study must tell us not only something about the environment, but especially something about the way people relate to one another in order to cope with the environment and how they perceive the features of the environment.

How Groups Are Formed.   No two individuals in any local group or community are ever socially alike. Distinctions are made which emphasize age, sex, wealth, certain skills and specialties, or membership in certain social groups, etc. Nevertheless we can ask what kinds of people group themselves together, using combinations of these attributes as criteria. We shall want to know how individuals become members and how they retain their membership. If we ask these questions in relational terms, we shall get at the social network of a community. Another way of asking the question is: what roles do the people play in a given community, and what expectations do the members of the community have of incumbents of these roles?

The most easily recognized social grouping in a society is, of course, the family. But it is important to recognize that the roles played by father, mother, children and relatives are not the same in every society. On the contrary, anthropological literature is replete with examples that show that the institution of the family has many forms. Sometimes this form is determined by the nature of the marriage arrangement. Marriage itself is more often conceived as a uniting of two individuals, with individual choice often playing a minor role. Thus one must ask: how does a marriage come about? what is expected of the mated pair and other relatives? and how do families live together? If we know answers to these questions, we can better understand the function of the family in a given community. This will also help our understanding of the patterns of child-rearing, patterns of responsibility among relatives to children and to one another. Also one may see that some people are considered relatives, while others, though genetically related in the same manner, are not so considered.

We shall have to ask questions as to the importance of the familial relationships in the community as a whole. Certain families may be very important, while others may be marginal in the prestige hierarchy of a community. Furthermore, in the network of social relationships in a community we have to discover how important family ties are as compared to certain associational ties. There may be a certain shift in the importance of the family as an individual matures, or during certain times in an individual's life cycle. Among some people, for instance, the family moves into the background as occupational or ritual groups become more important.

Non-Family Groups.   Knowledge of other formal groups that focus upon certain activities which are central in the life of a community, such as economics, education, religion and government, cannot be underestimated. Yet informal groups that come into existence as people gather to gossip, loaf or drink are also very important, because they become part of the gossip chain which has so much to do with the formation of public opinion.

Furthermore every community has some means of controlling the behavior of its members. This may be done by specialized formal institutions such as tribal courts, constabularies or councils of elders, etc. Often, however, informal groups, whose membership is not immediately discernible, but who can be detected over a protracted period of time, importantly control behavior.

It is important to assess the relative influence of the formal or informal groups, especially in community affairs where both may be competing for the control of the community. On the other hand, when the formal institutions of a community are very well established and quite rigid and inflexible, we often find that informal social relationships compensate for its overt rigidity by fulfilling the necessary functions not carried out by the formal institution, especially in changing situations. All of this will be of vital importance to the missionary, for an innovation may best be introduced in one community through the informal, and in another through the formal, social group, depending upon its relationships to the rest of the community.

Conduct-Making and Conduct-Controlling Groups. Formal and informal groups, too, have structure. Thus we must discover the leaders and the followers in such groups. If we merely rely upon the word of other people, we may be misled as to the nature of leadership. Often, leaders are not those in duly recognized authority positions, but are the opinion-setters who work in the background. This can only be observed in the field situations, and no prior rule can be established as to what constitutes leadership. Leaders may be recognized by virtue of their ability to influence behavior. Thus we would observe those who act as spokesmen and those who are most often consulted for advice.

An innovation will often have to be introduced through the leaders of a community. But not all leaders may serve the purpose. If a society is stratified or hierarchically organized, leaders from the different levels will have different viewpoints. Thus a recognition of a hierarchical organization would suggest that the best place to introduce an innovation which concerns the whole community is at the top. On the other hand, a society which is not so structured will demand broad representation on the village or community level.

Influences from Outside the Community. So far the community has been viewed as a more or less autonomous unit. But such communities are indeed rare today. Most communities have had contact with representatives from other social structures which they may view with distrust, or which they may welcome. One such relationship exists between local communities and the nation through government officials. The contact personnel may be local, or outsiders. Whatever the nature of this relationship, it is important to recognize it, and to make it part of the community analysis, for it may serve as a most effective way of introducing changes, if such a government official has high prestige. In other communities, the government official might be viewed with hostility, as in many villages in India where he is identified with the tax collector.[8] Thus role expectations of the people of a community in relation to outsiders will give us a clue as to the nature of the relationship. Conversely, the role expectations of outsiders toward the community is similarly important and must become part of the analysis of a community.

Most communities also have their own network of relationships which connects them to other communities, such as trade with neighboring villages, tribes or urban centers. We must know the importance of these in introducing new ideas into a community. Adair and Vogt have described the effect of military service on the Navaho and Zuni returned veterans and showed that they became important agents for technological change in one group, and introduced new forms of internal organization in the other.[9]

Groups Communicating Ideas.   Social structures may also be viewed as the primary channels for communication. But we must not take for granted that the same channels and techniques of communication of one culture necessarily exist in another, or that they would function effectively if these were transferred from one culture to another. We must then analyze these channels. They may follow naturally from our knowledge of social relationships, and the expectations that people have of certain role incumbents. Here we only call attention to such channels as gossip between men or women in their social gatherings, the weekly market or religious festivals. Sometimes a village crier serves the purpose, while elsewhere signals such as church bells may serve. Sometimes there will be village scribes, traders, story tellers or key persons such as headmen, chiefs, priests, shamans, teachers, all serving as the centers for communicating messages to the group. These channels are important, because they can be used to disperse knowledge as well as spread distrust and hostility to any anticipated development program.

We further have to consider the fact that every communication has at least two aspects: the tangible physical, and the less tangible social-psychological aspect. The former is easy to apprehend, but the latter varies considerably from culture to culture. For instance, a poster using a pig to illustrate the essentials of animal husbandry in a Moslem community would certainly defeat its purpose. Similarly, we must know how important the personal contact for communication is as against formal business-like relationships. These may influence the meaning implicit in communication content.

Cultural Values in a Community.   Perhaps one of the most important aspects in the study of a community are its values. In recent years so-called "values research" has gone ahead and we can more systematically look at the values which are important in a group. Although man acts and reacts in terms of certain biological and environmental determinants, he also acts in terms of cultural value patterns. These are vital in the *selecting, regulating* and *goal-discriminating* processes of a community. As Vogt puts it, "It is as if the value-orientations of a group function as selective 'screens' or 'filters' in the diffusion of cultural materials . . . , and then as 'automatic pilots' which permit cultural changes and elaborations in certain directions but not in others." [10]

We know that many cultural items diffuse from one culture to another. This, however, tells us nothing about the mechanism which is at work by which such items are accepted, rejected or modified as they move from one culture to the next. Value-orientations play an important part in the process of transferring cultural items through the influence they exert on perception. Wright tells us that the Chinese, like others, distinguish between right and left, but differ in the kinds of symbolic associations they traditionally assign to them. The left is associated with the east, the male force, springtime and the place of honor. This linkage posed some problems to missionaries in connection with the passage of the New Testament which states that Jesus is seated on the right hand of God. Translators stuck to the literal text and created the impression that someone other than Jesus occupied the place of honor on the left.[11]

Value-orientations or cultural screens are, in part at least, the consequence of historical events in the life of a group. For this reason an analysis must contain not only what is happening today, but also what significant events have taken place in the past: natural catastrophes, unusual persons, certain kinds of contacts with the world at large or combinations of all these may shape the values or points of view in a community.

How to Detect and Focus Values.   The question then arises how to study or detect these values or clusters of values around certain focal issues. The data for the study of this aspect of culture must come from overt and verbal behavior as it occurs, or it can be induced through the interview.

From among cultural situations one can select "choice situations." In other words, from what we know already about the human ecology, and the social structure, we know that there are alternative ways of behaving within the limits set by social, ecological and biological determinants. After recognizing such choice situations or describing the presence of actually perceived alternatives, and then observing concrete behavior, and asking people why they have done thus and so, we have moved a long way toward the isolation of cultural values.

Particularly useful among choice situations are those involving crisis and conflict. The former disrupts certain relationships, such as those of man-to-man, nature-to-man, man-to-universe, and demands action if the group is to survive. Some of these crises situations may be recurrent, and a culture may have ready-made responses for them. Others may be new, and choices are made on the basis of experiences to which they are superficially connected. Secure as much information as possible about conflicts arising out of generational differences, where an older generation may hold to older value-orientations while another is already committed to certain technological innovations learned in mission or government schools.

Still another technique is to record the day-by-day statements made by people of a community, and subject that material to a content analysis. Especially important are statements made by people in a community which are approving or disapproving of actual behavior. This can best be obtained by living among the people of a community and permitting them to express themselves without suggesting personal opinions. The goal-discriminations made in a community may be obtained in a similar manner. A more precise technique is to ask people about their aspirations for themselves, and for their children. The latter method in particular gives insights into the goals of people.

Analyzing Religious Values.   Viewing a community in terms of its values implies that there are very few aspects of daily living which do not also have a value aspect.[12] I want to call attention to the religious aspect of culture, which is often overlooked by the technician innovator as entering on the social and the value level. Among many people, religion is not only a belief, a creed or ritual but also aids in the adjustment of people to the unknown and uncontrollable. For instance, sometimes much of sickness and health is associated with spirits, with supernatural powers, which can only be controlled through magic, spells or ritual.

Traditional religious values also support the social status system of a group and provide the sanction for maintaining it. Changing these without adequate substitution may have detrimental effects.[13] The beliefs themselves are important, and if understood properly can greatly facilitate a program of change. Aside from beliefs, instrumentalities such as certain curing practices involving paraphernalia and ritual must be understood in their meaning and function. Finally, the role of those persons in the community who exercise these rituals, be they priests or shamans, must be appreciated. The vested interests of such practitioners make them powerful members of a local group. Often change is opposed precisely because it is said that it is against the will of God or some spirits. For instance, Tannous tells us that the installation of a village pump by outsiders in an Arab village failed, though it was a much needed sanitary improvement. But after patiently explaining that iron pipes do not spoil the taste of water, or quickly drain away the water, and after it was demonstrated that it was a labor-saving device, it was rejected. When the technicians finally quoted from the Koran that cleanliness was required from every faithful Moslem, and that man should do his best to avoid the danger of disease, the innovation was accepted.[14] To recognize that religion has a non-spiritual function as well as a spiritual one, suggests that an analysis of the values surrounding the whole complex of religion may be the solution to the successful introduction of socio-economic change.

The Way the Young Are Reared. In order to complete our analysis of a community we must also take into account the ways in which the young are reared or enculturated.[15] There is no society that does not have some mechanism for enculturation in the form of a system of education. Sometimes these are formal structures like schools, but more often they are only a part in the total enculturation process. In many societies there are so-called rites of passage, all of which serve not only to give a certain position to the individuals in the community, but perhaps more importantly to teach these individuals their new responsibilities which are part of the new social position.

That the personnel involved in the enculturation process are important may be illustrated by showing the implications this had for a housing program among an American Indian group. The tribe itself decided to undertake a housing betterment program. It introduced white type houses which were assigned to nuclear families. However, traditionally Ute families are extended and often include grandparents, whose primary duty is to rear the young grandchildren. The consequence of this educational arrangement was that they moved into the new house with their children and grandchildren. The new houses, adequate for small families, thus were overcrowded.[16]

There is a related problem. Those values which individuals learn from early childhood onward, especially if they are reinforced by kinship interaction, tend to be held more strongly than those acquired later in life. Thus, a knowledge of these values learned in childhood may shed light on activties which might be particularly resistant to change. This would suggest that a program of change should not be initiated in this area of cultural behavior.

Conclusions from the Analysis. In summary then, we have seen that there are three basic relationships which we must analyze: the man-to-nature, the man-to-man, the man-to-values. Although we have taken these separately, for purposes of exposition, we must recognize that they overlap and are constantly interrelated. It is for this reason that we sometimes speak of cultural systems. But it would be wrong to think these systems are either closed, or that everything in a community is part of that system or equally relevant to a program for socio-economic change. There are loose ends, but the aim is to discover patterns. Insofar as we begin to see the patterned relationships, we are dealing, I think, with a model that will be of great value to the missionary because it will provide him with insights into those aspects of a community that might present greatest resistance to a program and, on the other hand, those aspects that might be most susceptible to a development program. Perhaps the most important consequence of this knowledge is that those concerned with socio-economic betterment may begin where the people stand in their thinking, instead of beginning with preconceived plans that do not correspond with the ways of a people, their perceptions and their goals.

Another advantage of this approach to the study of a community is that it will provide a method for analysis once a

program has been initiated. It will alert the missionary to possible unexpected shifts in relationships. Unlike an engineering
problem where one deals with fixed quantities, in human engineering the units of analysis, whether individuals, groups or
values, tend to be in a constant state of change; the direction-
ality is often far from clear. Therefore an ongoing analysis of
a community, it seems, is as important as a prior study of the
community in which change is anticipated.

Reflections on Doctor Lang's Plan. As Doctor Lang completed the above presentation, Father Lawlor addressed Bishop
Blomjous: "It seems that at least occasionally missionaries who
have served for many years in an area have erroneous ideas
about what the people hold on certain things. How does this
come to pass?"

"Mainly," Bishop Blomjous replied, "because we have no
general background of social anthropology. As Doctor Lang
indicates, such a background would be extremely useful in
order that the missionary might interpret the facts that he
observes, not with a Western eye but through the eye of the
African or the Indian or the Chinese."

"If only the missionary would condition himself to the realization," stated Doctor Gladwin, "that he cannot take it for
granted that he will by general previous knowledge of life draw
the correct conclusions from what he experiences in an area
of alien culture! As an anthropologist I naturally believe that
systematic anthropological training is very valuable—I belong
to the union! However, I don't think it is a magic key. Anthropology doesn't possess any mysterious expertise that does more
than make observation more systematic and sharpen the individual's sensitivity to cultural differences.

"A perceptive missionary who is prepared to ask a series
of questions systematically can come very close to gaining the
knowledge of his people that an anthropologist would secure.
It is my conviction that if we build our program for social action
on the availability of experts we are going to be bankrupt. I
think it is a dangerous philosophy to hold that we can build

solely on the expert. To a large extent the majority of missionaries will have to be their own experts.

"There is a call for a mode of attack. This, I think, is what Doctor Lang in very brief outline is intending to give us. I think if the missionary in going into the field is given the proper opportunity to learn the language, including some basic understanding of linguistic analysis, and to learn the local culture, he can be his own anthropologist."

"Let me say briefly," added Father Fitzpatrick, "that I think the crucial point in our discussion is the question of culture. If you can give the missionary a real insight into what culture is, an opportunity to acquire this insight, a lot of the things that we are asking to have done here would be settled. One of the difficulties I have experienced lies in explaining to our Americans not what a foreign culture is but what our own American culture consists of. Most haven't the faintest idea of the structure and the system of the culture in which they themselves have been living.

"I think we must give our missionaries in the seminary an introduction into the nature of culture and an understanding of it. There should be, then, an orientation into their area culture before going to work in their assignment."

"I would like to put on record here," said Father Considine, "the plea of certain experienced men in the field, not that every missionary be trained as an anthropologist but that for every mission area we provide a missionary anthropologist to document a body of systematized anthropological data.

"A Bishop in southern Africa makes the assertion that in his territory the missionary practice on a number of important points would be different today if the pioneer missionaries who entered his area 90 years ago had the knowledge of the significance of local folk practices that his missionaries possess today. Basic errors, he says, have been made in the interpretation of these practices, errors that involved the condemnation of practices which could well have served as supports for Christian living.

"The proposal has been made that many parts of the Catholic world would do well to set aside one or two priests with four or five years of field experience, still young enough for university training, to study social anthropology and then document the culture of their areas for the benefit of their confreres not only of the present generation but for those to come."

"We must recognize," noted Louis Miniclier, "the increasingly important contribution of the social scientists. Probably every organization operating on a large scale in other cultures could increase its effectiveness if it employed on a regional basis a cultural anthropologist or another social scientist as an adviser and trouble-shooter."

For recommended reading, see Bibliography No. 4 and Periodicals, page 264.

REACTION TO THE
INTRODUCTION OF CHANGE

A Keener Insight into People. The priest desires to possess the most effective possible insight into people in order to accomplish best his work for souls. His spiritual training serves him well in this regard. But more and more priests are finding profit from studies in the behavioral sciences provided by our Catholic universities. Thus churchmen gain knowledge from the lessons on life presented by social anthropology, from the cultural and cross-cultural data assembled by sociology and from the behavioral data gathered by psychology.

For inter-cultural work such as the missionary career represents, the missionary's problem is often not one of gaining a knowledge of man's behavior *in general;* it is, rather, a question of knowledge of the behavior of a given specific people in the sector of the world where he is to exercise his apostolate. Pin-pointing education to meet this situation is not easy because societies vary so under each varying combination of circumstances. Hence the best equipment that can be recommended for a missionary is the attainment of a capacity for an intelligent insight into peoples whose customs differ from his own, an obtaining of the keenest possible knowledge of human behavior.

In complex modern societies such as is encountered in countries like Japan, it would seem that a missioner is best prepared by cross-cultural data, a great deal of it to be obtained from qualified teachers on location, regarding family, community, business, political contingencies, the life of the spirit. Such teachers are found in the disciplines of sociology, commerce, political science. In less evolved societies, such as the Indians of the Amazon or the natives of New Guinea, the social anthropologist would seem to be the man best geared to provide the help—if the missionary can find precisely the right man or his books. The pity is that, too often, gathering the necessary data must be limited to casual, unsystematic snatches of information picked up by the missionary without qualified assistance.

In seeking aid in this general field of learning about and teaching other peoples, the wise heads advise us not only to acquire abstract principles but to acquaint ourselves with numerous examples, which the sociologist calls learning situations. Doctor Thomas O'Dea, formerly Professor of Sociology at Fordham and now at the University of Utah, makes a contribution in valuable examples by citing four cases, two successes and two failures, which demonstrate efforts to improve the economic condition of local communities.

"The introduction of technological or socio-economic change in communities," declares Doctor O'Dea, "involves also a changing of people. In this regard I would like to emphasize the social-psychological dimension.

"As Carl Taylor indicates,[1] a project of change should represent a genuine felt need, a feasible proposal, and real participation by the local people. Let me emphasize the dimension of psychological depth.

"We must not have a highly intellectualized and verbalized notion of what learning means or of what attitude means in this context. We are trying to change very fundamental and often not very well-voiced orientations of people and this is not just an individual process; it is a group process. By working together in this situation, the people learn not only how to master techniques, not only how to solve the problem at hand, but they learn in part how problems in general are solved. They build up attitudes and social structures in the course of doing this, which place them in a position to handle another kind of problem the next time."

Doctor O'Dea's presentation follows.

A Study of Men's Attitudes toward Economic Cooperation

We begin by stating that those who wish to mobilize communities for intelligent self-improvement must be concerned with the process of changing fundamental aspirations and definitions of both what is desirable and what is feasible. They must in a word be concerned with effecting changes in people's attitudes.

Let us look at four small communities in which change was attempted, in order to see more concretely what this involves. In two of these communities the change was successfully carried through. In two of them it failed to be brought about. In two—one of which was successful and the other not—such change arose intrinsically. In the other two—likewise one successful and the other unsuccessful—it was introduced on the initiative of outsiders. As a result of examining these four cases briefly, it is hoped that some positive statements may be made about what is involved in changing people's attitudes.

Rimrock and Homestead. In the December 1953 issue of the *American Sociological Review,* Professor Evon Z. Vogt of Harvard University and I published a small study in which we compared two villages in New Mexico in which we had lived as participant observers and made community studies.[2] Each of these villages had a population of about 250 persons. One of them, the one in which I lived, was a Mormon community, which was given the pseudonym of Rimrock in the study. The other, settled by migrants from western Texas and Oklahoma in the 1930's, was called Homestead. The Mormon village, homogeneous in culture and religious affiliation, had been established in the late 1870's by missionaries from the Church of Jesus Christ of Latter-day Saints interested in proselytizing among the Navaho and Zuni Indians, and was gradually transformed into a residential agricultural community. Homestead was composed of people from one region of the country and hence its residents shared a common culture, but it was much divided in terms of religious belief and church membership. In both communities the family farm was the basic socioeconomic unit. One difference between the two communities was apparent to the casual observer. Rimrock people lived in a village clustered around the church, while Homstead farmers in the great majority lived on isolated farmsteads away from the center of the village.

This apparent difference was significant of deeper differences. The Rimrock Mormons engaged in irrigation farming so characteristic of Mormon communities and developed by the Mormons into a major strategic technique for living in the semi-arid region west of the 100th meridian. Homestead settlers engaged in dry-farming, a risky venture in that high area of the southern portion of the Colorado Plateau, where the prevailing elevations stand at 7,000 feet and where a steppe climate allows an average annual precipitation of 14 inches that, moreover, varies most unreliably from year to year. The two villages are forty miles apart, and with the man-made exception of irrigation in the former, may be said to share a common ecological setting.

Sharing a common environment, these two communities also faced common problems, but the difference in their individual responses was striking in the extreme. Both villages faced what was called locally a "tight land situation," which meant that there was, for a number of reasons beyond our present scope, no room for much needed expansion. Both villages had village streets that were badly in need of repair. Both villages required some local recreational forms which were met in each case by intrinsic responses. Finally, both villages were given an opportunity to expand local school facilities. Let us now look at the way these common problems were handled in each case.

1) **The Tight Land Situation:** *a) Rimrock.* "Rimrock Mormons, feeling themselves 'gathered,' dislike having to migrate to non-Mormon areas. However, after World War II the 32 returned veterans faced a choice between poverty and underemployment or leaving the community. This situation became the concern of the Church and was discussed in the upper lay priesthood bodies in the village. It was decided to buy land to enable the veterans to remain. The possibilities of land purchase in the area were almost nonexistent, when unexpectedly the opportunity to buy some 38 sections presented itself. At the time, the village did not have the needed 10,000 dollars for the down payment, so the sum was borrowed from the Cooperative Security Corporation, a Church Welfare Plan agency, and the land was purchased. The patterns revealed here—community concern over a community problem, and appeal to and reception of aid from the general authorities of the Church—are typically Mormon. However, Mormon cooperation did not end here. Instead of breaking up the purchased land into plots to be individually owned and farmed, the parcel was kept as a unit, and a cooperative Rimrock Land and Cattle Company was formed. The company copied and adapted the form of a mutual irrigation company. Shares were sold in the village, each member being limited to two. A quota of cattle per share per year to be run on the land and a quota of bulls relative to cows were established. The cattle are privately owned, but the land is owned and managed cooperatively. The calves are the property of the owners of the cows. The project, which has not been limited to veterans, supplements other earnings sufficiently to keep most of the veterans in the village." [3]

b) Homestead. "In 1934 the Federal Security Administration, working in conjunction with the Land Use Division of the

Department of Agriculture, proposed a 'unit re-organization plan.' This plan would have enabled the Homesteaders to acquire additional tracts of land and permit them to run more livestock and hence depend less upon the more hazardous economic pursuit of dry-land pinto bean farming. It called for the use of government funds to purchase large ranches near the Homestead area which would be managed cooperatively by a board of directors selected by the community. The scheme collapsed while it was still in the planning stages, because it was clear that each family expected to acquire its own private holdings on the range and that a cooperative would not work in Homestead." [4]

2) **The Gravelling of the Village Streets:** *a) Rimrock.* "The streets of Rimrock were in bad repair in the fall of 1950. That summer a construction company had brought much large equipment into the area to build and gravel a section of a state highway which runs through the village. Before this company left, taking its equipment with it, villagers, again reacting through the Church organization, decided that the village should avail itself of the opportunity and have the town's streets gravelled. This was discussed in the Sunday priesthood meeting and announced at the Sunday sacrament meeting. A meeting was called for Monday evening, and each household was asked to send a representative. The meeting was well attended, and although not every family had a member present, practically all were represented at least by proxy. There was considerable discussion, and it was finally decided to pay 800 dollars for the job which meant a 20 dollar donation from each family. The local trader paid a larger amount, and, within a few days after the meeting, the total amount was collected. Only one villager raised objections to the proceedings. Although he was a man of importance locally, he was soon silenced by a much poorer man who invoked Mormon values of progress and cooperation and pledged to give 25 dollars, which was 5 dollars above the norm." [5]

b) Homestead. "During the winter of 1949–50 the construction company which was building the highway through
Rimrock was also building a small section of highway north of
Homestead. The construction company offered to gravel the
streets of Homestead center if the residents who lived in the village would cooperatively contribute enough funds for the
purpose. This community plan was rejected by the Homesteaders, and an alternative plan was followed. Each of the
operators of several of the service institutions—including the
two stores, the bar, and the post office—independently hired
the construction company truck drivers to haul a few loads of
gravel to be placed in front of his own place of business, which
still left the rest of the village streets a sea of mud in rainy
weather." [6]

3) **Recreation:** *a) Rimrock.* "The Mormons have always
considered dancing to be an important form of recreation—
in fact a particularly Mormon form of recreation. Almost every
Friday evening a dance is held in the village church house.
These dances are family affairs and are opened and closed with
prayer. They are part of the general Church recreation program
and are paid for by what is called locally 'the budget.' The
budget refers to the plan under which villagers pay 15 dollars
per family per year to cover a large number of entertainments,
all sponsored by the Church auxiliary organization for youth,
the Young Men's Mutual Improvement Association, and the
Young Women's Mutual Improvement Association. The budget
payment admits all members of the family to such entertainments.

"Observation of these dances over a six months period did
not reveal any tension or fighting. Smoking and drinking are
forbidden to loyal Mormons, and those who smoked did so
outside and away from the building. At dances held in the local
school there has been evidence of drinking, at times fighting
has resulted from the presence of non-villagers. But on the
whole the Rimrock dances are peaceful family affairs." [7]

b) Homestead. "As in Rimrock, the village dances in

Homestead are important focal points for community activity. These affairs take place several times a year in the schoolhouse and are always well attended. But while the dances in Rimrock are well co-ordinated activities which carry through the evening, the dances in Homestead often end when tensions between rival families result in fist-fights. And there is always the expectation in Homestead that a dance (or other cooperative activity such as picnic or rodeo) may end at any moment and the level of activity be reduced to the component nuclear families which form the only solid core of social organization within the community." [8]

4) **The Construction of a High School Gymnasium:** *a) Rimrock.* "In 1951 a plan for the construction of a high school gymnasium was presented to the Rimrock villagers. Funds for materials and for certain skilled labor would be provided from state school appropriations, providing that the local residents would contribute the labor for construction. The plan was discussed in a Sunday priesthood meeting in the church and later meetings were held both in the church and in the schoolhouse. Under the leadership of the principal of the school (who is also a member of the higher priesthood), arrangements were made whereby each able-bodied man in the community would either contribute at least 50 hours of labor or 50 dollars (the latter to be used to hire outside laborers) toward the construction. The original blueprint was extended to include a row of classrooms for the high school around the large central gymnasium.

"Work on the new building began in late 1951, continued through 1952, and is now (in 1953) nearing completion. The enterprise was not carried through without difficulties. A few families were sympathetic at first but failed to contribute full amounts of either labor or cash, and some were unsympathetic from the start. The high school principal had to keep reminding villagers about their pledges to support the enterprise. But in the end the project was successful, and it represented an important effort on the part of the majority." [9]

b) Homestead. "In 1950 the same plan for the construction of a new gymnasium was presented to the Homesteaders
as was presented to the Morman village of Rimrock. As noted
above, this plan was accepted by the community of Rimrock,
and the new building is now nearing completion. But the plan
was rejected by the residents of Homestead at a meeting in the
summer of 1950, and there were long speeches to the effect
that 'I've got to look after my own farm and my own family
first; I can't be up here in town building a gymnasium.' Later
in the summer additional funds were provided for labor; and
with these funds adobe bricks were made, the foundation was
dug, and construction was started—the Homesteaders being
willing to work on the gymnasium on a purely business basis at
a dollar an hour. But as soon as the funds were exhausted,
construction stopped. Today a partially completed gymnasium,
and stacks of some 10,000 adobe bricks disintegrating slowly
with the rains, stand as monuments to the individualism of the
Homesteaders." [10]

The Role of Group Attitude in Change.   How are we to account for the enviable success in one case and the tremendous
failure in the other, in terms of their respective responses to
these challenging problems? In the study quoted the authors
suggest that the differences are to be understood in terms of
the culture and social structure of the two communities. In the
terms we have used here we may say that in one case there
existed attitudes favorable to cooperation for self-help, and
that these attitudes were embodied in the organizational structure of the Mormon Church which was a live organization in
which villagers really participated. The Mormon Church structure is one of a lay priesthood embracing all adult males not
deemed unworthy and auxiliary organizations which activate
women and youth. Hence in Rimrock attitudes and social
structures capable of and predisposed to cooperation existed.
Moreover, a genuine indigenous leadership was present. These
assets are the precipitate of Mormon historical experience out
of which they emerged. Moreover, the strong cooperative tra-

dition which embodies these values is expressed in explicit Mormon religious tenets.

Mormon attitudes were such that any call for cooperation for the common welfare was felt by the individual to oblige him unless he should be able to show cause why it should not. The Mormon was accustomed to thinking of betterment as a positive value and of group action as a way of achieving betterment.

In Homestead, on the other hand, there were no real social bonds that extended far beyond the individual farm family. These attitudes no doubt derived from the experience of life in Texas and Oklahoma, and they were also reinforced by the experience of migration to, and settlement in, Homestead. Settlement has been fundamentally an individual family affair. The attitudes learned by Homesteaders in their past experience implied, "Every family for itself." The social structure with its weak extra-familial organizations reflected this state of affairs. In contrast to the Mormon, the typical Homesteader felt that a call for the general welfare did not oblige him unless he could be convinced that such was in fact the case.

Importance of Learning by Doing. Let us note again that the Mormon community has in the Church a structural embodiment of its basic attitudes. It had ready to hand an institutional structure through which the cooperative action toward which the people inclined could be made effective. The past experience of the Mormons was a series of learning situations in which they developed attitudes favorable to cooperation. Moreover, such learning situations had produced the kinds of organization and the presence of genuine leadership necessary for future initiative. In Homestead no such organization and leadership existed. As extra-familial cooperation made no strong demands upon the conscience of the individual, so also there existed no social structures beyond the individual farm family that could mobilize the people for action.

It is most important that what we are talking about here be understood in more than a formal sense. We are talking about two very profound aspects of human life. Fundamental attitudes are learned in group experiences and they are a basic part of the structure of individual personality. We stress again that the most important aspects of this learning are not verbal. It is learning by doing or, better perhaps, learning by living the attitudes learned in terms of common activities. Such learning is often reinforced by verbal communication as well, but mere verbal communication without this deeper stratum of learning by living will be of little practical effect.

Taylor's Four Stages as Test.   It is interesting to look at these cases in terms of Taylor's four stages. In Rimrock all four stages are to be found, but their order is not quite the same as in the Indian communities with which Taylor is concerned. Taylor's fourth stage is seen as first in Rimrock: "The fourth step in Community Development is the creation of groups or community aspirations and the determination to undertake additional improvement projects." The Mormon experience has long since created this in Rimrock. Such a precipitate of past learning is not to be found in Homestead. Moreover, the kinds of attitudes which Homesteaders have developed in their past learning make it very difficult for them to carry through new experiences that would alter their attitudes. Note the circular causality in the processes in both cases. Attitudes make possible activities, activities create and reinforce attitudes. In Rimrock favorable attitudes make possible successful activities which reinforce favorable attitudes; in Homestead unfavorable attitudes cause activities that fail, and failure reinforces unfavorable attitudes.

Cornell Project in Peru.   We now turn to the third example. A few years ago the Cornell-Peru Project selected an ancient estate in the high country of Peru which it turned into a laboratory for the study of social change. This estate, the Hacienda Vicos, inhabited by over 2,000 Indians, represented a continuation of a social form that went back to the conquest by the Spaniards. According to the rigidly traditionalistic hacienda system the Indians are serfs and the patron a lord, supposedly their benefactor and all too often their exploiter as well. The

Indians worked three days a week without pay for the hacienda and received in return rights to farm a few acres as well as to use water, graze animals and gather wood. The hacienda is the center and circumference of the peon's life, and church services and the celebration of various fiestas take place there. There the Indians are born, they work and raise their families and engage in what meager recreation is available, there they die, and there their remains are laid away in the earth. In times of distress the peons turn to the patron and always they leave all important decisions to him.

Hacienda Vicos, with 35,000 acres, was in a state of decay when the Cornell-Peru Project acquired it. Its lands were eroded and its people hungry and suffering from disease. It had passed from one lessee to another over the decades, and the Cornell group conceived the idea of purchasing it and operating it under the traditional system, assuming to itself the role and function of the patron. In this way the going system would not be disrupted and the confusion and anxiety resulting from such disruption could be avoided. Moreover, the social scientists saw that this method of operation would give them a chance to understand the life of the Indians and its problems as these exist within the customary patterns of life. Acting as patron, the staff of the Cornell-Peru Project felt that they would be able to persuade the Indians to change their farming techniques to more improved methods and lead them to a higher standard of living. They intended to plow back the returns of increased production into further improvements. They hoped by working within the old established forms of social life to lead the Indians to a better life and develop among them the capacity for self-help and self-reliance. In the words of John and Mary Collier, "The change would develop from the bottom up, not be imposed from the top." [11]

The hacienda offered a formidable challenge to such aspirations. Only 2 percent of its people were literate and most of them spoke the Indian language rather than Spanish. The Colliers state, "Hunger was their chronic condition, and drinking almost their only recreation." Epidemics were common. Moreover, the neighboring mestizos looked down upon them and they returned the condescension with distrust and suspicion.

Old Institutions Bar Change. The Cornell group enlisted the cooperation of the Peruvian Government and its agencies and set out to increase food production as the first step. Blight had recently so devastated the potato crop that peons were eating seed potatoes. They were in fact digging them up out of the ground to eat them. They were also selling their cattle and stealing from the hacienda. The staff took the proper scientific measures to survey the problem, obtained blight resistant seed as well as insecticide and fertilizer from agricultural experimental stations and offered these things to the Indians at cost. The response was disappointing, for few Indians bought any and not much attention was paid to the innovations. The staff saw that the people had no money to purchase these things and proceeded to work out a credit plan which proposed to give seed, fertilizer and insecticide in advance, in return for receiving half of the crop at the time of harvest.

The staff utilized the weekly meetings of the *mayorales* who were the leaders of the community and served as foremen over the other peons in their work. The *mayorales* listened to the new plan of the staff but shook their heads, declaring that it would not work. It soon became apparent that these local leaders were not merely sceptical. Behind their doubt lurked real hostility, for they feared that such a change would threaten their own leading positions in the community. Vested interests were being placed in danger and the *mayorales* in defense of their own statuses were resisting.[12]

Not only were the attitudes of the people formed in a long history of hacienda life unprepared for the innovations of the staff, but the social structure was such that the leaders of the peons felt their position threatened. Change very often threatens some people in the community. When it threatens those well established in the social structure, they can become a formidable force of resistance and opposition.

Patience and Prudence at Work. Yet the Cornell-Peru staff decided to present the idea to the weekly meeting of the peons that was customarily held for the assignment of work. The Indians seemed to take to the proposition and excited discussion took place. But when one of the *mayorales* spoke in opposition the common opinion changed and turned cool. Of the 125 men present only 9 signed up to cooperate. Later on, an additional 22 signed up privately.

Yet the majority held aloof and opposition increased. Rumors of a fantastic kind, possibly instigated by neighboring landowners and mestizos, spread, insinuating that this was some plan to cheat and exploit the peons. It was even suggested in one of the rumors that the gringos intended to fatten the Indians on potatoes and then boil down their bodies for oil for American machinery. And in a situation where the people saw in change the threat of the unknown, such rumors found credence. Hysteria developed in the face of an unstructured and threatening future.

The project managers answered this response by having the Peruvian scientists who were working with them attempt to counter these fears. One of them visited scores of people in their homes and in the fields to explain matters, and as a result signed up 9 more. This brought the total number of participants to 40, but of these only 17 actually took seed and entered into the deal proposed by the Cornell-Peru group. The Colliers state, "Most of these (participating) were the poorest of the poor; against the disapproval of their wives in some instances they decided to take the chance to save themselves from starvation and improve their position." [13]

Good Crops and Fair Treatment Win. The participants were expected to follow scientific measures and were instructed on techniques. Despite some mistakes the project went forward. The majority looked upon those who cooperated as deluded and knew they would be disappointed. But when the harvest came it was the participants who won the day, for each of them had doubled the usual yield of potatoes. Each man divided his crop into two piles, one for himself and the other for the patron. The project staff then did what was perhaps most unexpected to the Indians. They invited the farmer to take his choice of piles. It is hard to think of anything better calculated to build up a relationship of trust. The next year 85 peons, including one of the *mayorales* who had been actively opposed, took part and some of the neighboring mestizos asked to be allowed to come in on it. The third year 135 Indians took part. By 1955 sharecropping was abolished. The Indians had become skilled enough in the new methods to take the full risk of buying seed and carrying out the agricultural operations.

This reform led to others: branding cattle to control stealing and quarreling over the identity of cows; rehabilitation of buildings including dwellings; and eventually the construction of a school and a health program. Even the attitudes of the neighbors changed and respect replaced the old condescension. Now the weekly meetings of the *mayorales* and the peons involve genuine discussion where both can air grievances and make decisions. Of course, the first difficulties were not the only ones, but the direction of development has been consistently toward self-reliance and a better standard of life. At the same time, the experimental hacienda has been a worthwhile laboratory for acquiring scientific knowledge through observation and experiment with respect to social change.

Analysis of Success.   In this case we have an example of deeply embedded attitudes and strongly entrenched social structures. The peons had no abilities for initiative and there had not been for generations the kinds of learning situations in which they could have been developed. They had no reason to believe things could be made better. They had every reason to distrust change. The structure of the hacienda was the only one they or their forefathers had even known for a very long time. Constantly reinforced attitudes and their concomitant social structures become extremely fixed, and this was certainly the case here. Moreover, vested interests (the feelings of the *mayorales* that their meaningful function required things to remain the same) in the leading positions opposed the changes proposed by the staff.

What is most surprising about this whole case is that, despite all the disadvantages under which they had to labor, the staff acting as haciendado were able to make a revolution and to make it while working not to break down but to utilize the existing social structures of the traditional hacienda system. How they did this is worth a moment of attention.

Fulfilling a Strongly Felt Need. The staff acting as patron had some structured position in terms of traditional attitudes for initiating change. But they had the connecting link with the people—the *mayorales*—against them. They were forced to circumvent this level of structure and used Peruvian colleagues to appeal directly to the people. As a result they got only the poorest group to be interested. Having to rely on the poorest members of the community, in initiating change in opposition to established leaders, is to be in a very weak position and possibly one that might have been untenable had the staff not had the structured position of patron.

Moreover, the staff did not engage in conflict with the *mayorales,* which might have produced a revolutionary situation and destroyed the old structure without establishing a new one in its place. Rather it combined patient explanation with carrying out the plan with those willing to cooperate. The cooperators were those without rank and prestige and as such were just those people in the village least likely to influence others. But this weakness in social position of the cooperators was compensated for, not only by the staff's position as patron, but especially by the genuineness of the need the plan had set out to fill. These people were hungry. A doubled harvest could not but be impressive to men in those circumstances. Taylor's admonition of the necessity for meeting a real need was certainly well illustrated by the conduct of the staff here. Note that they took the time and effort to figure out what was feasible and realistic in the circumstances. Imagine what a poor harvest would have meant!

Demonstrating against Exploitation. Moreover, the staff utilized the occasion of the harvest as a learning situation for replacing old attitudes of distrust with feelings of confidence. Cooperation demands reciprocal attitudes that will form a fabric of mutual trust. When the staff not only gave the peons half of the double harvest but gave them their choice of piles of potatoes, age-old attitudes were undermined at their very foundations. This upset the old expectations of exploitation. It is a dramatic example of a good learning situation.

Had the plan not filled a real need or had it been unsuccessful, nothing would have been accomplished and eventually the Cornell-Peru people would have had to pack up and go home. Realism in terms of people's needs, realism in terms of what actually can be done in the circumstances, patience with established attitudes, intelligence in utilizing opportunities to get across new attitudes, skill in using existing social structures and scrupulous fairness—these elements went a long way to make the efforts of the staff a success.

Demonstrating against Authoritarianism. It must have been difficult for the staff to utilize its position as patron to get its project started without "pulling rank"—acting too authoritarianly—when the going was tough. It must have been a real temptation to enter into open conflict with the *mayorales*. But the staff did not make these mistakes or if it did it corrected them in sufficient time. Agents of change must avoid a crystallization of antagonistic attitudes toward them in a large section of the community, although some such crystallization in some parts of the population cannot always be avoided. The balance of forces is what is important, as well as keeping open the pathways to further learning. Too great a reliance on authority or too much willingness to enter into conflict might well have hardened the attitudes of the great majority against the plan. A real sensitivity to what differences in culture and social structure meant concretely enabled the staff to gauge its way without serious mistakes that could have threatened the whole plan. Moreover, as the participators increased they were involved in the actual working out of the projects to be undertaken, although this was not possible initially. Thus they gradually learned to share initiative with the patron, which was something unheard of.

Application of Taylor's Four Stages. If we examine this case for a moment in terms of Taylor's four stages, we note all four are to be seen, but that at the beginning the plan could only meet his criteria very inadequately. A real need was easily discernible but the first planning had to be done by the staff. The attitudes of the people as well as the scientific nature of the first step in this case made real involvement impossible until a plan had been drawn up. Even after that, anything like a complete mobilization of resources remained impossible until several successful harvests had their psychological effect. Yet, as time went on, Taylor's first three stages began to be seen in terms adequate to his own criteria. Moreover, the fourth step —that of preparing the group to be able to take initiative and creating new aspirations—was also being brought into existence.

This case illustrates very well what has been said about the importance of group learning situations. It shows, moreover, how agents of change can utilize even quite inappropriate structures in trying to achieve this, and it suggests some of the problems that such utilization can entail.

Failure among Papago Indians. Our final example is one in which enthusiastic and idealistic Indian Service personnel attempted to introduce a change in farming technique among the Papago Indians some twenty years ago.[14] These officials discovered that Mexicans in the State of Sonora used a system of digging basins which later served as gardens to preserve meager rainfall and provide sufficient moisture to crops. They thought that such a system would improve productivity on their own reservation and decided to introduce the system there. This was meant to supplant the traditional system long in use, a system that involved flooding the fields where the arroyos spread out and thereby utilizing the small rainfall. The Papago Indians built low earthen dikes to spread the water from arroyos over the area to be planted as well as to divert water from the gullies. When rain came these constructions took care of water distribution without human labor and attention. The new idea as it worked in Sonora made use of flood waters by holding the water in an artificial pool and letting it seep into the ground creating moisture at a considerable depth. After this the ground in the pool or *bolsa* (meaning purse or pocket in Spanish) is plowed, harrowed and seed sown. The soil is cultivated and kept loose to prevent moisure from drying out.

There seemed to be good ecological reasons to believe that this system would be superior to the older traditional one. It appeared to offer a more secure water supply and the learning of the new technique did not seem very complicated. It involved learning to use retainer dikes in place of the traditional spreader dikes. The Indian Agency members decided to introduce the new way and, moved with sincere desire to improve the life of the Indians, actually put a good deal of emphasis upon it and thus to a considerable degree staked their own reputation on its prospects.

However, the new system also demanded that the new gates be operated in time of rain by human operators. This was not convenient for the Indian farmers and caused difficulties. A way out seemed to offer itself by having people reside near the gates. But other Indian families who had long-recognized grazing rights to the land there objected. These families had relinquished some of their grazing land for the construction of the *bolsa* and did not feel that they should be asked to give up more. This stalemate discouraged the cooperators or *bolseros*. But the officials who had constructed the *bolsas* convinced people to carry on. Moreover, some people began to use the *bolsa* as an irrigation scheme. Since the *bolsas* were unevenly levelled this also caused difficulty. Furthermore, in constructing the *bolsas* topsoil had been removed to make the dikes, thus removing the most fertile earth from the gardens.

Productivity from the *bolsas* was low and the experience was not an encouraging one for the *bolseros*. By the end of the war no one in Papago was farming a *bolsa*. However, in 1946 after seven years of effort that eventuated in failure, a new extension agent came to Papago and he made an attempt to salvage the plan. He got an important member of the District Council to cooperate. At the agent's instigation this man bought a tractor and set out to put his own *bolsa* assignment in good order. The first year grasshoppers ate his crop despite the fact that the agent supplied him with grasshopper poison. In 1947 the councilman tried again, and again his crops failed and the next year he did not try. The plan had failed again.

Observations on the Failure. Several important observations can be made with respect to this unsuccessful attempt to introduce economic and technological change. First of all, did the *bolsas* meet a felt need of the Papago people or did they represent simply a brainstorm of the "Anglo" officials? Secondly, was the *bolsa* method really applicable to the Papago ecology and did the introducers find out all they needed to know in this respect before starting? Actually the *bolsa* system had worked in commercial farming in Sonora, and Papago people were engaged in subsistence farming. The attitudes of commercial farmers are likely to be quite different from those of subsistence farmers in terms of orientation toward work, toward returns and toward change. Also the ecological setting in Papago was not really the same as in Sonora, with respect to times of frost and sources of water and in other important respects. Finally, technological problems were not all handled well, as can be seen in the removal of the topsoil.

Actually, in giving up the *bolsa* system, the Indians simply went back to a way of farming which they knew better and from which they got more production with less expenditure of effort.

Taylor's Four Stages Not Applied. Carl C. Taylor's pre-

requisites of meeting a felt need and feasibility of the innovation were not met in this case. Moreover, the administrators
did not involve the local people in the planning. They went to
Sonora themselves to see how the *bolsa* system worked but
they did not take any Indians with them. Had the Indians been
involved in the planning, it seems highly likely that many of
the functional difficulties that later plagued the system could
have been foreseen and avoided. The Indians could have helped
adapt the idea to local conditions. As a result the Indians were
not wholeheartedly motivated to participate, and therefore the
kind of situation in which they might develop new attitudes
was not created. As a matter of fact, the Papago farmers always
looked upon the *bolsas* as something belonging to the "Anglos"
and their culture, and so they were never integrated into the
ongoing Papago social structure.

The project failed for a large number of reasons. Basically
it was because the technique was not fully understood by those
who introduced it, and because they did not really enlist the
Papago farmers in the planning in a way that would have permitted them to make it their own and also enabled them to
adapt the technique to local needs. It had not been realistically
related to a felt need and it had not created real Indian participation. None of Taylor's criteria had been met. The innovation had not been related to and involved within the Papago
social structure in a way comparable to that by which the
Cornell-Peru staff had related their proposals to the ongoing
hacienda social system. The outside agents had failed completely to involve the Indians in any real sense. Unlike the
Cornell group, they did not utilize the social structure of the
administered group to create conditions that could provide a
real learning situation, in terms of the group developing new
attitudes while adopting and adapting the new methods.

Lessons from the Four Cases.   These four cases illustrate
the kinds of situations under which change succeeds and fails.
Whether the change be intrinsic or extrinsic in origin, its
chances for success are dependent upon the kinds of attitudes

and social relations accepted as customary by the people to whom it is introduced. When previous experience has created attitudes and the social institutions that embody them, which are prepared for innovation as in the Mormon case, change can be successfully introduced. Where, as in Homestead, this is not the case, failure is almost bound to result. In such cases, successful change requires some outside agency to supply what the community itself does not have. The outside agency must, however, utilize realistically the existing attitudes and social structure or it too will fail.

We found in Peru that even in what looked like the most recalcitrant configuration of attitudes and social structure, intelligent action calculated to introduce realistic answers to real needs, when combined with equally realistic measures to provide appropriate learning situations for the changing of attitudes, can bring success, whereas in the Papago situation failure to meet problems brought failure of the efforts after change. Since mission personnel will often be placed in the position of acting as such outside agents of change or as cooperating partners of such agencies, the understanding of these problems and of what is involved in changing attitudes is correspondingly very important.

Conclusions for Missionaires. In addition to the main points already sufficiently stressed in the foregoing, some remarks addressed to mission personnel may be added in conclusion:

1) It is important to know how to analyze the situation in which change is to be introduced in terms of the strategic elements—the operating variables—involved. This calls attention to the need for organizations concerned with mission work to pay attention to the social sciences and to the training of all personnel in some acquaintance with what is involved in social science fields. It further points to the need to have *some* people in the organization who are experts in these matters and can be utilized by people in the field as resource persons. Ongoing research to build up a fund of experience and knowledge and to

train individuals by participation is important in this respect, and larger mission organizations should give such matters serious thought. Programs of cooperation with universities and other research agencies offer many ways of working out this kind of thing concretely. One way is to be found in systematic observation and critical analysis of actual field experiences.

2) It is most important for mission personnel, especially religious, not to overestimate the importance of verbal communication. It must be faced that the highly verbal educational processes so characteristic of Catholic seminaries often create a tendency to "overintellectualize" and see things too much in terms of abstract categories. This can lead to failure to comprehend the real attitudes among people and to overestimate the manifest content of verbal communication. People who are the products of such education must often make a special effort to sensitize themselves to the other levels of human thought and feeling.

3) It is also important for mission personnel to understand that social groups are functional wholes and that as such their integration is of quite another kind than the integration of abstract ideas. Moreover, changes introduced with what seem like good verbal reasons may work in the concrete situation to elicit quite unintended responses unless there is a real understanding of the variables involved in the concrete situation itself. Here too, "overintellectualization" can create blinders, and as a result of blinders, blunders.

4) The kind of sensitivity meant in points 2 and 3 above applies especially to the understanding in some depth of strange and foreign cultures in their concrete settings.

5) Mission personnel must become aware that much of the training of the religious is highly paternalistic and does not make the person who has gone through such training sensitive to the process of eliciting real cooperation. Clerical dress and religious habit can serve as an unvoiced "trigger" for eliciting dependent attitudes that can interfere with the kind of cooperation Taylor has pointed out as necessary.

6) Those who would act as agents of change must not yield to the subtle temptation to control every phase of the process "for the people's own good" because only they, the agents, "really understand what is necessary or right." They must be able to relinquish initiative as they develop it in others. This can be difficult for those whose educational training has been highly paternalistic.

7) And finally in relation to the first point these needs may demand some educational changes in preparing personnel for the field. While religious are taught to ask self-critical questions with respect to certain kinds of moral issues, they are often not given the kind of training that would make them good critical observers of themselves operating in the kind of a situation that acting as agents of change requires. Here, too, introduction to social science techniques through participation in real field research is something that needs serious consideration. The idea that the fruits of a body of knowledge can be appropriated and used without real appropriation of and mastery of the concomitant techniques and ways of seeing the problems can be highly deceptive.

For recommended reading, see Bibliography No. 5, page 268.

Socio-Economic Improvement of the Family

Mr. James R. Dumpson is the first Negro to reach the high post of Commissioner of Welfare in New York City. In addition to his consuming engrossment for many years in the social welfare problems of the largest city in the world, Mr. Dumpson found it possible, shortly after World War II, to spend a number of years with an international commission in Pakistan, where he obtained invaluable insights into the special tasks which face missionaries in underdeveloped lands.

"I feel at ease and not the least on the defensive as I present my contribution on the economic improvement of the family," Mr. Dumpson explained, "because I do so within the context of the knowledge of contemporary social work strengthened by my Catholic philosophy of life.

"In the young profession of social work, an honest search is under way to assist individuals, groups and communities in the achievement of a better life adjustment. American social workers are at times shaken and react with defensiveness when challenged by the other disciplines on certain dearly cherished concepts. And the defensiveness is heightened because for many there is not agreement on the origin, nature and destiny of man."

Christian Concept of the Family. With this Christian comprehension of the principles governing the social field, Mr. Dumpson is well prepared to point the way to the young missionary in matters of economic betterment of the family.

"One of the most typical examples," he stated, "of close relationship between Revelation and natural ethics is furnished in the Christian doctrine of the family. Very few new principles were supplied by Revelation. About the only social innovation in the New Testament was the establishment of the absolute indissolubility of marriage. This was in addition to Christ's religious act of raising marriage to the dignity of a sacrament.

"Christianity can be said to have revived the human tradition or concept of the family basic to all civilized peoples. Indeed, no institution is closer to nature than the family. It is an elementary society supported closely by primal instincts proceeding from the development of human life itself. A fairly identical family organization is found both among civilized peoples and those peoples closest to nature.

"The term 'family' has, it is true, certain different connotations from society to society, from country to country. However, irrespective of this difference, the well-being of the individual is inextricably bound to the family group. My approach, then, recognizes the family as the basic unit in any society. Irrespective of the cultural characteristics of the society or of the particular stage of its social or economic developments, the family is the chief medium of assuring and improving the dignity and well-being of the individual. This is a fact whether we are viewing the more highly developed societies or the peoples of our more immediate concern, in underdeveloped countries."

Intrinsic Inferiority Not Implied. All-important in this day, when burgeoning new nations are highly sensitive to any implication that we accuse them of social inferiority, is the point made by Mr. Dumpson, that differing family practices do not necessarily imply inferior practices.

"It is important to stress the essential content of the phrase 'underdeveloped countries,' " he said. "The stranger to these countries must recognize that the characterization of a people as 'underdeveloped' springs from a norm of societal development that is of Western definition. It reflects the Western value system.

"But no country is completely and totally 'underdeveloped.' Countries of the Middle East, as countries of the Far East and in Latin America, are economically and industrially underdeveloped. But there are other areas of human endeavor in which they are in a stage of superior development. Their cultural heritage is replete with values, patterns of relationships and practices that might well be incorporated in Western patterns of living.

"I suggest that any approach to improving family living in the so-called underdeveloped countries include a conviction that no one culture is intrinsically better than another. Nevertheless we start with the premise that change must occur if the individual is to realize his full potential and his rightful destiny.

"Where change is indicated, it must be remembered that to effect it for one cultural factor or value is to set in motion a rearrangement of the entire value constellation with the possible danger of causing personal or group chaos and disorganization.

"The missionary, I would say, should avoid engendering conflict about those values that are not immediately important or those that are outside his area of function. As a helping person he must know that constructive change in a person or group is brought about principally through inner-felt need, which often creates internal dissension and unrest. And it is always brought about by contact with difference, the difference represented by the missionary whose effectiveness is enhanced by the value placed on him as a person by those whom he would help."

Interdependent Social and Economic Program. The program for family betterment which follows is outlined by Mr. Dumpson and represents the imaginative thinking found among social work leaders. It is grounded on the principle that one cannot seek to raise the levels of living of a people without recognizing that economic and social progress are interdependent. Each makes its contribution. Ideally, the social policy of a country should rest on the indivisibility of social and economic progress. In planning for economic development, each element should include planning for a corollary element in social development.

Hence the essential necessity of the missionary's interest in the influences that affect the life of the family economically. He cannot turn his back on the economic with some such comment as, "Economics is only for the materialistic-minded." The world of economics impinges vitally on the same family life which religion seeks to build and guide. To seek to ignore it disdainfully would represent in effect some form of crude Manicheism that would construct two separate worlds of good and evil.

Basic Components of Family Living. Socio-economic development of the family presumes a clear delineation of at least nine basic social components of family living: 1) food, 2) housing, 3) health, 4) nutrition, 5) education, 6) employment and labor, 7) leisure, 8) family civil rights (human freedom), 9) religion.

But much more must be included. One must record the total body of experiences that affect both the material and moral well-being of the family.

Particularly in underdeveloped countries there are considerable non-monetary factors in the economy, of which we may mention a few:

1 *Self-supplied needs:* foods raised in the family garden, cloth woven at the family loom;
2 *Institutionally-supplied needs:* goods and services in terms of education and health available through organized efforts of government or voluntary charitable organizations;
3 *Mutual agencies:* goods and services available through social security programs.

These non-monetary factors promote family betterment in proportion to the strength of the economy behind them, but to a great extent they depend as well on the capacity of the given family to employ them:

1 the educational level of the family;
2 family resourcefulness in using the *total* family income;
3 the degree of practicality in the goals of the family;
4 the degree of loose family spending habits, or the existence of inter-family group competitiveness which results in continually mounting debts.

Moral, social or psychological elements figure greatly in these non-monetary factors which influence what the family produces and what it refrains from spending. Thus it is important, in considering socio-economic family development, to think of non-economic factors such as:

1 the quality of social relations and personal adjustment within the family;
2 the levels of appreciation of cultural and educational values;
3 the degree of opportunities enjoyed through possession of human rights; the absence of discrimination because of race, sex, caste or religion.

The missionary will see immediately that family betterment touches large phases of life quite distinct from the popularly conceived yardstick of remunerative jobs.

Organization for Socio-Economic Betterment. Let us turn to consideration of the essential guideposts (A-F) to organized efforts in improving the socio-economic condition of the family.

(A) First, we must protect and preserve the various sources of livelihood available to the family:

1 protection of ownership or tenure of land;
2 protection of the family's craft or of the village's cottage industries;
3 assistance in the development of programs to improve methods of work;
4 stimulation of local markets for homegrown or homemade products;
5 facilitation of production to accommodate the increase in family size.

All of these represent building on indigenous sources of income available to the family in rural areas.

(B) Secondly, in urban areas where paid employment supplants self-employment our efforts turn to securing and improving working opportunities. The means include:

1 attention to wage scales;
2 conditions of employment;
3 fringe labor benefits;
4 services and facilities to substitute for absence of the mother from home;
5 protections and safeguards for women in employment.

The Migrant Problem in Socio-Economic Betterment. (C) A third consideration concerns areas in which migration is active. Proper provisions should be made at both ends of the trajectory of movement as well as at any of the stopping places en route. Family breakdown, neglected children and consequent social pathology accompany rapid urbanization and industrialization and destroy family well-being in both the urban and rural areas involved. Migration must be recognized by the missionary as one of the normal and legitimate occurrences in the life of peoples. Considerations include the following:

1   At the point of departure, efforts must be made to prevent
    family disintegration as the breadwinner leaves for the urban
    center, creating a social and emotional void in the family
    structure.

2   The person who leaves the quiet countryside for the city faces
    serious problems of social adjustment. Village civil authori-
    ties as well as missionaries sometimes have a tendency to be
    impatient and unfeeling in dealing with departants, treating
    them somewhat as disloyal citizens who are foreswearing the
    home grounds for an alien base. This is, among other things,
    socially unsound and harmful.

    Every possible safeguard should be offered in the way of
    guidance to minimize the dangers. In the Belgian Congo, a
    liaison exists between rural missionaries and city parishes to
    insure immediate contact at the journeyer's new base. This
    liaison takes the form of an identification card which each
    Christian is expected to show the urban missionary on arrival,
    and which sometimes provides a place for certification that
    the migrant has kept up his spiritual duties.

3   Labor hostels are provided along routes in certain lands to
    issure migrants proper care while travelling. Again, local
    workers, civil and ecclesiastical, are tempted to deny any re-
    sponsibility for such people. This must be recognized as so-
    cially and spiritually unsound.

4   At the point of arrival, sharp distinctions are made between
    migrants, who are by their nature short-term workers, and
    immigrants, who presumably are permanent new citizens. It
    is understandable, however unfortunate it may be, that neither
    of these categories gets the attention given to old resident
    families of a community, but the migrant gets the lesser atten-
    tion and hence the grave social and spiritual harm that migrant
    families suffer throughout the world.

Institutions to Offset Family Deficiencies. (D) Fourth among
the considerations for improving the socio-economic condition
of the family is the network of social services and social security
programs requisite to offset the social and economic deficiencies
in families, particularly in countries in the throes of industrialization. Such programs include:

1   means of income during periods of seasonal or more pro-
     tracted unemployment;
2   public health measures;
3   medical services;
4   rehabilitation services;
5   low-cost housing;
6   maternal and child welfare services;
7   nutrition and health guidance;
8   institutional care for physically handicapped and dependent
     children.

(E) Fifthly, a program of organized family guidance should
be provided for socio-economic betterment. The areas of special
need are usually the following:

1   budgeting of the income;
2   preparation of available foods to secure highest nutritive
     value;
3   provision of supplementary food for children, usually through
     school lunches;
4   the development and encouragement of voluntary coopera-
     tive societies for farmers, craftsmen, consumers in general,
     with an eye to better use of family purchasing power.

Adapt Rather than Discard. (F) Sixthly, in providing for
family socio-economic development, emphasis must be placed
on retaining the values inherent in the cultural heritage of the
people. Steps in this direction may include the following:

1   Families should be helped to adapt rather than to discard
     customs and practices that have in them potential social and
     moral support for better family living.
         In Pakistan, for example, the parent-child relationship as-
     sures affection, warmth, protection and acceptance to the
     naturally dependent child. As socio-economic forces take their
     toll in familial relations, as economic individualism increases,
     as urbanization proceeds, Pakistan families must retain their
     characteristic human resiliency, their warmth, integrity, co-

hesiveness, social stability, while adapting themselves to the
new social and economic environment.

2 Families need to be encouraged to support their own indigenous self-help groups while improving their local institutions
and traditions.

In many economically underdeveloped countries we find a
number of established mutual-aid and self-help efforts of local
origin, supported by voluntary groups. The indigenous leadership in them may often be recognized and utilized. Their status
with their people should be enhanced and their leadership
strengthened by the missionary's improved programs.

Respect the Family Structure. Mr. Dumpson, in chorus
with other perceptive sociologists and mission leaders, emphasizes as basic to all betterment efforts the maintenance of a
proper respect for family structure, and calls for due regard
for the traditional structure patterns that the Westerner of
superficial experience is ready to write off without hesitation.

"In Pakistan and in the Indian sub-continent generally," he
stated, "the people have maintained a social structure that
assures strong support to the family. Known as the joint family
system, it provides, despite weaknesses and limitations, security,
stability and shared responsibility.

"Marriages are arranged by the elders and the new husband
and his bride move into the family group of his parents. Thus
new families are incorporated into an established family, usually a unit that is economically, socially and psychologically
experienced in family living. Social supports within this extended kinship tend to prevent family breakdown and disintegration.

"True, these families are now being forced to adapt themselves to the tremendous economic and social changes in process. These people are deeply concerned about finding ways to
continue the family as they have known it, as an institution. If
they must adjust its structure to basic economic forces, they
want assurance that they will not be left detached, isolated and

disintegrated. No effort of the missionary will gain more positive response than a demonstration on his part that he understands the importance intellectually and emotionally of the family as an institution. Whatever know-how he can contribute toward stimulating moral and socio-economic growth within the desired family framework will be deeply appreciated.

"In suggesting policy for such efforts, it must be pointed out that the stage of social and economic development and the socio-economic problems vary from country to country. Policy, I submit, needs to be related to the particular setting in which it is to be applied; it must be related to the socio-economic, cultural and ethnic context of the people. This fact places on both social workers and missionaries the responsibility of familiarizing themselves, first of all, with the culture of the people to be served and then with the local socio-economic environment."

Family Structure in Africa. It is one thing to advise the adaptation of the family social structure when referring to the rich, complex cultures of Asia; but what of the less evolved cultures of Africa? Bishop Joseph Blomjous of Mwanza, a leader among the White Fathers and the hierarchy of Tanganyika and East Africa, came out quite cateogrically for a similar policy on his continent.

"The fundamental problem in the African set-up," declared Bishop Blomjous, "is the difference in the concept of the family in the tribal milieu as compared with the Western concept, often called the nuclear family. One of the most important things for young missionaries to grasp is the full significance in African family life of the extended kinship relationship.

"I would like to point out a mistake which many missionaries make who conclude that the Christian family ideal can only be achieved through acceptance of the Western concept of family, the nuclear family. I don't believe that a basis for this thinking can be found anywhere in Scripture or theology. There is surely a way of realizing the Christian ideal also in the pattern of the complete family or extended kinship family.

"It is a pity when missionaries, as sometimes happens, seek to destroy the extended family because they think the nuclear family is the only way to establish Christian life. I remember attending a Christian life conference in the Belgian Congo. Practically all the papers seemed to aim at one goal: 'Let us get rid, as soon as possible, of the primitive African family concept and put in its place the Western family concept. Then we shall have a basis for the Christian family.' This is surely not true.

"The more or less Westernized type of family which we find among Africans in urbanized areas is often under heavy social and economic pressures to provide proper family stability. In the extended family system of the old tribal life, social and economic pressures are eased by the tribal relationship.

"As an example, in African tribal society orphans do not exist. It is impossible to be an orphan in Africa; if you lose one father or one mother you automatically acquire a new father or a new mother; custom specifies exactly which uncle or aunt immediately becomes your new and authentic father or mother. Most of the Bantu tribes have no word for orphan.

"The missionary should give serious thought as well to the role in the African family played by the older generation. If you destroy too quickly this role, you destroy an important stabilizing factor in society. A contributing factor in increased juvenile delinquency in the big towns of Africa is the disappearance of the stabilizing educational force of the older generation in the extended family system."

Is the Nuclear Family for Africa? It is worth our while checking these thoughts of one of our missionary leaders against the opinion of a representative voice among today's social anthropologists. Felix M. Keesing, Professor of Anthropology at Stanford University, in his new book [1] has interesting comments on the independent nuclear family of contemporary America.

"Perhaps never before in human history," says Keesing, "have socio-economics called for so much family mobility. A young couple today is expected to be able to rear children without a wider circle of relatives who act as mutual helpers and who, in the case of old people, are either dominant or dependent. Larger family ties, to the extent that they are exercised, have become rather a matter of opportunity and personal choice—and they are a familiar butt for jokes.

"Social relations within the modern nuclear family have become intensified to a point apparently never reached before in family organization. . . . Under the best circumstances, husband-wife relationships may perhaps be evaluated as richer and more intimate than could possibly occur in a larger kin grouping and composite household. But often two individuals who marry cannot rise to the demands and possibilities of such a monogamous, close-living unit. When their religious beliefs, finances and personal situations allow it, increasing numbers make use of legally sanctioned mechanisms for separation and divorce."

Features of the Extended Family.   What professional appraisal does an academician like Keesing give the extended family? The *extended,* or *joint,* or *multiple,* or *great,* family represents a merged group of nuclear units of parents and children. The most typical practices regarding residence either require all the brides to go to live with the husbands' people (so-called patrilocal, or "father-place," residence) or all the husbands to go to live with the brides' people (matrilocal residence).

"Practically all human groups in past and present," explains Keesing,[2] "have had some form of extended family household system of which nuclear families form constituent units. Such a system has been characteristic of Western society until the last few generations and is still widely familiar, especially in rural places. . . . In general, within such larger groupings, there have to be meticulous definitions and rules governing the behavior of individuals. . . . Young parents take their place among a number of persons working collectively, and are usually subject to direction by the elders to the point where, in terms of our values, there is no personal freedom and initiative, little privacy and slight authority over their own children.

"Over against this, they enjoy economic and status securities in such a larger group which young parents in the modern system rarely have, and so the tensions which are so marked among youthful fathers and mothers struggling to make their way in their own setting are minimized.

"At times of crisis such as births, sickness and death—events which usually disorganize, stun and bewilder the modern small family—the situation is likely to be met with little fuss and fumbling for such events are much less unusual and there are many hands to help. Children have the security of a large kin group, and a wide range of persons participate in their training. As the old people die off and parents become grandparents, they in their turn attain to authority, responsibility and prestige."

Such considerations make it clear why an experienced churchman like Bishop Blomjous warns the young missionary against labelling the extended family as a crude tribal institution of darkest Africa, or of labelling the nuclear family as the perfect instrument for all young parents everywhere because it is a product of the modern West. It may be true that the nuclear family is due to prevail in almost every area that is modernizing because, despite its burdens on parents, it fits the socio-economic requirements of the times. Nevertheless the missionary is urged to entertain respect for the extended family.

The New Position of Women and Children. "Missionaries must be aware," Bishop Blomjous told us, "of the changing position in African families of both the women and the children. In tribal societies, the woman is an economic asset. When a family moves out of the tribal set-up, the woman may become an economic burden. In the old set-up, the woman worked in the field and was otherwise a contributor, but when she goes to an industrial area as housewife to a man with a modern job she devotes herself entirely to the home and her man must support her. A major problem in urban areas is the great amount of time a young wife has to herself and the restrictions she feels toward having no self-earned income. Too many get into questionable occupations, including such things as operating home stills for brewing moonshine beer."

Problems arise in the changing rural economy as regards the children. "In many African families," explained Bishop Blomjous, "the children are needed for herding the cattle. When the government and the missionaries open schools, the children should attend. But who is going to herd the cattle? Here is one of the many reasons why parents oppose education. It is not because they don't understand the advantages of education; they contend that their whole economy is geared to the use of children for herding cattle."

Women and Children in Western Kenya. Father John de Reeper of the Mill Hill Fathers is now an Assistant to the Superior General and a professor at the major seminary of his Society in the suburbs of London. As a veteran field missionary, he is an experienced observer of the profound family changes wrought in western Kenya by the new socio-economic pattern that developed in the years following World War II. This pattern applies to many similar areas in Africa and elsewhere.

"The process of industrialization," stated Father de Reeper, "creates new problems, not only for the men folk who are in the thick of things, but for the women and children as well. Let us try to picture such a process in East Africa, where I witnessed it myself.

"After the war, thousands of African lads who had been in the army were demobilized. Most of them did not want to resume the customary tribal life of herding cattle, beer drinking, loafing and attending endless palavers. Part of their army pay had been kept back by the British government and this was paid out to them on demobilization.

"With that money some bought lorries and started a transport business, others took to garage work, again others erected mills for grinding maize and millet, others started brick making, got into the building trades, opened bicycle shops. In a couple of years, the aspect of the placid farming and pastoral country was changed into a beehive of small industrial activities.

"The effect on the men, which we must not leave unmentioned, was to make them more industrious, more mercenary, more money-conscious. It was surprising to see how many developed into good businessmen, builders, mechanics and the like. Of course there were failures and some of these had to go back to farming and stock raising, if they still had land to fall back on. Others drifted into labor centers where they were absorbed into the amorphous mass of job seekers, lost more often than not, to the tribe, the family and the Church."

The New Woman. "The women," continued Father de Reeper, "who up to now had been the only providers of food for the family, either found themselves where they had no gardens to cultivate, or, even if there were gardens about, realized that they were not required to work them or that they could no longer grow the food their husbands wanted. For in the army the men had become accustomed to a much healthier and more varied diet than was produced by the women at home. Once back home the men demanded similar food, more meat, fish, so-called European vegetables, such as carrots and cabbage, and a variety of jams and beverages.

"For the women this meant less garden work and a necessary reliance on financial support from the husband. This financial support by the husband is an entirely new feature in African home life. Heretofore the woman had a free hand in the spending of money because whatever little cash she had she obtained herself by selling the surplus crop of her garden. But now she depended for every expenditure on her husband. He, on his part, had no background that taught him to be a money provider. This novel break with old traditions called for quite a bit of give and take from both parties before the proper balance could be found.

"Thus the need for prudent family administration has become quite apparent and courses in domestic science have become a must for all new style African spouses. Here is a need which the missionary should seek to fill to insure well-conducted modern African homes.

"Estranged from farm work, new African wives lack useful occupation. They have no idea how to fill their days unless they have learned to take pride in a clean house, well-dressed children, hygienic and tasteful preparation of food, all of which activities are arguments for domestic science courses. Without such occupations, trouble lies ahead. Idleness in the tropics holds still greater dangers than in our temperate climate."

Parental Support of Their Children. Father de Reeper, a seeded philosopher of East African family life, made the charge that a certain danger faces the youth of Africa because the parents lack a tradition to provide their young people with things in life that in this new day African youngsters are bound they are going to possess. His argument runs as follows:

"At present there is a veritable craze among African boys for more education. They will do anything to get into a school and to get out of the school all that they can. I remember on one occasion, when the principal of a secondary school gave the boys a free day, the class prefects came in the name of the boys and protested. 'We have not paid school fees to get free days!' they shouted.

"Behind this attitude is the fact that most of the boys get their school fees by their own labor. This effort is praiseworthy, of course, but it engenders at an early age an unhealthy greed for money and a spending liberty which leads to dangerous consequences. They take jobs in local industries, and if they have to earn their entire support the process opens the way to many abuses—exploitation of cheap labor, underpayment, unwise mixing with adult labor and similar consequences.

"The obvious solution, of course, is the training of parents to look after the present-day needs of the children. They must be taught that it is their responsibility to educate their children and to provide the substantial part of the needs in clothing, school fees and the like. It is our experience that this is becoming more and more the tradition, with relatives and friends sharing in the burden.

"Here in America and similarly in Europe, it is a commonly accepted fact that young men pick up money for their private benefit by delivering newspapers, running errands and similar spare time jobs. This principle of fending for oneself exists in Africa. For ten years I looked after an area of European farms in the Kenya Highlands. For the seasonal work of picking coffee, tea and pyrethrum flowers, thousands of boys and girls simply disappeared from their homes for a couple of weeks or months and flocked to the farms to pick up money for clothing and school fees.

"Once it happened that a boy in my seminary was hauled away by the police because during the holidays he had stolen a cow from his father's herd and sold it to pay his seminary fees! His father was a heathen who did not believe in seminary training. Another time, a Christian shopkeeper came to me to protest that his son had stolen money from the shop for school fees. The boy retorted that his father had refused him the money for the fees and he had helped himself to it, for, he cried, 'Are not all my father's things also mine?' I wonder how you'd have answered that!

"The boys certainly should be encouraged in their proper ambitions, but the parents must not default on their duties. When they do, both the parents and the youngsters are harmed."

Women and Catholic Principles.   It is well to recall that the Church's position on the place of woman in the newer societies of the world is not merely a matter of opinion among leaders on the spot. These leaders are guided by established Catholic principles. The World Union of Catholic Women's Organizations plays an important role today in presenting these principles to governmental and non-governmental bodies around the globe. An experienced unit in this work is St. Joan's International Alliance of Great Britain.

In 1937 St. Joan's Alliance presented to the League of Nations of that day a document bearing a statement of Catholic thought on human rights as applying to woman, that was circulated at the time as an official document of the League.[8] It stated: "No administration can be called just which governs a territory where a woman is treated as a chattel to be sold by her father or alleged proprietor to a polygamist or anyone else. We claim that every woman must be permitted to choose her own partner in life despite any contract entered into in her name by any other person."

At the time, St. Joan's International Alliance recommended the following as the Catholic position on woman:

1 Education to be free and compulsory for both sexes;
2 The woman to be given her maturity at the age of 21 or before;
3 No marriage contract to be made for a girl under 14;
4 Consent of the two parties to be a condition of valid marriage;
5 Appeal against coercion to be made generally known and easily accessible;
6 Bride-price to be discouraged and registered monogamous marriage encouraged;
7 A widow to be free to dispose of herself and her children as she thinks fit;
8 All State regulation of prostitution to be abolished and third-party exploitation of prostitution severely punished;
9 Facilities for decent family life to be provided in connection with labor recruitment and in urban areas.

When the United Nations Charter was formulated at San Francisco in 1945, Catholic women's groups worked on the Liaison Committee which asked that the new world organization "guarantee to every citizen, irrespective of sex, social standing, creed, race and birth, freedom from fear and want, freedom of speech . . . marriage and worship and freedom to earn; and equality before the law." The final text left out all reference to religion but recognized the place of woman. The

Charter reads: "Faith in fundamental human rights, in the dignity and value of the human person, in the equal right of men and women and of nations large and small."

Economic Questions Touching Women. Economic questions relating to women apply in principle to underdeveloped areas just as they do to the evolved peoples. Equal pay for equal work is proposed for world acceptance at least in principle and is then to be fought for as a practice. Actual practice in the socio-economic field allows for difference of opinion but basic economic questions touching the welfare of women are:

1 the age of retirement;
2 pensions;
3 working conditions for women with family responsibilities;
4 "protection" of women workers;
5 part-time work for women.

In 1949 the Trusteeship Council of the U. N. on a petition from St. Joan's Alliance recommended that "uncivilized practices, such as child marriage, should be expressly forbidden by law." The General Assembly received a resolution calling for "absolute prohibition" of such practices.

The French Government has been active in legislation to improve the status of woman in Africa. The Mandel Law in 1939 forbade the marriage contract before a spouse's 14th year and made consent indispensable for validity. The Jacquinot Decree in 1951 permits a woman of 21 to marry without bride-price and allows girls under 21 to marry without consent of parents when the bride-price demand is excessive. Both these decrees owe much to a French White Sister, Soeur Marie-André, who was a graduate lawyer of Lille University before entering religion.

A world convention condemns as "practices similar to slavery" the following:

"Any institution or practice whereby:
"1 a woman, without the right to refuse, is promised or given in marriage in payment of a consideration in money or in

kind to her parents, guardian, family or any other person or group; or

"2   the husband of a woman, his family, or his clan has the right to transfer her to another person for value received or otherwise; or

"3   a woman on the death of her husband is liable to be inherited by another person."

Build with the Family Woman. "Women can often do much more than men in the socio-economic field," declared Father John Dijkstra, S.J., of Indonesia. "They are the wives of the wage earners. By their hands is spent the greatest part of the national income. Many of them are workers themselves, though very poorly paid in Asian countries. The workers' and farmers' movement certainly must have a women's section. Here is a wonderful opportunity for zealous women and girls. They must understand their responsibility in achieving a better way of life for themselves and their families. This they will accomplish through courses in adult education, home economics, nutrition, child care. It is up to the missionary to educate the Catholic woman to see and do her duty."

For recommended reading, see Bibliography No. 6, page 270.

Socio-Economic Aids
to the Farmer

The Man with the Key. During recent years, a number of American missionaries have studied tropical agriculture in the College of Agriculture at Southwestern Louisiana Institute, prompted in their choice of a school by the presence there of a gracious and solicitous teacher, Doctor T. J. Arceneaux. Doctor Arceneaux, through his service as a government technician in Africa, is deeply convinced of the importance of the missionary as a guide to better living for the peoples of the underdeveloped world. In a previous chapter we have quoted him briefly on this. We now develop his thought.

"The missionary," he explained, "often labors among people who are agricultural workers, making their living from the soil by following primitive methods of farming. Such conditions, if not improved, are certainly not conducive to very high standards of living. Such environments, if not modified, cannot normally develop into strong and lasting Christian communities.

"In his capacity as a missionary and as a leader the priest can very well be the contact between the people he is serving and the agricultural officials, who are generally eager to improve conditions in the area in which they are serving. To perform this very vital function, the priest need not be a highly trained agriculturist. Yet he should have enough knowledge of basic scientific agriculture to recognize the problems and then to be able to discuss them intelligently with the technical experts assigned to his area by government or other agencies. In such a capacity he can be of unlimited value to his people in the development of a stable rural community.

"Many very competent agricultural workers are to be found in some of the underdeveloped areas of the world, and they are eager to reach the people. In many places they can and should be reached through the missionary priest. This, in my opinion, should be *the main agricultural task of the rural missionary priest.*

"Intelligent cooperation on the part of the missionary priest in the agricultural development of his mission area can be greatly improved by a little agricultural training. This is the program in which we have tried to participate at my institution during recent years."

The Scope of the Problem. Words of Pius XII on the farmer are quoted frequently. "The farmer," stated His Holiness, "is the foundation of the nation, whether considered for his outstanding economic contribution, or his sanity, or for his vigor and morality. . . . There is no more mistaken idea than the notion that the man who tills the soil does not need a serious and adequate education to enable him to perform the various duties of the season after the fashion of the times."

As is the case in considering the other divisions of this study, we must make it evident, from the start, that the economic factors of agriculture must be paralleled by the social factors. Doctor Goncalves, a sociologist from Brazil, while thoroughly sympathetic to the technical, called as well for attention to a "knowledge of the human beings concerned."

"Agriculture, of course, is important," he declared. "Agricultural techniques, extension work, all have their place. But behind them and above them the missionary should endeavor to know how to deal with human beings. That is why I put emphasis on short or long courses in rural sociology and other applied social sciences. In Brazil, for instance, 70 percent of the people are farmers and 30 percent of the clergy come from rural areas. But in the seminaries there is too little instruction about human society in rural life. I think this is a very important matter to correct."

Taken in its broadest sense, agricultural betterment embraces the following:

1   the promotion of continuous improvement in agricultural production;
2   more effective marketing;
3   home utilization of production;
4   improved management of all the resources of the farm, including the directly agricultural and the complementary factors such as woodlands, orchards, waters and wild life.

Home economics extension programs deserve consideration:

1   improved techniques and practices;
2   education in farm management;
3   primary processing, marketing;
4   rural health through child-care training.

There are, then, the so-called supporting agricultural services:

1   the training of rural extension workers;
2   seed multiplication and production of nursery stock;
3   applied and basic research;
4   irrigation and drainage;
5   marketing services;
6   agricultural banks;
7   promulgation of land tenure policy and legislation;
8   protective institutions for labor conditions and prices.

In the field of rural sociology the long gamut includes:

1 rural schools;
2 rural public health and medicine;
3 social welfare, family guidance;
4 rural leisure programs, cultural programs, folk arts, wider participation in religious life;
5 communications, mass media, rural library services.

The Missionary's Image of the Farmer. Basic to the missionary's approach to his task in a rural area in any part of the world is the mental image he builds regarding the ultimate goals—economic, social, cultural, spiritual—of the people among whom he works.

He may accept a traditional concept, that these are simple and backward people whose ancestors have always been simple and backward, whose descendants will always be simple and backward so long as they remain in this milieu. He may find that to all appearances this is precisely the impression these people have of themselves. He may be told that the national political regime and the industrial interests act accordingly, regarding his region as an area for subsistence farming, the source of a labor pool for the cities and industrial centers, a locality from which the more alert and ambitious emigrate early in life and to which they return only to visit their loved ones.

Acting on this assumption, he can give himself to serving the populace devotedly as children of God, greeting them, guiding them, engaging in small talk with them, consoling them in grief, in suffering and in want, calming them in anger, sharing the laughter of their joys and the happiness of their festivities.

When young men and young women propose taking work in the city, he may warn them of the dangers and send them off with his blessing. When an intelligent youngster whispers to him that he is unhappy in the countryside, that he dreams of working his way through college and becoming a lawyer or doctor in the city, he may agree heartily and whisper back, "By all means go, son; there is no future here."

But then, he may talk with the village teachers, the local government officers and with his mission superiors, and reach the conclusion that as a helping person he has, if not a direct duty, at least a splendid opportunity to better the living conditions of the region. He may unite with others in an area-wide program that may employ community development techniques and aim at the transformation of local society and of the countryside. Or he may propose more limited objectives, with the economic and social goals outlined above as guides.

Certainly, everything which the missionary determines to do will prove a vital contribution toward a better world society and toward a stronger Christian society. It is hard to say that a missionary can be accused of impropriety or of weakness if he limits himself to the exclusively spiritual service of his flock. Nevertheless, it seems inconceivable that an observant man would not see that by a negative position he may fail to give to his people all that they need to strengthen their temporal condition, even as a means of strengthening their spiritual condition.

"Foster respect for farming," urged Monsignor Ligutti, a great protagonist of building faith and hope among farmers in the future of their countryside. And, very much to the point here, it is the missionary who should undertake to foster this respect.

"The missionary, figuratively a farmer," observed the Monsignor, "must come to know the person of man, the social man. The simple principles of our training must apply to our missionary practices. It doesn't make any difference what the program might be, whether a housing program, an agricultural program, a soil conservation program, we must decide to interest ourselves in the need as an *Alter Christus,* as one called to be all things to all men, as one charged by the precept *instaurare omnia in Christo,* to restore all in Christ. The accent is on *all.* The missionary must conceive his task as not *only* baptizing, *only* marrying, *only* burying, but also as helping to build the social foundations of the community."

To return, then, to the attitude which the missionary should assume toward his farming region, let him see it as an area that is backward, true, but practically never as without hope of betterment. Farming communities must exist to the end of time; we betray our task if we systematically encourage the young men to run away and if we leave the farmers to blunder on in their inadequacies.

Missionary Agriculture in New Guinea. A frontal attack on bad agricultural conditions in their mission field has been launched by the Divine Word Fathers from their base at Madang on New Guinea, in the southwest Pacific, the world's largest island. Father Otto Shelly, S.V.D., of husky farmer stock from the state of Indiana, was assigned by his community to prepare himself as an agricultural specialist. He supplied us not merely with details of the local problem but with basic data on training programs for agricultural missionaries.

"In New Guinea," explained Father Shelly, "we have insufficient food, particularly for the mountain people in whom I am interested directly. There is lack of protein in the food and there is no material for clothing. There is wholesale erosion, and there is quite a bit of land unsuitable for tillage because it is swampy. In short, we face poor agricultural conditions in general.

"Among the New Guineans there is lack of proper crop selection and of animal selection. This means that the crops grown are not nutritional, they are not disease-resistant and they are not as productive as others might be.

"The general situation, then, is complicated by a very high rainfall of 120 inches per annum.

"The Divine Word Fathers determined *to act jointly* in the area in meeting the need. *The Government at present has no program.* Someone had to be in charge of our program, so I was sent home to agricultural college to prepare details. The missionaries are very anxious to cooperate in the plan that touches their people so closely.

"Our program, by present development, is as follows:

"1   A farm at a mission station as base for agricultural exten-
      sion work. On this farm the natives work in their traditional
      fashion, digging the soil with their sticks. I, as the missionary
      technician, or one of my confreres joins these men as they
      work and without any direct interference we show them little
      practices, one at a time, that gradually lead to a different
      type of agriculture. This practical field method, we think,
      disturbs these people the least as we seek to introduce
      changes.
"2   Short courses at various spots in the area to farmer volun-
      teers.
"3   An organization similar to the 4-H Club for the younger
      folk.
"4   A news sheet out of the center for the missionaries and for
      the natives who can read, in order to provide the program
      with a means to keep us coordinated."

Making Farmers Better Farmers.   Father Shelly's task, as
is that of his companions in New Guinea, represents a frontal
approach to improving the farming techniques of the New
Guineans.

"You seem to imply," we said to him, "that you have no
revolutionary program for your people. You speak of showing
them little ways of improving things as they work. Evidently
you aim at changes but not big changes in their ways."

"This is not the case," he replied. "Our ultimate goals are
definitely revolutionary. But we are keeping in mind the missionary axiom that big ideas in the way of change frighten people who live in little worlds. We'll show them just one tiny
move at a time.

"We not only hope to bring about a transition from poor
methods to better methods in traditional farming, but we aim
to shift our people eventually from traditional to progressive
farming, according to the best thinking of the Western world.

"Progressive farming calls for something much more than

the improvement of agricultural methods. It means so altering their approach to running a farm that they free themselves from being wedded to a static combination of agricultural practices, including a set annual program of crops to be planted, and adopt a dynamic pattern of continuously changing production such as the knowledgeable farmer in the United States employs."

"Are you in favor of boys from backward mission areas being sent to agricultural colleges?"

"Certainly there are advantages. A young man who would get such a schooling would secure an overview of the whole agricultural picture and a view of complete rural living on a level much higher than the local. The boy with brains and vision would thus get an opportunity to train as an outstanding agricultural leader.

"But caution is required in such a move. Few rural youths are qualified for entrance into such colleges, and if they fail their future is jeopardized. They can acquire such ideas at school that even though they stay in agriculture they are lost to their local countryside. Even when they return home, they can be in trouble through having ideas so far ahead of the local folk who are running the farms that they end by only causing friction. If government technicians and the missionary will guide them, such college grads can serve their people to good purpose."

"What about giving young men practical non-collegiate training in progressive farming and in the processes of a dynamic agriculture?"

"I would see good in that. A good type of practical secondary education can be provided for skilled farm workers and future farm owners. Opportunities should be provided to keep the locality abreast of the most recent agricultural developments that can be useful in the area. Such a plan offers a chance to train farm workers in the operation and on-the-spot repair of some of the simpler of modern mechanized farm equipment.

"Such steps, however, are not of great value unless they are part of an over-all, well-established program of extension education. With this type of program, the community can be made progressive-minded and newer ideas can be successfully initiated. A local or regional training center for young farmers requires a substantial budget and cannot be self-supporting by any schemes that require the students to cover the expenses of the center through their labor. A capable manager and a personnel well trained in good techniques are essential."

The Demonstration Farm and Alternatives. "Is the type of farm you mention in your program," we asked Father Shelly, "what is known as a demonstration farm?"

"Not exactly. A demonstration farm aims to present at a single center the best in progressive agricultural methods and prove their value over traditional methods. Such a farm can furnish visible evidences of the agricultural potentialities of a region. A so-called experimental farm can do much the same job.

"But there are serious limitations to these farms. First of all, very few farmers are able to copy the methods used; they need independent training, not always possible, on where and how to begin even if they are stirred sufficiently to want to try. When they see so many practices at once, backward farmers are apt to conclude that such methods require financial resources and managerial ability beyond their capacity.

"The usefulness of a demonstration farm is limited by its concentration at a single location. Instead, individual model practices widely scattered on many small land units have greater utility. Then, the cost of a demonstration farm is too great for the results achieved unless it serves other purposes as well."

"Do you have alternate suggestions in place of the demonstration farm?" he was asked.

"Many technicians favor much smaller holdings of five to ten acres. These can be employed, for instance, to demonstrate truck gardening methods. A few acres can be operated as a model unit for teaching the care of milk cows, other units can teach care of hogs, or chickens. Priest managers can operate such limited efforts and have time to do missionary work and help develop a community improvement program. There is much in favor of modest plans to teach a few simple farm and home practices which will give immediate results."

"This brings up the principle of local short-course training in specific subjects, doesn't it? Evidently there are advantages in such less ambitious tactics," was commented.

"Quite right. There is much more elasticity to such procedure, which allows the capable missionary to make a certain contribution and permits a continuing program in which visiting government officers and others can play a part. Among other things in its favor, this is a relatively inexpensive way to be helpful.

"Such small centers can serve for brief regional training courses which technicians can conduct. They can provide bases for in-service training of young farmers of the neighborhood. Care must be taken, however, to work according to a plan and not to be superficial. The missionaries or the agricultural officers involved must have a clear understanding of what they intend to teach and make sure that the new ideas are put to practical use."

Father Shelly found ready corroboration for his view that ambitious training centers for young farmers cannot wisely be considered the normal pattern for assistance by the missionary. Full allowance is made for situations where the missionary alone is prepared to act and where such action is imperative. Nevertheless establishment of such schools by missionaries is regarded as exceptional.

"For many years," explained Monsignor Ligutti, "I used to believe in Catholic agricultural schools. I don't any more. I think that usually they are a waste of money. The Catholic missionary serves his people best when he secures the aid of the technicians to improve the status of his farmers. The practical demonstration people should be called in, to help better

the production methods, the distribution methods, the cooperatives of the community."

"I agree entirely with Monsignor Ligutti," stated Father
William Gibbons. "We should be much more active in using
the technical advice and help of the secular arm. We find the
U. S. Department of Agriculture as well as the FAO extraordinarily cooperative. I hope the young Padres now going to
the field will call upon them unhesitatingly."

"I agree wholeheartedly with Monsignor Ligutti," added
Doctor Goncalves, "that at least in Latin America we should
not spend our scarce mission money to build agricultural
schools. Our experience in Brazil should prompt the missionary
to link his people with institutions and technicians who will
train their local farm leaders."

Missionary Specialists in Rural Life. This categoric opposition to formally established agricultural schools under
missionary auspices by no means eliminates the need of knowledgeable missionary personnel as regards agricultural and non-
agricultural problems in rural life. A frequently voiced opinion
calls for at least one such specialist in every missionary diocese
that counts a considerable rural population within its embrace.
Doctor Arceneaux presented helpful proposals on the preparation of such personnel as regards agricultural techniques.

"First of all," noted the Doctor, "I feel that, previous to
receiving any special training in the problems which face farmers, the priest, or Brother, or layman should have some experience in the mission field. We have trained both the newly
ordained, who have come to us before going to the field, and
those who have been some years in action. The latter, I would
say, have definite advantages in comprehending exactly what
they should get from our course, to make of themselves not
dirt farmers but, rather, helpful missionary guides of dirt
farmers.

"Secondly, I would recommend that when there is a choice
the priest assigned for this special work should have been raised
in a rural milieu. The majority of our missionaries, it appears,

were brought up as city boys and frequently they succeed very well in projecting themselves into the problems of the country. But the man whose earliest recollections go back to day-to-day farm life has the advantage of an insight that is a valuable asset.

"Thirdly, I would note that consideration should be given to training missionary specialists in the specific regional problems of the field where they will labor. Most of the mission areas of the world are in tropical or subtropical lands and in underdeveloped countries. Many of the good agricultural practices and rural traditions of the U. S. Middle West make no allowance for the difficulties encountered in mission lands. This, of course, is a bit of a plug for our college in southern Louisiana where we seek to face up to problems in tropical agriculture, but there are other schools that do the same.

"Fourthly, a word on the length of the course. It is my opinion that the priest who is given a year in an agricultural college has received the requisite minimum, despite the fact that in that period he cannot obtain the fundamentals in the various fields of scientific agriculture.

"Fifthly, I would note that while for most priest specialists one year of study is sufficient for practical purposes, responsible leadership in a region requires that a few key missionaries should possess a degree. I think of the priest primarily as a contact between his people and the agricultural agencies of the area. As you know, in some sections of the world a degree is very important. If the missionary can sit down with the agricultural authorities of an area, with the planners and the directors of experimental stations, and present his credentials as a college graduate from an accredited agricultural school, he will find himself in a very good position to speak for his people.

"Sixthly, I wish to enter a plea for agricultural libraries and extension work information centers in the mission field. I visited many research posts in Africa, and I was appalled by the lack of scientific publications even in government laboratories. Here in this country we have an abundance of such publications available at no cost, or very little cost. Certainly at the headquarters of missionary societies such publications might be accumulated to heighten the efficacy of their workers overseas."

Briefing Courses for the Many. Following Doctor Arceneaux's presentation of the requisites in preparing the specialists, Mr. Miniclier raised the question of guiding the missionary rank and file in effective cooperation.

"Doctor Arceneaux," inquired Mr. Miniclier, "you recommend a year's training for the priest specialist. Now, many missionaries won't get a year's training. With such a shortage of agricultural specialists around the world, is it not possible to give the main body of missionaries the abc's of agricultural problems in order that they will all help guide the rural people toward bettering themselves?"

"I don't want to minimize the value of any training, however short," replied Doctor Arceneaux, "that increases the amount of wise guidance that will reach the people."

"I have great respect for higher studies," commented Monsignor George Higgins of the NCWC Social Action Department, "but in my own field, that of labor, much of the best work is being done by priests who got their training in special short courses. I think we can safely recognize the distinction between careful technical training and the more quickly acquired general leadership training."

"I wish to call attention to the fact," interposed Father Shelly, "that in addition to the specific course of studies, long or short, that the technician or the missionary or the individual farmer takes at the beginning of his agricultural career or at given periods during it, there is a process of continuing education that goes on in agriculture as well as in any other life career. In agriculture the outstanding current activity of this sort goes by the name of agriculture extension services. If the rural missionary did nothing more than follow the agricultural extension literature in the nation in which he works, he would, in many cases, find himself with an intelligent grasp of the current farm problems."

Agricultural Extension Services. As Father Shelly indicated, the development of agricultural extension services represents a world trend of the past decade. Such services operate as the educational arm by which all technical sections of the national agriculture departments make contact with the farmer and his family. In the better developed countries, the typical extension officer covers an area embracing 300 to 1,000 farms and through this officer the specialists at headquarters provide training and advice. In a number of newer nations in Asia, agricultural extension has been incorporated into community development programs that aim at a balanced growth of the rural community, including agriculture, health, sanitation, education, youth work, home economics, and rural industries. Farmer-participation is a feature of these programs.

"In our mission work," explained Father Shelly, "agricultural extension programs have a three-fold purpose:

"1 to educate adults in new practices and methods and to show them how these methods are to be applied;
"2 to educate the youth in the phases of rural living and to help them appreciate rural life;
"3 to uncover local problems and to alert research organizations concerning them.

"We see ourselves working through the services to give the farmers greater confidence in themselves and to guide them in spending as wisely as possible whatever funds they have for the improvement of their operation. We aim to alert the country as a whole to the potentialities of rural people and the high place which their importance merits for them in the community. It is a misfortune that such a large part of humanity holds farming people in low esteem.

"From the directly Christian angle, the organization of agricultural extension can be utilized to improve Christian family living in rural areas. We should strive to provide deeper aesthetic and spiritual satisfactions at the personal, family and community levels among farming folk."

"Are there any Catholic missionary efforts, Father Shelly, aimed specifically at the farming world?"

"Aside from efforts of the Catholic Rural Life Movement there is nothing in the United States. Among the Protestants there is a well functioning organization. This is Agricultural Missions, Incorporated. It conducts a school for rural missionaries every January at Cornell University and a one-year course in rural service training at Cornell. A course of field training in extension methods is held each year in the Ozarks in cooperation with the University of Arkansas College of Agriculture. A seminar in extension education is held also each February at the U. S. Department of Agriculture in Washington."

"If I may," volunteered Father Eugene Higgins of the Maryknoll Extension Service, "I would like to emphasize the value of building up at regional extension centers a certain amount of audio-visual aids and other types of mass media, which are too expensive to acquire at the parish level but which can be of very practical value in teaching socio-economic practices generally."

"Good material in the audio-visual field," noted Jules Weinberg, "is available from a number of the international non-governmental organizations. The International Labor Organization is establishing regional film libraries. There is one in India and their films are pretty good. They cover a broad range of labor and socio-economic problems. The CIO has lending facilities that are available to any responsible group. Simple equipment in this field is to be preferred in order that it can be operated even in the back country. You don't have to go into these things in a big way to accomplish good."

The Demographic Factor in Agriculture. Production of food could not be considered without referring to the world population problem so much under discussion currently. Father William Gibbons, S.J., speaks and writes authoritatively on the subject.

"The demographic factor underlies the agricultural picture," he observed. "One of the reasons why we simply have to shift into progressive or modern agriculture, or whatever you want to call it, is that there is a demand for foodstuffs that the old methods cannot fill. While one man used to produce for his family, or perhaps for an extra few people, we now have to urge one family to produce for the many, for the simple reason that there is not enough land.

"Local leaders must consider the statistical aspect in any given situation before undertaking an over-all program. We must see what the net result is going to be. As Father Shelly has obviously implied, when you shift from traditional to progressive agriculture, you begin to produce more with less man hours. When you produce more with less man hours, you can feed more people with less work. Eventually you are going to displace large numbers of the population for which there may or may not be agricultural or related employment in their rural areas. In the very shift, you are producing the forces, the economic push, that lead to the so-called rural exodus.

"Yet the demographic factors themselves, the growth of the population, have made this trend essential. As we look around the world, we realize that the world today has to change its methods of agriculture precisely in order to produce enough food to permit fewer people to labor in agriculture and a greater number in non-agricultural production. The poorest sections of the globe have as many as two out of every three people growing food, while in the United States we have something like one in every fifteen at this task. The missionary must visualize intelligently the place of his rural area in the world scene."

Father James J. Berna, S.J., an economist, followed this thought through to its fuller conclusion.

"Economists believe," stated Father Berna, "that an agricultural revolution must precede the industrial revolution. Agricultural production must grow in order to provide both food and the industrial raw materials required by industry. Ideally timed, the development of agriculture will be rapid enough to furnish food for the men who will work the factories, and agricultural raw materials for the factories, while industry will develop rapidly enough to furnish factories for the new labor freed by progressive agriculture, and to consume the new raw materials. Both agriculture and industry should provide sufficient money return to the men they employ, to furnish purchasing power to the millions of people involved, in order that they may go into the markets and buy and thus keep a healthy economy in being."

For recommended reading, see Bibliography No. 7, page 273.

MISSIONARY GUIDE-LINES ON LAND REFORM

The World Problem of Land. There is no part of the globe in which a missionary will work that will have no rural problems. The beginning of wisdom as regards these problems lies in the recognition that the abnormalities in this field are the normal lot of a great portion of the human race, and that their solution is to be found not in makeshift steps conceived solely on the basis of local thinking but with the lessons of world society and of the world Church before our eyes.

World efforts at facing these problems fall into a number of categories: 1) regional development programs, 2) extension work, 3) land reform, 4) rural resettlement programs, 5) agricultural credit, 6) agricultural cooperatives, 7) agricultural price and income support, 8) crop insurance, 9) community small industries, 10) farm labor unionization.

We are unable to cover all these categories in this book. We have referred to development programs and extension work in the previous chapter. We shall speak of agricultural credit in the later chapter on cooperatives. Income support will be considered in the chapter on community small industries. Farm labor unionization will be considered in the chapter on labor. In the current chapter, we shall consider land reform.

The temper of the free world since World War II, hopefully stirred by United Nations agencies as well as by governmental and non-governmental organizations and leaders, including our Popes, has called for reforms of the global abuses concerning land. However, except in revolutionary settings, which represent force if not open violence, progress in land reform has been slow.

The Factors Involved in Land Reform. The obstacles to land reform are admittedly great. First of all, we must recognize the resistance of vested interests. Secondly, it is difficult to secure effective legislative implementation. Thirdly, all who are close to operations understand better than ever the tremendous strength of custom and tradition in the villages, which stand in the way of clearly recognized reasons for change. Fourthly, agrarian reform policy, despite the evident need for new socio-economic institutions, lacks the aid of ideological and political principles necessary for intelligent and consistent introduction of better systems. Finally, the financial means are lacking for the state or for peasants themselves to acquire ownership of much land.

An analysis of land reform presents us with the following eight factors: 1) redistribution of land, 2) land registration, 3) consolidation of fragmented holdings, 4) improvement in tenancy relations, 5) control of rents, 6) changes in land taxation, 7) land reclamation, 8) land improvement.

Land reform programs usually need to be accompanied by the strengthening of other related institutions. These include: 1) credit facilities, 2) cooperative organizations, 3) marketing facilities, 4) extension services, 5) the supply of agricultural tools and other requisites, 6) the provision of administrative and technical personnel.

Land Reform in Western Europe. A review, particularly through United Nations agencies,[1] of world activities in land reform during the 1950's makes it clear that land reform is not limited to gravely backward countries but touches many nations of Western Europe. In France, Germany, the Netherlands, Sweden and Switzerland large-scale programs of land consolidation have been in progress and substantial increases in productivity have been obtained. European countries with well-functioning institutions have carried on land purchase operations by credit or grant arrangements, without recourse to special legislation. In Scandinavian countries, where family-farm ownership is well established though not everywhere prevalent, the family-farm pattern has been enlarged by measures to help tenants purchase their holdings. In Denmark and Sweden tenants have the right of preemption on the land cultivated by them. In Switzerland young farmers, agricultural workers and tenant cultivators are under certain conditions assisted by the government to acquire their own farms.

In Italy the land reform legislation enacted in the after-war years is being systematically applied. In several areas, notably about the River Po and in the far south of the peninsula, Catholic cooperation in this program has rescued these areas from Red control. By 1957 some 1,800,000 acres had been expropriated, of which 1,350,000 had been distributed to more than 100,000 families. As a result of 1952 legislation in Greece, some 3,000,-000 acres of land have been expropriated and settled by landless cultivators and cattle breeders. Another 230,000 acres in rural properties have been distributed to something over 5,000 families.

Land Reform in Latin America. In underdeveloped regions of Latin America the goals have been: 1) abolition of landlordism; 2) the reduction of intermediaries between landowner and cultivator; 3) the redistribution of large estates; 4) tenancy reforms antecedent to eventual transfer of land titles. Relatively little progress has been made in the region as a whole. In Guatemala the government has limited rents of agricultural land to 5 percent of their value. But, as in other countries, tenants' poverty and inadequate administrative machinery are obstacles to effective enforcement. In Nicaragua rentals are reported which are sometimes as much as eight times the amount allowed by law.

The most extensive Latin American land reform activity in the '50's was the Bolivian program. The basic plan was redistribution of latifundia (large estates) in family-farms and cooperatives. Prior to 1953 some 600 landowners possessed half of Bolivia's total agricultural land. The Agrarian Reform Law of 1953 gave land to 14,000 landless Indians, but a pastoral letter of the Bolivian Bishops dated March 2, 1958, points out that three things went wrong with this worthy plan.

First, the government transferred the land merely by taking it away from the legal title holders without providing them any specific guarantee of compensation.

Secondly, the Indians, suddenly thrown on their own with no knowledge of agriculture beyond simple sustenance farming, which means raising only enough food to care for themselves, have brought about disastrous retrogression in the areas of the divided estates. A dairy farm near Cochabamba that used to yield 125,000 quarts of milk yearly, in 1957 produced only 26,000 quarts, because the Indians are not trained to produce an excess for sale. Another farm that employed 400 *campesinos* and when parcelled possessed 840 head of cattle, 600 hogs and 16,000 sheep, in 1958 possessed only 25 cows, 20 hogs and 1,000 sheep in the same area. The Bishops reported strong evidence of a drift toward economic distress if guidance is not supplied the Indian families.

Thirdly, the Bishops charged that the reform of 1953, "though acceptable in its guiding principles, degenerated in practice into an agrarian revolution of the Communist type." The pastoral continues, "From this agrarian revolution new landlords have arisen, harsher and more grasping than many of the former ones. They impose on the *campesinos* a yoke heavier than that of old." The Bishops took pains not merely to condemn; they called for properly guided application of the reform. "Let us save Bolivia, setting aside merely negative, destructive criticism," they urged. "Let us set an example of discipline, hard work and honor."

Land Reform in Asia. In Japan and India extensive farm consolidation programs are under development. The control of farm rents, which has been legislated in a number of Asian countries, has proved to be a very complex task. As in the case of control of eviction and lease periods, custom proves here a very serious obstacle. In Burma the transfer of rice-land to the cultivators continues. Ceylon, in January, 1958, introduced the Paddy Lands Act which established a complete change in landlord-tenant relationship. The tenant cultivator is assured the right of permanent, transferable and inheritable occupancy of paddy land. The local cultivation committee and the government commissioner exercise the rights of the landlord, who actually receives only a controlled rent, which is not to exceed a quarter of the total yield of the paddy.

In India comprehensive state legislation concerned with tenancy rights is being implemented. But, as in other less-developed countries, the main obstacle to effective enforcement is the general illiteracy of tenants, their weak economic positions and their lack of organization. In some areas the right of the owner to resume the cultivation of his land counteracts to a considerable extent the efforts made to give security to the tenants.

Land Reform in the Middle East. In Egypt, by 1957, the Land Reform Law of 1952 had expropriated some 500,000 acres and redistributed them to family farmers. Progress was claimed in the establishment of cooperative societies among the new owners, in improved landlord-tenant relations, in minimum-wage fixing and farm labor unionization. Yield and production are reported higher in the redistributed areas, while the big landlords have also intensified use of their remaining holdings. Improved use has been achieved on one-sixth of the total cultivated area of Egypt.

Iraq in 1958 established a Council for Agrarian Reform for expropriation with compensation of all properties above a given acreage, but the law permits this expropriation either for state projects or for individual cultivators.

Tenancy is widely prevalent in the Middle East, with absentee landlordism and speculation by middlemen. Hence, the tenants as a whole enjoy little security.

Land Reform in Africa. African tribal laws have provided traditionally for the holding of the lands of the tribe jointly. This creates today the complex problems of customary tenure systems. A power above the tribes, which means the governing authorities, is urgently needed to direct wisely the transition from the communal ownership to individual ownership wherever it appears. In varying degrees this control is exercised in the areas under Belgian, British and French authority, with the control due to pass to African direction upon attainment of independence. European authority seeks to avoid rapid disintegration of the tribal system, on the grounds that this can lead to usurpation of the land by a few individuals with money, to the detriment of the majority of Africans.

Individualization can be observed in many territories. In Southern Rhodesia, for instance, land custom still prevails but the powers of allocation traditionally exercised by chiefs or headmen have been withdrawn in favor of native commissioners. The Native Land Husbandry Act of 1951 has given a strong impetus to registration of land rights in individual owners' names. In the more congested areas of Northern Rhodesia a more exact demarcation of family holdings is becoming the practice. The cultivation of cash crops in Tanganyika, particularly among the enterprising Chagga people around Mt. Kilimanjaro, is leading to individualization. In Kenya Africans as well as whites are moving toward the enclosure of arable lands or grazing grounds. Individual ownership is noticeable in former French African areas. Even in Portuguese Africa, less advanced than other areas, the law allows certain individual Africans to own lands.

Land Reform in Communist Countries. In the Soviet Union, during the 1950's, the state farms (*sovkhozes*) have greatly increased in importance over the collective farms (*kolkhozes*). The collective farms, then, have been amalgamated into larger units so that the number of collective farms has been reduced from 235,000 to 86,000. Yet in 1955 the collective farms still accounted for 80 percent of the sown area in the U. S. S. R., while the state farms embrace 16 percent of the sown area. Although private exploitation is negligible in the over-all structure, nevertheless this 4 percent of private farms (family plots of collective farm members, urban gardens and individual holdings) are responsible for 45 percent of the potatoes and vegetables produced in the Union, 46 percent of the cattle (including 56 percent of the cows), 40 percent of the pigs and 83 percent of the goats.

Viewed as a whole, collective farming in Communist Europe decreased during the 1950's. Other Eastern European countries have not accepted the imposition of collectivization as have the peasants of the U. S. S. R. In Poland the revolt of October, 1956, reduced collectives from 10,000 to about two or three thousand. However, party authorities are fighting to reinstate the collectives. In the Hungarian revolt of 1956 collectives were reduced by half but are being restored. Except in Bulgaria and Czechoslovakia, so-called "inferior" types of cooperative farms are being employed as preparatory to imposing full-fledged collectivization on the peasants.

Red China promulgated an agrarian reform in 1950 which by 1953 had eliminated the landlord class, to a large degree by murdering or enslaving the landlords. It redistributed the land in a mild cooperative system which operated until 1955. Then the so-called "advanced" type of cooperative was introduced. Of the 110,000,000 rural households of Red China, 91 percent were reported as bound together in cooperatives, of which 62 percent were of the "advanced" type and 38 percent of the elementary type. Then came the notorious "people's communes." These communes embrace up to 10,000 households. They are intended to develop industry and agriculture simultaneously. In addition to producing crops, they build irrigation works, roads and communications networks, set up small factories and establish schools. In short, as efficiency machines they are planned to represent a challenge to the world. But for individual family and community living, the data supplied regarding them presents them as hideous distortions of all that is socially desirable.

The Missionary and Land Reform. From the foregoing world review of land reform, it is evident that every young missionary should approach his task with keen appreciation of the importance of land problems in current human society. A timely warning from Doctor Goncalves prompts us not to approach this subject without recalling the wider and more basic aspects of the problem.

"Land reform," commented Doctor Goncalves, "is too often discussed as representing principally a matter of division of the land. This is not the whole answer. Land parcelling is but one part of the picture. Experience around the world reveals that there is need as well for careful, well-timed, guided programs of rural development, rural resettlement programs, agricultural credit, extension services, education of the farmer and his family. Land reform involves a very complex operation.

"A very important matter for the missionary to consider is the attitude of the landlord toward his tenant and of the tenant toward his landlord. Communism has been establishing a conviction around the world that the landlord should be destroyed. In Brazil I spoke to the tenants in an area one night, and the next morning in talking to one of the owners I commented that I could not reconcile the Cadillac in which he rode with the poverty of the farmers who were producing the coffee that he sold. This owner reported me to the Bishop as a Communist and declared that persons such as I should not be permitted to roam the peaceful countryside.

"This situation is not difficult to understand: the Communists have succeeded in spreading their doctrine on landlords, the Church has not succeeded in spreading its social teachings which condemn unfair landlords but recognize a proper place

for landlords who work to build modern society on social justice. The only thing the owner in his ignorance knows how to
do is condemn everybody who seems to go along with the Communist call that he be destroyed. So, likewise, the only thing
the worker in his ignorance knows how to do is to echo the
Communist call for the destruction of all men who employ
other men.

"The missionary has a role here and it consists in doing more
than talking. Is this not the time to demonstrate Catholic social
teaching by examples? I think we should set up pilot projects
where conditions provide the opportunity to illustrate Catholic
teaching. For each pilot project we should supply technicians,
resources and a dynamic missionary leader. This missionary
should be rural-minded and properly trained to serve as an
active catalyst who would command the respect of technicians,
farmers and the general public, so that prestige would be won
for our Christian way of life."

Action Built on Principles.   Father James L. Vizzard, a
California Jesuit with a master's degree in economics from
Georgetown and teaching experience at the University of Santa
Clara, provides us with a clear statement of principles on the
specific subject of this chapter, land reform.

"Throughout the world," stated Father Vizzard, "the phrase
'the land to the tiller' is becoming the battle cry of the landless.
The demand for land reform is one of the most urgent problems of our time. Let us get clear on our principles. We formulate the following four conclusions as basic principles for land
reform.[2]

> "1   Man's first and most fundamental right in regard to material
> things is an adequate supply of the physical necessities with-
> out which he cannot maintain life and health—e.g., food,
> clothing, shelter. The actuation of this right is the first de-
> mand on the world's resources. No system of property,
> therefore, or actual division of property, is just which does
> not promote the fulfillment of this right.

"2   Private ownership of productive property is both legitimate and necessary: *legitimate,* because of man's natural, God-given dominion over material things; *necessary,* because it is required by the welfare of the individual, of the family and of society. The actuation of this right is the second demand on the material resources of the earth. No actual division of productive property is just, therefore, which does not make possible the fulfillment of this right for as many as the actual extent of such property will allow.

"3   This right of private property is necessarily limited both by the end for which it is intended, and by the fact that *all* men possess the same right in the same way and in the same measure. Therefore, whether there be much or little productive property to divide, *concentrated* ownership cannot be justified by appeal to the right of private property.

"4   Land is the fundamental form of productive property, and here, more than anywhere else, the principles of limitation must be applied. Individual, family and social welfare demand the widest possible diffusion of farm land among individual owners."

The Basic Philosophy on Land. These four conclusions enunciated by Father Vizzard provide our Christian philosophy on land. His brief study on the subject quotes St. Thomas Aquinas and the modern Popes as his authorities. First, the land of the earth should, above all else, serve to provide food, clothing, shelter. Secondly, the land of the earth, to serve its purpose best, should be available for private ownership. Thirdly, the land of the earth, since *all* men possess the same right in the same way and in the same measure to private ownership of it, cannot justifiably be concentrated in detrimental fashion in the hands of a few. Fourthly, the land of the earth, which as farm land is the fundamental form of productive property on earth, should possess widest possible diffusion among individual owners.

"Innumerable complexities are involved in these conclusions," noted Father Vizzard. "I wish to note in particular that the first principle enunciated must never be lost sight of as the key goal. The most fundamental and most urgent of all rights of men with regard to material resources, and this means of all the world's farmers, is that they have proper food, clothing and shelter. The application of the other principles is subordinated to their efficacy in the fulfillment of this basic aim, highly important though the other principles be in their own right."

A few of the complexities to which Father Vizzard referred may be reviewed here briefly.

"Is the right to individual ownership of private property limited to the family," asked Father Richard Lawler, S.J., "or can it be extended to larger groups such as the native tribes of Africa?"

"Communal land tenure in Africa," answered Bishop Blomjous, "is a form that in Catholic philosophy is classed as private ownership of land because it is the ownership of more or less the extended family living on the land. It is not at all ownership of the land by the state. Naturally with the changing economic and social conditions in Africa there will be a change, which I hope will be slow, from this communal land to a stricter form of private ownership, namely, individual ownership. I don't think, however, that there is any question of state ownership of lands involved in African communal land tenure."

The Concept of Private Property. "As a sociologist," interposed Doctor O'Dea, "I'd like to use the occasion of this question to make some comments.

"The Roman Catholic Church, a universal institution, has nevertheless in some aspects been rather closely related historically to the development of Western culture, and the specification of Catholic positions on these things has been very highly influenced by the development of property notions in Western culture—Anglo-Saxon fee simple, Roman law and so forth. I don't think it is very sound, therefore, to make general statements about the nature of man and then jump to his rights to private property, if we employ strictly Western European cultural patterns of private property as the standard of judgment. We must be more universal in our outlook.

"We of the West tend to look at property as a bundle of established expectations with respect to several aspects which are very relative in the individual cultures of the earth. First of all, in speaking of property we refer to rights of access, of use and of disposal or alienation. There are various ways in which these rights may be viewed other than the way we bundle them together.

"It is quite possible to define the right of access in different ways. In feudalism, during the Middle Ages, the right of access was defined variously and parcelled out with reciprocal expectations with regard to the self, to the free farmer, to the lord and so forth. So likewise as regards the right of property use. None of these people had the right of alienation. It was only in the 15th and 16th centuries that society began to get new notions of property, later called capitalist concepts of property, that made provision for alienation. There is a discussion of this in Karl Marx's *Das Kapital* where Marx talks about the Duchess of Sutherland who was very busy converting Scottish clan property into capitalist property.

"We cannot identify the position of the Church with any local cultural institution. If we are going to insist on private ownership in land as a final solution, do we define private ownership in its local cultural sense or in some universal sense? Owning stock in General Motors is not really ownership in the particular sense implied in talking about ownership of land, with its implications regarding access, use and alienation. Between 1905 and 1916 in Russia Stolypin decided to break up the old communal farms and to substitute private ownership farming and the growth of the kulaks. The Bolsheviks came in, continued this policy for a while and then turned to collectivization. I see no reason to tie up Catholic doctrine with any specifically Western cultural practice but, rather, to allow for equivalently satisfactory practices in other cultures. The word 'property,' I think, is a fetish. It is a high-level abstraction which we over-particularize when we use it. When talking at the world level, it would seem wiser to throw it out and speak clearly about right of access, right of disposal, right of security or whatever the equivalents may be, in other cultures, to the value concepts in our right of private property."

Land Security to Every Farmer. Doctor O'Dea made it clear that he regarded our Western concepts of private property as confusing our intent, when we apply our principles regarding land to the various culture areas of the world. Monsignor Ligutti concurred so far as the varying concepts of property were concerned.

"As one who has traveled in different parts of the world," explained the Monsignor, "I can testify to a wide divergence in property concepts. In each of the states of Brazil there are completely different viewpoints on property ownership, because the various places were settled from different parts of Portugal with their different land-holding traditions. In Syria and the Near East generally you find a still different way of owning. In Africa, of course, you get different answers to your questions from every tribe you visit."

"Definitions of private property," noted Father Fitzpatrick, "are inevitably culturally relative because it depends upon what you mean by property and what you mean by private."

"What we find in many papal documents," stated Father Edward Murphy, "is not so much an insistence upon private property as we understand it, but rather an insistence upon some kind of ownership which gives security. The type of ownership may change from culture to culture. It may be communal ownership, which is a perfectly legitimate kind of ownership, if it guarantees the individual farmer security, a means of subsistence and opportunities for improvement."

"Instead of speaking of the purposes of private property," commented Father Edward Malone of the Maryknoll faculty, "we might address ourselves to the purposes of the *bona materialis,* the material goods which in every culture we wish to secure to the owner. We seem to look upon private ownership as if it were a part of Divine Revelation; we seem to imply that God demands private ownership of farms as an essential. Our aim should be to realize the same personal and social consequences for the farmer everywhere, without necessarily a Western conceived form of private property.

"We don't want our missionaries going in and demanding redistribution of land in order to give everybody a little plot merely because the books seem to say that this is an end in itself. The true end must be the enduring welfare of the farmer family."

The Meaning of "Widest Possible Diffusion."   The principle of the greatest good must serve as the criterion in interpreting the term "widest possible diffusion" as found in Father Vizzard's fourth point.

"In Indonesia," explained Father Dijkstra, "we have had, traditionally, a communal ownership but a still more basic ownership of the land by the government that is looked upon as the original possessor. Now by Western education this is changing to private ownership in the Western sense.

"The government is moving very cautiously. In Middle Java private ownership of farm lands is recognized but the authorities do not yet dare to apply to the small farmer the consequence of private ownership, the land tax.

"Now, the peculiar fact in Indonesia is the strong Communist backing for private ownership. None of us are deceived —the Reds are merely interested in destroying the traditional system of property ownership. Once this destruction is complete, it will be simple to move in on the weak small holders, unless the government is strong enough and alert enough to protect the small holders. For the Reds, the system of private property is only an intermediate stage before eventual communization. In Indonesia, if we are not careful, the principle of widest possible diffusion of ownership could lead to Communism."

"The demographic question raises some very realistic problems regarding land division," noted Father William Gibbons.

"In many rural areas the population is growing and hence the number of male sons. When ownership passes through the male line, the number of adult sons becomes greater than the number of available farms large enough for a reasonable income. We may be moving into an era, in the more densely populated parts of the world, when a new concept of land ownership will be needed. We cannot assert, certainly, any absolute right by individual family x, y or z to a specific piece of land when all available land has been preempted."

"Despite my suspicion," intervened Father Vizzard, "that protests against the harm of land division in some regions are really attempts to block any serious programs of land reform, none the less we all must recognize that there can be circumstances that require that land be held in large estates. The principle is not sound, that all large tracts must unqualifiedly be fractioned."

"I think the situation in Chile illustrates this problem very well," commented Father William Coleman, a former director of an agricultural school in Chile. "Individual estates in Chile may be judged to be too large, but many persons who have had experience in rural Chile conclude that the Chilean land tenure system is pretty good. The poorest person in Chile is the person who owns a small piece of property. He is almost helpless. Soil analysis shows that the soil generally is very poor. An economic commission, which sought to establish that a system of small farm ownerships would support the population, failed to prove its point.

"I don't think the division of land is the present solution in Chile. It would only move the country toward famine. My experience in trying to buy land for our agricultural school made it clear that it is impossible to exploit land unless you have a quantity of it, because of the need to possess concomitant irrigation rights. Theoretically, a state-owned irrigation system can serve small farmers but only the wealthy can provide it in Chile. If you owned the best piece of land in the country, you couldn't do a thing with it without irrigation rights.

"I think the approach to land reform in Chile through the parcelling of land is an oversimplification. As Doctor Goncalves de Souza has explained, owner-tenant relations need attention to give proper dignity and freedom to the tenant and his family. Chile's still more urgent preoccupation is what to do about all the people who are going to the city."

The Missionary's Land Reform Program. What should be the rural missionary's attitude toward land reform? The subject is much too important to the populace in many areas of the world for any priest devoted to his flock not to give it serious consideration. Father Vizzard offered a program:

"The missionary at the local or regional level can, by contacts with owners, workers, government officials and the general public, help prevent opposition and break down opposition to land reform. He can, further, lend a prudent guiding hand to promote appropriate steps toward a program. Ordinarily, he should not participate as a technician but as a catalyst.

"First, the missionary should strive earnestly to inform himself on local conditions through sound instruction from properly qualified sources. Agricultural practices and institutions are the outcome of particular and often unique circumstances of climate, soil, geography, history, tradition, culture and even religion.

"Secondly, the missionary should recall that land reform must follow a pattern of broad social-economic-cultural change. Single isolated measures of land reform, undertaken without complementary steps in a wide range program, will almost invariably prove inadequate to solve anything and can even lead to more serious difficulties.

"Thirdly, the missionary must bear in mind that land reform requires careful preparation. Sudden changes are almost always bad changes. For instance, a government program of widespread expropriation and redistribution of land without adequate preparation, may so disrupt production as to cause

famine. This has actually happened in some areas of the world.
"Fourthly, land reform usually requires a series of steps. All
changes should be made in the direction of fulfillment of the
basic principles and objectives that I have enumerated, but
these objectives can rarely, perhaps never, be achieved at one
time.

"Fifthly, land reform calls for education of all involved concerning the local problems and for enunciation of forthright
moral principles to be recognized by all. The local weaknesses
need to be uncovered: i) land holdings which are too small;
ii) fragmentation of holdings, sometimes with a single farm
family possessing 12 or 15 small particles of land; iii) defective
tenancy practices; iv) defective titles to land or water rights;
v) problems from communal tenure; vi) too large holdings,
latifundia; vii) absence of development capital for improvements; viii) excessive tax burdens.

"Sixthly, successful land reform calls for many non-agricultural institutions, such as more schools, the organizing of
credit unions, the provision of health and leisure programs."

"Father Vizzard," observed Doctor Gladwin, "has very
wisely warned the missionary, particularly the young missionary, to approach this field of land reform with judicious caution. Certainly it involves problems that demand a great deal
of technical expertise and of human understanding. The great
good to be accomplished will have a commanding appeal to
every zealous missionary. Let him tackle the problems vigorously but guard against disasters through imprudence that can
only hurt religion."

For recommended reading, see Bibliography No. 8, page 274.

BUILDING A STRONG
RURAL COMMUNITY

Socio-Economic Factors in a Community. A writer recently described the community as the "human whole" and noted that studying the community "lies today in a borderline between science and art." The experienced missionary prides himself on the ability he acquires with the passing of the years to get to know communities. In a large mission parish he may have 50 towns and villages. After a while each of them has for him a distinctive personality.

Since our present considerations concern the socio-economic, we remind the missionary that he must occupy himself, not only with the spirit of the community's inhabitants, but with the more plebeian yet strongly influential physical aspects of the community.

Father Eugene Higgins of the Maryknoll Extension Service provides us with an analysis of these physical aspects.

"A book written in Spanish," he said, "carries the title, *Housing Is More Than a Roof.* We may say, as well, that a village is more than a number of buildings and streets. Village planning is concerned with programs which are intended to provide for the orderly disposition of the many interrelated requirements that are necessary for the proper care and development of the body, mind and soul of man. An intelligent coordination and evaluation of the factors involved in village planning helps the young missionary to see what makes a village tick.

"Missionaries should understand the great opportunity they possess in working at the village level. 'Start at the bottom' is one of the dictums of national development. Missionaries are right there on the spot—at the bottom. National strength develops from well-nourished, well-housed, well-clothed, well-cultured villagers who form the very foundation of the social and economic structure of the nation. When well disciplined in Christian living, they likewise form the backbone of spiritual strength for religion throughout the world.

"A knowledge of the factors involved in village planning pays good missionary dividends even if the missionary never sits down with a village planning committee. It provides him with a more alert administrative sense, a greater sympathy for the problems of all, non-Christian and Christian, who make up the village community. With this knowledge he will be more sure-footed in avoiding any proposals to his flock that will prove divisory in the community, since he will understand clearly that Christianity is best served if it becomes known as a stalwart supporter of everything that serves the true interest of the whole community and not merely of the Catholic segment."

Physical Components of a Rural Community. The urban community is due for consideration in a later chapter. Father Higgins' components of the rural community line up as follows:

1 *Land, forests, mines, commercial waters:*
    i proper type land to provide an administrative, business and residence center for the community;
    ii surrounding farm land for local food supply, money crops, animal industry;

    iii forest areas for commercial timber, for extraction en-
terprises (rubber, oil, nuts, etc.) or for orchards;

    iv deposits, ferrous or non-ferrous, for commercial min-
ing;

    v river, lake or coastal waters for transportation or fish-
ing.

2 *Water:* adequate supply of drinking water, of water for crops,
animals, business establishments.

3 *Sewage disposal.*

4 *Heat, light and power.*

5 *Transportation:*
    i pedestrian facilities, streets, roads, highways;
    ii public conveyance provisions (bus, railroad, boat, air-
plane).

6 *Communications:* telephone, telegraph, press, radio, television, motion pictures, audio-visual aids, according to national economy.

7 *Institutional facilities* for:
    i public administration;
    ii divine worship;
    iii education;
    iv cultural life (library, museum, arts and folk culture);
    v health and medical care (hospital, clinics, public or
private medical personnel);
    vi social welfare;
    vii leisure and recreation;
    viii interment.

8 *Industry:* agriculturally related enterprises or non-agricultural industries.

9 *Merchandizing:* wholesale enterprises, retail shopping areas.

10 *Housing.*

It goes without saying that we shall not cover the entire
gamut of the above components. Which of the dozens of subjects listed should be given top consideration by the missionary,
from our present angle of the socio-economic, must remain a
moot question.

"I believe," stated Doctor Arceneaux, "that in community

planning education is the real basis. I suggest that the village school be considered very important in the community for all this planning. I am thinking not only in terms of the regular instruction given in the schools; I include adult education as well. In other words, the schools should be centers for the diffusion of ideas. Government and the religious authorities should cooperate in an area to make the schools accomplish their maximum."

Certainly the school has this great function to fill. So important is it that a separate special study of all the functions of education in the missionary Church is proposed as the best answer. To serve best the study of our socio-economic problems, we have selected community public health, nutrition and housing for consideration in this chapter.

Missionary Concern for the Physical Elements. "Let us recall once again," observed Doctor Thomas Gladwin, "that we are considering the joint concept of the social and the economic. From my experience in the islands of the Pacific I would warn against being carried away with material improvement in such fashion that it drags in its train a lot of social disruption. You put in a water supply, let us say, and the necessary adjustments requiring the relocation of dwellings and changes in the way of life in a village can be enormous, if the procedure has been directed merely from the angle of the water with no regard for the ways of life. The missionary, first and foremost, is to concern himself with men's souls. That means he is highly sensitive to the import of social custom in men's lives. He must make it very clear that in every situation he takes care that the social factors are not injured in the search for material gain."

"On the other hand," interposed Monsignor Ligutti, "I wish to enter a mild protest against the easy-going missionary who seems hopelessly unconcerned about improving situations. His watchword is, 'People don't want it.'

"Down in the Cherokee District in Panama the women cook on three stones on the floor. 'Why not lift up this crude cooking apparatus off the floor?' I asked a missionary old-timer. 'The women don't want it,' he answered. A younger man chuckled and the two of us decided to ask the women. The very first we approached answered, 'Oh, I've been after my husband to do that but he's too lazy.' All of the others favored some sort of improvement."

"The ordinary practical man going into a town or village needs to have certain basic concepts," observed Father William Gibbons. "The State of California, which is currently the most rapidly changing demographic area in the United States, has set up a special structure at state and local levels to train men to know the state, its problems and their solutions. In some small way this idea may help us. In this matter of building Christian life into village life, we too often seem to know too little about the villages."

"I think we need a deeper concept of what a village is," remarked Father Considine. "A village is not an accident. In most parts of the world it represents a great deal of the philosophy of life of the people even in its physical layout. I would say that this is one of the things that many of us going into new lands overlook. It has a lot to do with our introduction of Christianity.

"In Latin America, for instance, the layout of every town represents the consistent expression of a philosophy. Each town has a central square, on one side of which is the equivalent of our town hall and opposite the town hall stands the Catholic church. Other institutions in town have their place. If the North American decides he'd rather build a new church on a better site half a mile down the road, what happens to town traditions? Perhaps they'll adjust, but he needs to appreciate the necessity of finding out."

"In Pakistan," added Mr. Dumpson, "the pattern of the village has similar significance. The missionary needs to know that the place in town where he locates his chapel has great significance as regards its dignity as a house of worship."

"At the same time," noted Father de Reeper, "we have to

be ready to adjust ourselves to less than the ideal. The villages in Africa are very different from our European idea of a village. Often our mission compound is the equivalent of what in our part of Africa passes for a village, a small nucleus of dwellings. When a missionary starts a station, he can't just pick the best spot, with good soil, near a well; the ideas of the chief and of government officials all figure. Let's get basic notions of what we need for building Christian society and do the best we can according to local conditions."

The Missionary and Community Health. Of the ten components listed in this chapter as figuring in community planning, the seventh concerns itself with what are termed institutional facilities. Eight categories of institutions are enumerated as having a place in the town's life. They concern the individual from birth until his death and burial in the village cemetery. Important among these categories is community health and medical care.

How interested is the missionary in community health? Curiously, to a question phrased in this fashion, many a missionary would hesitate to answer. He is likely to say, "I conduct a dispensary in my station and the Bishop has a hospital operated by Sisters who do grand work but, frankly, I've never really considered myself involved in problems of community health."

Because this view is still encountered among missionaries, this socio-economic study aims to place emphasis on the new approach to the role of the medical apostolate that characterizes mission effort in many parts of the world. Medicine traditionally has figured prominently in the apostolate. Social medicine is a newly coined term for an activity that has long been practiced in mission lands but which has not been known by that name.

"Bishop Blomjous," we asked, "how widespread is the acceptance of the idea among missionaries that medicine is no longer merely curative but should be regarded as playing a preventive role as well?"

"More and more," replied His Excellency, "our hospitals are being regarded not only as centers for curative medicine but also as bases for health work and preventive medicine. At the same time, up to the present in East Africa we can expect no recognition by the people for any health work efforts unless we have a hospital. In backward areas a public health program needs the prestige of the hospital to secure acceptance."

"In Indonesia," volunteered Father Dijkstra, "our hospitals have the tendency to grow too big. Then the Sisters and the nurses have the tendency, by force of circumstances, to stay in the hospitals. This is too bad. We need hospitals but we do our best to get as many as possible of the Sisters out into the homes, into the environment where they can exercise tremendous influence among the people in the promotion of the government's public health program."

Preventive medicine is the order of the day. Where a few years ago major attention went to lowering the death rates, in many countries now principal effort is centered on the reduction and prevention of sickness. There have been important gains on three fronts: 1) in the treatment of disease through the so-called wonder drugs; 2) in the development of health centers providing integrated curative and preventive services; 3) in the use of rural mobile field units for both curative and preventive programs.

Public Health in Mission Lands. Graciously assisting us to obtain a sound missionary outlook on the use of medicine in strengthening the community were Dr. August Groeschel, Director of New York Hospital and Associate Professor of Public Health and Preventive Medicine at Cornell University Medical School, and Doctor Duncan W. Clark, Professor of Public Health and Environmental Medicine and Nutrition at Long Island University.

"Don't be surprised," noted Doctor Groeschel, "that the medical world differs even at such an elementary level as in its definitions, quite as happens in so many other fields. One school, for example, gives us the following as its concept of health: 'Health defined as a state of complete physical, mental and social well-being—and not merely the absence of disease and infirmity—is a basic component of the standard of living and is therefore a fundamental requirement for community development.'

"Quite another statement comes from the head of the New York Department of Public Health: 'With respect to positive definitions of health, it is believed that health is a relative term which describes only that degree to which an individual is able to operate as an effective person within the particular circumstances of his own heredity and environment. In short, the philosophy of the Department is based on the fact that all living things, including men, are inevitably disease-ridden and mortal but that within these immutable limits some diseases are preferable to others.' This is the party line of our New York Department."

Doctor Clark provided a brief practical survey of public health.

"The public health problems in the underdeveloped countries, which are your mission countries," he noted, "cover a very wide range of medicine. They fall particularly into these areas: 1) communicable disease, 2) nutrition, 3) maternal and child health, 4) family health, 5) environmental sanitation, 6) health education, 7) personal hygiene, 8) health records and statistics, 9) organization of health services, 10) education and training of health personnel."

Cooperation against Communicable Diseases. In regard to the first, Doctor Clark said: "A great deal of technical effort is going on at present in underdeveloped countries by small technical teams, which bring local health hazards and communicable diseases under control without the personal cooperation or the understanding of the masses of the people. But in the activities that lie ahead much more of the enterprises will call for personal understanding. This is where community leaders such as missionaries are needed.

"The almost startling effects of some of the programs are

well known to you. We have moved from the day of malarial control programs to malarial eradication. Given the funds, the administration devices and proper cooperation, eradication may be accomplished within the next few years.

"In this eradication of communicable diseases, missionaries may be guides and instigators at the several operational levels of preventive medicine.

"The first level is the promotion of health or well-being of a community to a degree that lessens susceptibility to disease generally. This can be done by health education.

"The second level is one of specific protection. Vaccination against certain diseases is an example, and the vaccination campaigns need leadership support.

"The third level is the fight for early detection and treatment. Your aid in defeating tuberculosis lies in this field.

"The fourth level is the prevention or limitation of disabilities that may occur when a disease already contracted is poorly treated through local ignorance or negligence.

"The fifth level is the follow-up level, the provision of rehabilitation, which is really the use of medical, social and other cures in the restoration of people who have been gravely ill or injured."

Doctor Clark's appeal was for an appreciation by missionaries of the long-term good to mission lands that would accrue from their participation in a control of the major killers among infectious diseases. For the first time in history the possibilities are great for an effective tuberculosis control program. Hundreds of Catholic leprosy centers are profiting from the advent of the sulfones that make it possible to abandon old methods of leprosy control. Confidence and collaboration replace fear and blind hostility in the attitude of the victims. A missionary task still remains in the mental and physical reeducation of the cured patients and in rectifying the attitude of the general public toward these patients.

The fight against bilharziasis, a debilitating disease in Africa and the Western Pacific, is less further advanced. In the Philippines alone, the annual loss, caused by this species of fresh-water snail which renders men unable to do their work, is a million and a half dollars. New methods to combat it have been found and need promulgation in the afflicted areas.

Analysis of the Role of the Medicine Man. Doctor Clark and Doctor Groeschel both advise the Catholic missionary that, in order to serve properly the communities of non-Western culture by the introduction of Western medicine, care should be taken to apply the principles of social anthropology. Doctor Groeschel illustrated the process involved by describing a cartoon.

"My favorite cartoon on the course of modern medicine in Africa depicts the interior of a thatched hut with a native lying on the floor, obviously very sick. His wife is kneeling anxiously at his side looking at the local medicine man, who is completely equipped with an elaborate headdress and ferocious mask and a large ugly-looking baton. The medicine man has stopped midway in his ritual dance around the patient and addressing the patient's wife he says, 'I will dance around him twice again and if he isn't any better I will have to bring him to the hospital for X-rays.'

"This story is not without point in that it illustrates, in an admittedly crude fashion, the need for recognition of good in existing cultural patterns and the adaptation of our methods with consideration for these patterns in so far as this is possible."

Doctor Clark drew upon the writings of Professor Firth of London in order to urge the missionary to give proper value to the seemingly ridiculous carryings-on of the medicine man among underdeveloped peoples.

"It is important to note," stated Doctor Clark, "that tribal peoples in Africa and Asia have gone a long way in rearranging their ideas on healing. Even the local medicine men do not reject Western medication but seek to intermingle this with their particular healing rituals.

"How explain this? Professor Firth proposes that we consider how the doctor in the Western world takes care of the person who is ill. The doctor makes a brief visit, performs a quiet examination, prescribes medicine and with a courteous word to others in the house is on his way. It is all quite businesslike and we in the West are favorably impressed through it being so.

"But now witness the village healing expert in tribal Africa. He serves as a professional spirit medium as well. When he visits he goes through an elaborate spiritual ceremonial, but he often includes massages and applications involving primitive remedies. He visits his patient daily and spends considerable time with him. However, physical diagnosis is not his line. He interprets the cause of illness as an evil spirit. Sickness represents suffering inflicted through someone else's error or villainy. Diagnosis includes locating the culprit. The theory of illness, since it involves spiritual as well as physical causation, calls for spiritual as well as physical therapy. The foreign doctor can, the Africans agree, contribute to the physical but not to the spiritual relief of the patient or give any psychological reassurance to relatives or friends. The profound influence of a system that gathers all the neighbors and makes the patient the focus of social as well as physical interest will not readily be abandoned unless a substitute for the African variety of spiritual reassurance is supplied."

The Priest as Community Caretaker.   "This, clearly," continued Doctor Clark, "should be the role of Christianity, which in higher and nobler form must meet the tribal African's need at this critical juncture by correcting his confused ideas. The doctor cannot do this: it is not his function. It is not enough for secularists to debunk the notion that an enemy has brought the illness; the patient in grave illness still needs attention and solicitude, and this should come from a representative of religion.

"In our part of the world, which in my specific case is Brooklyn, the Catholic priest fulfills quite beautifully the role of community caretaker, a traditional role in at least two situations, namely, guidance of members of the community at times of crisis, and shepherd of the sorrowful in successful grieving. If crises are not handled well and grieving is not successful, both mental and physical illness can occur; so here is the role of the priest at a specific level of prevention, as truly in Africa as in Brooklyn.

"There are two implications in this consideration. The first is that Catholic missionaries can profit from the scientific efforts of psychiatrists. The second is that the priest in his missionary work recognize certain of his functions, which make him no less a priest, as paralleling the vocation of the social worker. The missionary seminarian in the course of his training feels, I know, that he profits from making himself familiar with the work of the doctor and of the hospital. He would also profit, I believe, if he acquainted himself by brief contact with the task of the social worker and the welfare field. One purpose would be to experience his own feelings and the feelings of the victims in crisis situations."

The Missionary's Part in Public Health. Doctor Clark and Doctor Groeschel quite realistically avoided any recommendation that the missionary, while he must hold himself responsible for the establishment of dispensaries or of public health programs or hospitals, should occupy himself personally with such work except under unusual circumstances. Sisters, Brothers and dedicated laity are the sources of a voluntary staff, while local employees (nurses, midwives and so forth) should be given proper status and paid satisfactory salaries. Nevertheless, on analysis, the role of the missionary in public health is an extensive one. Here are the principal recommendations:

1   *Health education program for the general public.* Certainly in public health no man is an island; the paltry staff that can be provided by most communities would get nowhere without public cooperation. In this field it seems best to emphasize direct educational methods which make the layman an active participant, organized to use his initiative in correcting specific local health weaknesses.

2 *Promotion of maternal and child health centers.* Major emphasis around the world by UNICEF of the United Nations and many national governments has been given during the past decade to these comprehensive health services. They specialize in catering to the needs of mothers of families, particularly as regards pre-natal and post-natal care during the period of childbirth, and to the needs of the children themselves.

Since these centers have, in some countries, become bases for birth control propaganda, it is important that Catholics be directed to take a positive and not a negative attitude toward them. They render excellent service when rightly conducted. The missionary should encourage their proper operation, substitute his own centers when wrong information regarding the marriage act is taught and if at all possible avoid abandoning this field to devotees of unacceptable practices.

3 *Promotion of care of pre-school children.* In many countries the one-to-five age-group experiences as high mortality as the infant group. Public health programs in backward areas need special support in fighting unsatisfactory nutrition, sanitation and communicable disease control as regards this group.

4 *School health program.* Will the school teacher or the district nurse be held responsible for the school health program? The missionary, as the operator of a school, may be brought into this world question which needs answering always in favor of the child. The school provides a convenient place for surveillance of children against communicable diseases such as tuberculosis, tooth decay, mental defects, malnutrition.

5 *Family health service.* The family unit is basic for health promotion. The missionary who is able to arrange his own home-visiting service, possibly directed by Sisters, is often able to make it multi-purpose—promoting health, Christian family practices, catechetical training, family relations counselling.

6 *Health program in community development.* Village health programs must be simple and inexpensive and depend greatly on voluntary assistance in an ordered program in which the populace can participate. Mother and child centers and similar projects lack trained staff and must depend on auxiliary workers such as can be enlisted in community development pro-

grams. The priest, as catalyst, has a role cut out for him in promoting a community spirit that will prompt generosity.

7 *Village sanitation.* The basic aspects of sanitation belong to engineering or environmental hygiene (safe water supply, problems of excreta, development of insecticides). But, again, a great field for auxiliary activity remains for local initiative, possibly inspired by the missionary, because paid personnel is impossible to obtain in backward areas. In one section of India, two technicians, a sanitary engineer and a health inspector, undertook with some success to set up a rural sanitation program for a population of 100,000. They created a local team of 25 persons who were given three aims: i) to teach the farmers how to construct simple types of wells and latrines; ii) to train voluntary well drillers and sanitary inspectors for the villages; iii) to carry out a health education program to insure public and individual support.

8 *Nutrition education.* The public in the Western world accepts the arguments for proper food production and distribution to insure a nutritional diet. Education in nutrition in mission lands means: i) helping people to understand nutritional needs; ii) encouraging grassroots leadership to change food habits with full regard for the local economic, social and cultural factors. Introducing green vegetables offers a problem if local people believe that all green vegetables are poisonous, as is the case in the great areas of the Amazon Basin. Items of food cannot be advocated simply because they are nourishing; they must be attractive to the taste; they must be easily and inexpensively obtained.

Supplementary feeding programs, such as those of Catholic Relief Services, UNICEF and CARE, are easier to promote but are only a phase of the problem of nutrition.

9 *Encouraging professional careers.* The doctor is the central figure in medicine and public health, and practically no country on the globe has its proper quota of doctors. Since World War II something over 100 medical schools have been added to the approximately 550 in the world; if the annual output is 50 per school, this addition of 5,000 new doctors yearly will still prove inadequate.

Concepts regarding the functions of nurses in many countries are such that girls of social station are discouraged from following this career, and in only a few countries is the training professionally adequate. The world shortage in nurses is tremendous.

The missionary in most instances will be able to encourage the pursuit of a career of medical service only at the humbler auxiliary levels, unless he is dealing with well-educated young people. Nevertheless he will render great good if he can fix his sights on choice subjects among his flock who might devote their lives to medicine.

Proper Family Dwellings.   In this chapter we are reviewing the essential life requirements in the rural community. The three basics among these requirements are food, clothing and shelter. Let us give a thought to shelter.

The gap between the cost of a minimum standard dwelling and the amount a low-income family can pay for a dwelling continues very wide, and in many countries it is widening. Thus shelter for the poor remains today a major public concern. Suggestions for the missionary are presented by Doctor Rafael Mora-Rubio of one of Colombia's strong Catholic families, a Community Housing Specialist, who has served with the Inter-American Housing Center (CINVA) at Bogota and who is now attached to UNESCO at United Nations Headquarters, New York.

"Looking at a map," stated Doctor Mora-Rubio, "one easily observes that most of the so-called underdeveloped countries are located in the tropical zone. Poverty, malnutrition, bad health, inadequate shelter, lack of education and therefore low levels of living are common to all of them. These conditions prevail particularly in the rural areas, where modern facilities cannot be provided easily and where people often find it difficult to eke out a living. Asia, Africa and Latin America, to a greater or lesser extent, are in these circumstances. They represent 70 percent of the total world population.

"This means that the problem of rural housing in most underdeveloped countries is that of tropical housing. Therefore, the approach to the problem has to be a special one. Housing standards cannot be based on those of developed countries in the temperate zone. Social organization, habits of living and cultural factors differ. It is necessary when making improvements not to disrupt suddenly the traditional patterns. Attention should be focused on: 1) the functions of the house; 2) the basic requirements for starting an improvement program."

How Does a Family Use a House? "A human biological unit, a family," said Doctor Mora-Rubio, "makes of a house a home. In the home it will live and provide independently for its subsistence. The functions of a home are primary and secondary.

"The primary functions are:

"1   to provide shelter;
"2   to serve as a dwelling place;
"3   to ensure privacy;
"4   to facilitate the activities of family living and the preservation of health;
"5   to safeguard the occupants and their belongings.

"The secondary functions are:

"1   the practice of religion;
"2   the entertainment of the family and their friends;
"3   the carrying on of household work;
"4   the meeting of cultural and educational needs.

"To provide shelter, rural people ordinarily use local materials such as earth, timber, stones, bamboo, leaves, grass or whatever else is found at hand. Some people believe these materials bad or inadequate, but this is not always true. Some may be defective, but their use can be improved through better techniques and methods. The United Nations, for example, has sponsored intensive research on earth as a building material. India has done important work improving bamboo houses, and the Inter-American Housing Center in Bogota has developed a simplified machine to produce stabilized soil blocks, the CINVA earth block.

"In many places in Latin America the concept of a house has been that of a place to rest and sleep; the other activities have been carried on outside the house, in the patio. In such circumstances, the house is little used in the daytime and therefore light and air within it are not given primary importance. This factor, together with the need for warmth at night in the mountain areas, accounts in part for the lack of windows and the low, narrow doorways. However, there are other reasons for lack of windows, as I shall explain.

"The patio is a very important component of the house in Latin America and a good deal of attention should be given to it. It is a mistake not to consider the patio as part of the rural house. There the children play, the wife works, the grain and other products are dried, the laundry is done, the small animals are kept and family activities are carried on.

"The function of the house as a dwelling place should have a bearing on its size. Its adequacy is decided by requirements of bedrooms, living room, kitchen and so forth. Overcrowding is measured by the number of persons per room, their age and sex. Overcrowding is acute in Latin America. In Argentine in 1947 40 percent of the rural families with children up to 21 slept in one room, and since 1947 the percentage seems to have risen.[1] This manner of sleeping is prevalent in other areas such as the Peruvian sierra, even when lack of space is not the reason."[2]

Provision for Privacy, Health, Family Life. "A certain measure of privacy," Doctor Mora-Rubio continued, "is required to provide sufficient scope for introspection, prayer, creative thinking and sex expression. The lack of windows is related traditionally to privacy, though this may be gained by curtains, doors or partitions. Trees, bushes, hedges, fences and walls are for privacy as well as protection from intruders. In some regions of Colombia the windowless rear of the house is toward the road, and the front faces the concealed patio, for greater privacy.

"The kitchen may be a component of the house or a separate structure. Here the housewife spends most of the day and since meals are usually served in the kitchen it becomes the social center of the house. A system of plumbing, involving the kitchen water supply, the toilets or their equivalent and the disposal of refuse, needs study from the aspect of sanitation.

"The effects of housing on health are a main concern of governments. It was epidemics in urban areas that first brought attention to housing, and the first housing regulations touched on health.

"For reasons of economy and protection, barns and out-houses are not usually constructed in Latin America. Thus animals, tools, equipment, the harvest, all end up in the house. The attic, the veranda and even bedrooms are used. Personal belongings and tools are hung from nails or pegs, since closets, pantries or shelves are seldom found. Animal corrals, pig pens and chicken coops are kept close to the patio. The dog plays an important role as watchman. Because of the dog, it is the custom throughout Latin America to shout greetings from a distance when approaching a rural house."

The Missionary and Dwelling Improvement. The missionary who is anxious to help his people improve their dwellings, Doctor Mora-Rubio explained, needs first of all to make a careful size-up of the local housing practices. Then he should proceed cautiously with a program that should become known locally as the people's plan, not his, with the people making the changes. His most important contribution may be the information he may secure for the people from the government or others on financing possibilities.

"Carry out a survey," suggested the Doctor, "or at least gather considerable information from the people that will acquaint you with the main defects in local housing. The investigation may suggest, for example, the need to replace earthen floors with other more hygienic material. If the house is built on stilts, it may be the accummulation of filth under it that requires attack. Perhaps the walls should be whitewashed, or the roofs should be made of better material, or latrines installed. Perhaps the delicate problem of introducing windows should be tackled. Overcrowding may be the main danger, calling for provision of more space and provision of shelters for animals outside the house. Maybe nothing short of building new houses is the answer.

"Once the physical defects have been assessed, careful consideration must be given to other factors, such as living habits, which are closely related to housing standards. So important are living habits that housing standards cannot be copied or adapted from standards prevailing in other countries or even in other regions of the same country. They must be based on investigation of the people's wants, opinions and attitudes.

"Perhaps it is the living habits and attitudes that must be changed. If so, any attempt at rapid action will lead to failure. A continuing process will be necessary so that little by little the desired changes may be obtained."

Changing Living Habits and Attitudes. "In Peru," explained Doctor Mora-Rubio, "the rural houses in the sierra consist of several structures around a patio. These include storehouses for the harvest. However, the storehouses remain empty most of the year, while the members of the family are crowded into the only bedroom in deplorable fashion. This maldistribution is largely due to habit and the low temperature. Stuffing all the sleepers into one room, with even the animals included to create warmth, represents a tradition which the inhabitant of the sierra has followed unquestioningly for generations. He inherited this mode of life and knows no other. How are these conditions to be changed? Perhaps the solution is to move the kitchen, supplied with a chimney, into the house. But research, careful thought and education will be necessary for such a step.

"What to us would be a very simple improvement, the introduction of windows, can be one of the most difficult in practice. If you build a nice house with windows, to your surprise you may find that they'll shortly be eliminated. How to encourage their use is a problem to be solved in each locality. Perhaps curtains will prove the answer; perhaps windows will be accepted only in the roof.

"Latrines are an important improvement but also entail difficulties. Some authority may force their construction and supply detailed instructions, but will they be used? In most cases the answer is negative. They will be adapted as chicken nests, or pig pens, or storage bins.

"There is one basic principle that can be accepted: the improvements that rural people are led to make of themselves with their own hands will remain. When this occurs a whole process has taken place; the interest has been aroused, the attitude is changed, the desire for improvement has been translated into action based on free will.

"We may contrast this healthy approach with the disastrous effects of paternalism. Once paternalism has been employed by political agents or by ignorant though well-intentioned philanthropists, it will be very hard to move the people to improve themselves."

A Practical Plan for Impoved Housing. Doctor Mora-Rubio's advice on housing improvement reminds us of the principles discussed under community development.

"It can be said bluntly," stated the Doctor, "that the main objective of the first step in the plan is success; you simply cannot afford to fail. An old Spanish saying goes, *'Obras son amores y no buenas razones'*: 'Deeds count and not good reasons.' Rural people in Latin America are generally skeptical. This is charged to their Indian ancestry and to their having been deceived so many times.

"Some urgent need connected with housing that is simple and inexpensive should be chosen. It might be the digging of family wells, which for the most part involve participation in hand labor by the people. Before starting, however, the problem should be discussed at a meeting and the participants should be called upon to suggest solutions, in order that the decision is theirs. The person who is launching the program should work out a feasible solution in advance and see that it is arrived at. It would be harmful to close the meeting without a concrete decision being determined upon and precise plans made as to what is going to be done and who is going to do it.

"Then the missionary planner should be prepared to function with the three principal groups of means that he must employ. These are: 1) the human element; 2) the tools and equipment; 3) the financing.

"Concerning the human element, the families with the proper attitudes and willingness to participate should have the first assignments. Those with sufficient knowledge of building techniques should be given their tasks, and the building materials should be securely available beyond hazard of non-appearance. Careful determination of the methods of financing should be determined before, not after, the proposal of housing improvements to the village folk.

"Many countries today, even the less prosperous, provide villages with modest financing schemes for housing under conditions for loan repayment which need to be studied. Farmers often do not know that such aid exists, do not know how to make application, find the procedures too complicated and discouraging. A friendly educated leader can be surprisingly useful.

"Many rural people have always built their own homes with the help of their neighbors. Now self-help housing schemes in some lands enlarge upon this idea by loans for materials, prefabricated house components at low prices, the provision of technical advice to promote improvements. In Chile over 600 homes were built by self-help methods at German Riesco, near Santiago, for victims of a huge fire. Popular interest awakened by their courageous efforts to overcome their misfortune prompted many among the better-off to aid them, a factor which sometimes can be enlisted by an enthusiastic leader.

"According to the region, different names are given in Latin

America to the cooperative effort which bands relatives, friends and neighbors in house building: the *minga,* the *junta,* the *convite.* This tradition, when properly organized, has accomplished a good deal, not only in house construction, but in providing schools, sports fields, roads, bridges.

"Family dignity, health and comfort can be measured by the manner in which the family is housed. Good or bad housing conditions leave an indelible mark on children and have a bearing on tomorrow's citizens of our communities."

For recommended reading, see Bibliography Nos. 9, 10 and 11, pages 275, 277 and 279.

THE MISSIONARY APPROACH TO URBAN PROBLEMS

World Trend to Urbanization. The number one urban problem today is urbanization, "the process whereby an increasing proportion of a country's population comes to live in urban localities."

"Urbanization and industrialization," explained Father Joseph Fitzpatrick, S.J., Director of the Department of Sociology at Fordham University, "are going to be increasing phenomena in the world of the future. A large number of missionaries are going to have to cope with them. Indeed, if the missionary body were to be distributed evenly among the population of the future, the great majority of tomorrow's missionaries would be urban missionaries because the great majority of the world's population is due to live in cities.

"The United States of America, as the most highly urbanized and industrialized country of the world today, has 15 percent of its people on farms, 20 percent in villages and towns and 65 percent in cities. The nations throughout the globe are marching in this direction."

Rapid, unplanned and uncontrolled city growth has given the urban areas of the globe a great crop of giant headaches: 1) steadily increasing overcrowding; 2) exaggerated metropolitan concentrations; 3) industrial overcentralization; 4) urban sprawl; 5) administrative confusion; 6) ever-expanding transport requirements; 7) over-taxed public utilities; 8) inadequate housing; 9) inadequate educational, health and sanitation facilities.

Urbanization, the experts tell us grimly, will continue to increase in most of the world for many years to come. Agriculture, if our rural areas are to be more prosperous, must modernize and employ methods and equipment that will greatly reduce the manpower requirements. Thus the cityward flow will be stepped up, and the prospects are that urban living conditions, burdened by the growing calls on urban facilities, will worsen rather than improve during the years ahead. The financial requirements to make things better are hopelessly beyond the reach of almost all of the countries of the globe.

The unapproved shanty towns built by squatters on the edge of cities without any rights of occupation are a world phenomenon. Municipalities wink at them rather than assume responsibility for services to poverty-striken groups that cannot pay taxes. Forced eviction merely brings social revolt. Providing quarters for new migrants is a practical impossibility without large sums, and even the longer established urban workers are often very badly housed.

This situation explains another phenomenon found in underdeveloped countries, the company town. Foreign private industrial enterprises plan, build, service and administer quarters for their employees either in or near cities or at isolated spots for the operation of iron, steel, copper plants and the like. Among the more celebrated are Mithrapur and Jamshedpur in India, Dahran in Saudi Arabia, El Mehallah in Egypt, Paz del Rio in Colombia, Huachipato in Chile, Chimbote in Peru. The company towns may have beneficial effects, since financially strong foreign industry initiates social welfare services that give ideas to neighboring communities. However, they represent some drawbacks: 1) they encourage exaggerated dependence of the worker and his family on industry; 2) they inhibit the growth of a civic responsibility; 3) they prevent the integration of workers with the general community; 4) they sometimes create a class of privileged workers in an area where many are under-employed. These disadvantages are eliminated when the company town is designed as a transitional segment of the community, with workers encouraged, by cooperatives and other self-help enterprises, to own their own homes and to assume responsibility.

Importance of the Human Factor. A statement by our American Government to the United Nations notes the current trend in urban problems "toward a closer coordination of physical planning and social planning." A similar report from the Netherlands states that development plans used to be regarded as strictly economic until "people began to recognize the fact that in various cases the primary economic ends of the welfare plan could not be attained because the factor 'man' as well as the social and cultural development of society had not been given sufficient attention." [1]

Thus civil governments recognize what the Catholic priest will quickly ascertain, namely, the need of a social structure to reach the people involved in the huge urbanization movement, if they are to be aided in their grave problems. The sense of participation in the community affairs, which are a normal feature of life in villages and small towns, is regarded as almost impossible to maintain in very large cities except in a vague way. However, in many such cities neighborhood and sectional groups organize themselves spontaneously to obtain services. Voluntary associations have sprung up to a surprising degree in African cities, often on the basis of tribal connections.

Very interesting is the degree of community cohesion found in cities of Latin America. The cities are divided into *barrios,* which often coincide with the Catholic parish lines. In several countries elected councils have appeared in these *barrios,* sometimes spontaneously and sometimes encouraged by the authorities. In Colombia they are called *juntas de mejoras,* in Costa Rica *juntas progresistas,* in Ecuador *asociaciones barriales.* They exert pressure for local improvements and in some instances organize the neighborhood for cooperative self-help activities. In Lima, Peru, they have at times organized themselves for cooperative labor and have even taxed themselves for neighborhood needs.

People Who Go to the City. "The institution that takes the greatest beating through urban migration," explained Father Fitzpatrick, "is the family. The major problem of the missionary is to keep the family strong as it faces the inevitable difficulties that arise when it moves to the city.

"Most of the cultural and social supports that keep the family strong in the rural areas are removed as the family finds itself in urban life. The extended kinship group of the family, strong by normal circumstances in the rural areas, is likewise a casualty when the migrant family takes up life isolatedly in the city.

"Trouble may center on the fact that the mother begins to work for a wage. She may have worked a great deal on the farm, but there her work was family-centered; it took place within the context of family relationships. When she begins to work for a wage outside her home this does a number of things. This compounds the problem of the dislocation of the family, already created by the absence of the man of the house who formerly was likewise nearby, working on the family farm.

"The farming man who takes a factory job that keeps him absent from his family all day, or all night by still more upsetting hours of the work shift, represents a source of crisis. The industrial system sets a rhythm that does not consider the demands of the family; it is rather the family that must submit itself to the demands of the economic system.

"City ways likewise call for an adjustment in the fulfillment of most of the basic functions of life. In rural areas, the child is born within the framework of the family, with the help of a midwife or a neighbor, much of the child's education is within the family, recreation in great part takes place within the family framework, the whole occupational activity is a family enterprise, sickness is taken care of by the family, old age is lived out within the family, death comes at the family hearth. In the city, a great many of these functions of life become commercialized and professionalized. City-born people very successfully live by the altered urban pattern, but those who have been brought up under the rural pattern suffer grievously from the transition. The missionary, and all who work to serve the migrant, must keep themselves keenly aware of this central fact."

Family Support by Association. "The shock of urban living can bring disaster," Father Fitzpatrick stated. "Family disorganization can lead to adult and juvenile crime. A loss of traditional moral values can bring loss of faith and of moral integrity and personality disorders. The strain of life can bring a mental breakdown that in the quiet of a rural setting would never occur.

"If the family is to override successfully these shocks, it must remain strong. The new society or culture in which it finds itself will not prevent it from becoming weak. It will remain strong only if the individuals involved, particularly the husband and wife, have learned to create a set of bonds that will serve both the family as a unit and its individual members in the new milieu.

"The missionary should counsel both parents and children to capitalize on certain benefits which can conceivably result from urban life. They should make a virtue of necessity by profiting from the breakdown of strong and even rigid family controls over the individual, by urging the individual to build within himself a new sense of personal responsibility. City life makes the individual freer from family and social controls. Prompt him to cultivate spiritual self-reliance, the capacity to depend on his own resources.

"But spiritually, socially and psychologically the family as well as the individuals must be kept strong. The couples in new city-made marriages must also be taught strength. For this the Cana Conference technique should serve as guidance before and after marriage.

"Further, meeting the need should not be confined to the individual family. We have learned, through the Christian Family Movement and through the Cana Conference, that an individual family will remain strong much more easily when it knows that it has the support of ten or twelve or fifteen or twenty other families. Thus we see that the question of community becomes rather important. If the missionary, while guiding an individual family can create a sense of community between that family and a dozen others, then they together may be able to cultivate the bonds of strength which will keep the family robust in the urban setting.

"Without knowing it, families that move to the city shift from a community form of life in the stricter meaning of that term to an association form of life. Social support for the family by such association can help it avoid problems of crime and delinquency.

"To create some sense of community or solidarity within the neighborhood itself is a rather serious problem. Where you have groups of immigrants who in the lands they left belonged to strong communities—as we did in the United States in times past—it is not too difficult to induce them to continue, for a generation or so, this old form. But this must inevitably break down, and we must be ready to help them find a new form fitting our modern urban life."

Reception of Migrants. The adaptation of rural migrants to city life is today a basic world task. Migrants, on arrival in the city, are in an especially vulnerable situation. Local government officers and voluntary agencies, including our Catholic missionary leaders, should meet their needs, since the migrants themselves are in such a state of mind that they are disinclined to avail themselves of friendly services, official or private, even if they hear of them. Both the community and the migrant need to recognize the value of a process by which they can adjust to each other.

In the United States currently, New York City faces an adjustment problem with three quarters of a million Puerto Ricans. Government and voluntary agencies are tackling the problem vigorously. Cardinal Spellman, with admirable decisiveness, has assigned hundreds of priests, Sisters and lay leaders to the process of melding them into the community. France has a current problem of 350,000 Algerians, 30 percent of whom have concentrated in Paris. The United Kingdom, with London the focal point, is receiving tens of thousands of West Indians, principally Jamaicans. But no Western nation has remotely the problems of Hong Kong or such other Asian cities as Karachi, Bangkok, Djakarta or Bandung.

In all of these areas a technique has been worked out that includes the coordinated enlistment of the employers, the churches and the general public, since officialdom has found out long ago that it cannot do the task alone. The missionary considers the spiritual welfare of the migrant his prime concern, but he understands well that matters touching socio-economic welfare bear directly on the spiritual and they also must often be his concern. The pattern employed in most countries is the following:

1   Migrants are met on arrival by friendly and instructed guidance people;
2   Advice and literature (for those who read) in the language of the arrivals is provided;
3   Accommodations in hostels and clubs for the better classes, in rentable quarters for workers, are indicated;
4   Job information is offered;
5   Language classes, schools and craft shops for improving skills are pointed out;
6   Healthful friendship and leisure contacts are indicated through religious and welfare agencies and social centers;
7   Emergency provisions such as medical and hospital service, clothing or feeding requirements are anticipated.

Physical Provision Is Not Enough. Housing for newly arrived migrants often solves relatively little; indeed, provision of the merely physical, while important in itself, is widely accepted today even among non-religious workers as plainly inadequate. For rural migrant housing projects, multi-purpose centers are set up in some countries with numerous goals in mind:

1   to advise on the use of apartment facilities;
2   to guide parents in buying;
3   to advise on job-seeking;
4   to provide day nurseries and kindergartens;
5   to organize home economics courses;
6   to organize after-school and after-work leisure programs;
7   to care for the aged.

Where large-scale uncontrolled immigration is in progress, communities have come to recognize that there is danger in piling strange families from distant areas into urban apartments. Frequently the so-called "socially maladjusted" element among them becomes a danger not only to morals but to life and limb. The urban missionary can well give heed to this question, since he will soon find that a major problem of newly arrived families is their dealings with their neighbors.

The Netherlands, which regards the problem as serious, proposes four categories of families, and housing accordingly:

1   "socially sound" families, which are given regular public housing units;
2   "relatively socially sound" families, which are likewise given regular units but are supervised;
3   "socially weak" families, which are housed in a special rehabilitation project with central bathroom and laundry facilities and with special social officers for training;
4   "anti-social" families, which are housed in still other re-education centers with low-cost equipment that cannot so easily be injured, under a staff with authority to direct living prac-

tices, particularly of the housewife, for the purpose of improvement.[2]

For the missionary, the factor of counselling and of encouraging, either by himself personally or by professional or volunteer staff, can mean the difference between vigorous, happy and spiritually loyal families and families that are disorganized, tepid and unfaithful.

Organized Guidance. "The experienced urban missionary," noted Father Fitzpatrick, "knows instinctively that his new families do not realize that they have problems to face. They fall victims to them and see too late what has befallen the loved ones for whom they are responsible. Our aim should be to help them early, through guiding the natural leaders among their own people.

"Our first step should be to alert them to the difficulties from which they quickly find themselves suffering. The principal problem of formed families is the children. The children begin to go around, as they must, with neighboring children longer in the city. Thus they learn a way of life different from what they were taught in the rural areas. Soon the child experiences a conflict with the values maintained by his parents. The missionary must in some way reach both the parents and the children.

"The parents should be advised not to look upon the development purely in terms of insubordination or lack of respect for their authority. They must, it is true, require obedience from their children, but the obedience must be won without the type of conflict that might conceivably lead to delinquency. The parents must be given an understanding of what the children are going through, and a certain amount of sympathy with them.

"At the same time, the children need to be reached. If possible, the children must be made aware that their parents find it hard to understand the new way of life which is different from that in which the parents were brought up; the love and appreciation of the child for the parent must not be permitted to cool. The child, then, has to learn how to live as a city dweller; to be confident in himself as a thoroughgoing city boy and a self-respecting Christian."

Community Education. "Some form of community education is needed," Father Fitzpatrick continued, "to serve both parents and children. A simple start is made by getting a few families together in the home of one family and gradually leading them to talk about the problems they are facing. This can usually be done best through the more mature neighborhood leaders whom the missionary seeks to instruct. Sometimes the Christian Family Movement can furnish the framework. In these little sessions, people become aware of the situations they have to face in the city."

"I think that in this matter of community education," commented Mr. Dumpson, "the missionary should acquaint himself particularly well with the social fabric of the areas of the city that make up his parish. He will instruct his lay assistants thoroughly on the spiritual ideals they will convey to the new families, but they will need to be checked likewise on their knowledge of the influence groups at work in the area, of the social castes among the population, of the factors that tend to unite the local people to make a better community as well as those that tend to divide them. His aim in community education is to bring about a genuine identification of the new families with the things that will bring them joy and satisfaction and not merely to warn them against the city's evils."

"In Japan," added Father Hubert Schiffer, of the Jesuits of the Catholic University of Tokyo, "we never have any difficulty getting city people together to talk on matters of community education. They are very anxious to discuss the training of their children, juvenile delinquency, the role of women. They are eager to have strong family ties."

"It seems to me," noted Father Vizzard, "that the Church has a most important opportunity in this area of work in the cities, because both the families and the community experience a real felt need for responsible guidance."

Catholic Identification with City Workers. "What is the role of the Church in areas of industrial development?" asked Monsignor Ligutti. "What do you say to this question, Father Fitzpatrick?"

"I think Mr. Dumpson's constructive comments on the approach of the missionary to community education of rank and file families in the city is a splendid indication of what the experienced social leader sees as possibilities. The Government of Puerto Rico brought one of Father Topshee's confreres in Antigonish, Father MacDonald, to the island to help in community organization of cooperatives and credit unions. Father MacDonald gave a splendid demonstration of the impact a competent priest can have in inspiring an urban working population to better itself.

"The Catholic Church should be identified, through its missionaries, with stirring the workers and their families to participation in betterment plans that are helpful to family and community life. By and large, we should be represented in social planning by experts who are Catholics rather than by Catholic programs officially launched as such."

"In Indonesia," explained Father Dijkstra, "there is tremendous migration to the towns and we missionaries have a system of assigning lay leaders to aid established groups of twenty or so families. These men are very helpful; they get to know their group very well and try to guide them wisely."

"This emphasis on the layman as the day-to-day helper of city workers," commented Father Frederick McGuire, C.M., "reminds us of the fact that at the moment we, in the United States, are not prepared to send out competent lay personnel on the same basis as we send out religious missionaries. There is as much to be done in the socio-economic field as there is in the catechetical field. The missionary should be a man who understands well the socio-economic problems, but it is teams of fine laymen, both native and foreign, who should operate in full partnership with the missionary in executing socio-economic programs."

"We should mention here," proposed Father Richard Lawlor, S.J., "the liaison that should be strongly established by urban missions with their rural counterparts which will enable them to handle migrants. In areas like the Belgian Congo a little central bureau exists in each city to which rural pastors send data on members of their flock who are heading for the city. One of the difficult and wearying, yet very consoling, aspects of the city apostolate is searching out these lost sheep who so often don't report, as instructed, on reaching the city."

"The Church in Puerto Rico has a system for following its folk who go to the United States," explained Monsignor John Illich, Vice President of the Catholic University of Puerto Rico in Ponce. "The families of emigrants put pressure on their members to contact the U. S. pastors where they work. At the New York end, the system of block leaders solves in principle the searching out of new arrivals in the metropolis. However, New York is so huge, each block is so huge, that to contact satisfactorily our Puerto Ricans in the concentrated areas a full-time operator would be required for each block."

"We have concerned ourselves thus far," remarked Father Joseph McGlade of the Columbans, "with city problems among Christians. In a city like Tokyo, where the population is overwhelmingly non-Christian, should the missionary become involved in problems touching the general population?"

"By way of reply," said Father Fitzpatrick, "I would note, first, that in countries such as Japan migration to the city badly disrupts the habits of country folk, who in their villages are extraordinarily attached to doing everything in consort with the community. The city leaves the man or woman extremely alone, and they welcome the good offices of the missionary.

"Secondly, I would say that any form of serious social disorganization, whether among Christians or non-Christians, is a grave threat to healthy moral or spiritual life. Whatever the missionary is able to do in such a case is an exercise of the corporal and spiritual works of mercy."

Church Cooperation in a City-Wide Program. "There is one country in the world," observed Monsignor Ligutti, "in which I know that Church people have assumed social obligations to work for all the people. This is the Belgian Congo, where the missionaries work in cooperation with the Belgian Government in an over-all social program which is best illustrated by the accomplishments in the capital city, Leopoldville. The example is very much worth our study."

Leopoldville, today a city of 350,000, certainly provides an unusual demonstration of the best missionary thinking regarding an urban social program, particularly as regards the employment of leisure in building urban life. Tribal Congolese poured by thousands into Leopoldville. The government turned to the missionaries to solve the hundred problems that the adaptation of these rural Africans to city life represented. The missionary program, which has been judged an outstanding success, embraced the following ten phases of development:

1   *Recreational activities.* Encouraged by the government, the missionaries centered their city-wide sports program in a major sports center that is fifty acres in extent. It includes swimming pools with a total surface of 40,000 square feet, football fields, tennis and basketball courts. A professional construction director among the Scheut Missionaries, Brother René Reygaerts, erected a huge concrete stadium that seats 75,000 spectators. The sports association currently directs leagues operating 60 football teams organized in every section of Leopoldville.

   Folk games, folk plays and folk dancing likewise are systematically encouraged. A charming practice among the tribes-people is skilled story telling. For this, groups of young and old gather around bonfires in the evening. Parties, socials, entertainments are cultivated and motion picture theaters are operated. To supply films properly adapted to Africa, the Scheut Missionaries established the Congo Catholic Cinema Center, unique in the world, since it has turned out over 100 films geared to entertain and instruct the Congolese.

2 *Youth work.* Boys' clubs and girls' clubs play a role in the Leopoldville program. The Scout troops are numerous, with a program aimed at vigorous health, mental hygiene, individual counselling, guidance in educational and vocational pursuits. As elsewhere in the world, outdoor life is emphasized. Four times a year there is a week-end camping expedition. The Catholic Scouts have a monthly paper in the vernacular (*Lingala*). The only European now in the movement is the chaplain.

The Y.C.W. aim at guiding Leopoldville boys 16 to 20 years of age who have jobs.

3 *Adult education and night schools.* Thousands of working people are enrolled for vocational training, handicrafts and night school courses. Men seeking advancement follow these courses assiduously for five and six years each evening after work. Large social centers for women teach sewing and domestic science, with special house-to-house visitations for on-the-spot home-making guidance.

4 *Social clubs and cooperatives.* Every parish in Leopoldville operates social and mutual aid clubs. Some are fraternal in nature, aimed to bring the diverse tribes into more harmonious relationship. The credit unions aim to give families the opportunity to borrow small sums for emergencies such as sickness and death.

5 *Cultural improvement.* The more alert in the population are keen for cultural improvement. Numbers join art appreciation courses, music courses, literary appreciation. Ecole St. Luc, conducted by the Christian Brothers, is an art school for painting, sculpture and wood-carving, with a seven-year course.

Drama in every form is encouraged, from simple group plays to huge community-wide pageants. Both men and women take with avidity to entertainment associations. Orchestras are quite numerous, group dancing ranks high. Christian choreography, employing the dance for religious expression, has been developed.

6   *Family programs.* Since family life is gauged to exert strong
influence on the thinking and activities of the Congolese,
the missionaries emphasize that home life should be characterized by pleasurable hours of leisure together. Parents
are urged to spend at least a part of their time with their
children. They are taught to make meals a happy gathering;
old customs that required men to eat separately are frowned
on. Birthdays, holidays, holydays are planned as much-en-
joyed occasions. Of an evening the mother and even the
father will join the family circle to solve riddles, play games,
tell stories, have neighbors in for song-fests. Pets, gardens,
barbecue pits, family picnics are encouraged.

7   *Spiritual activities.* Too seldom does the sociologist stress the
tremendous spiritual potential that lies in the employment of
leisure. In Leopoldville the parish priest emphasizes family
prayer, the block rosary. Attendance at daily Mass is the
practice of thousands. The family, then, is encouraged to do
good together, engaging in such practices as bringing food
to poorer folk about the city, visiting the sick and disabled.

In a number of parishes the Legion of Mary puts a blessing on many a worker's life. Other group efforts concern
themselves with the direct apostolate, with hospital service
and with volunteer teaching.

8   *Character building.* The Leopoldville program aims at the
establishment of a social environment conducive to purpose-
fulness in life, meeting the calls of daily living for recreation,
intellectual improvement, cultural satisfactions and spiritual
achievement.

Among the young everywhere, play is a major factor in
character building. Play, as elsewhere in the world, often
proves more stimulating than the classroom and more creative. The Leopoldville plan emphasizes learning to play
fairly, honestly and with initiative.

9   *Physical facilities for formation.* Every parish in the city has
a social hall and most are constantly in use. Every section
of the city has an auditorium with stages for theatricals and
meetings. Besides the great stadium, every section has its
gymnasium, swimming pools, playgrounds, facilities for club
work, library and reading room.

10 *Group leaders.* Full recognition is given to trained leadership. To form the Congolese, teams of expert lay directors
have been brought out from Belgium. Much of the initiative
which the Congolese of Leopoldville are displaying in the
current independence movement can reasonably be attrib-
uted to the spontaneity built into their lives by the Leopoldville leisure program.

The Fight against Depersonalization. Father Bernard F.
Meyer of Maryknoll, a veteran missionary from South China,
explained what the city does to men and how the evils may be
mitigated.

"There is general agreement," he said, "about the demoral-
izing influences to which the urban industrial worker is sub-
jected. He is commonly an immigrant from a cohesive and
organic social environment in which he had social status, a
sense of being valued as a person in numerous social relationships.

"In the city, his life tends to become depersonalized. This is
true also if he was born in the city. He no longer has roots in
an extended family, or in a neighborhood where he grew up
and of which he felt a part. All around him in the city are
strangers and he tends to move frequently so that he falls
among still other strangers.

"He tends to lose the sense of social ties or of responsibility
to others. He often feels alone against the world, even in his
own family. In the village, his community work was a social
contribution on which people depended, giving him added
status as a person. In the city, he holds an anonymous job; he
is merely a hand, a number.

"Why has this situation had such a serious effect on the
Church's influence with the workers? One reason would seem
to be that we priests took for granted the organic character
of Christian social solidarity. Our concern was mostly with the
religious belief and practice of the individual and little with the
Christian community as its framework. In a sense, we were

promoting the very isolation of the individual which urban industrialism has brought to a climax. We failed to realize how much the supernatural structure we erected depended on what was merely a natural foundation.

"We did not integrate the social foundation with religion by giving a religious motivation to social solidarity. When the natural social foundations became undermined by the depersonalizing influences of industrial urbanization, the whole supernatural structure of religion was weakened. In the village, a Catholic's sense of belonging to the Church depended largely on his sense of belonging to the social community. When he came to the city and lost his sense of community status, he easily gave up his religion also.

"There is a related consideration. Traditionally the only active role in the Church has seemed to belong to the clergy. The laity were the recipients of the priest's ministry. This was perhaps understandable when the organic solidarity of the social structure presented no problem. In this context the work of the Church was seen as religious only, and this was clearly the function of the clergy. Now, faced with the sad results of social disorganization, we are beginning to realize that the Church has also a social mission. Here the primary function belongs to the laity, who are the Church in society. In this social mission the function of the clergy is a subsidiary or supporting one, namely, to train the laity to carry out their mission."

Rescuing Man from Social Isolation.   Father Meyer explained what is not clearly understood by every missionary, namely, that the goal of the Church in reaching the worker is not merely to get him to join a Catholic group. Much more, it aims to change him socially so that religion will possess in his social ties a basis for operation.

"What," asked Father Meyer, "is the social mission of the Church to be carried out by the laity? Canon Cardijn, founder of the Young Christian Workers, says that in the urban industrial sphere with which we are concerned it is to rescue man from his social isolation. The natural social structure of more simple society is disappearing under the impact of technological change. Urban industrialism has produced a great new proletariat class.

"What makes the proletariat is not holding a subordinate place in society, or being propertyless, but being in a society with the feeling of not having active participation or recognized status. Without these, life lacks meaning. Thus the young individual in the proletariat is preoccupied, not with fulfilling any status role, but with self-centered satisfaction: food, sex and entertainment bound the horizons of his life. Substitute status is often sought in aggressive actions, such as acts of delinquency, joining movements of violence, or in the widespread practice of prestige-spending, found even among good people.

"In our effort to remedy this situation, we should apply a fundamental sociological principle that also applies to convert making. It we are to get people to change from undesirable to desirable attitudes, we must make them feel welcome in a group where the desirable attitudes are the accepted standard.

"A prominent leader in the Y.C.W. relates that in his early twenties he had a good job but spent his entire earnings on himself, even getting carfare from his mother. He went to Mass mostly at her urging. A friend invited him to a Y.C.W. group meeting. The group made him feel welcome. When he admitted to some in the group that he had not been close to his father for years, it was suggested that he invite his father to go to the cinema. Under the glow of his new friendships, he found himself consenting to this difficult step which succeeded in opening up a new sense of relationship with his father. It would not have come to pass had not the Y.C.W. group made him feel valued by them as a person. Beginning with that small act, the man went on to become a zealous apostle and leader."

Missionary Training for Social Leadership. The missionary has a task to do, noted Father Meyer, if the laity is to win the Christian allegiance of the workingman.

"The well-trained missionary," stated Father Meyer, "will understand:

"1   that a sound social, as well as spiritual, base is requisite to provide a Christian community serving the whole man;

"2   that in developing the social base of the Christian community the principal role belongs to the laity;

"3   that to train the laity for this role, the principles of group action should be applied.

"In other words, the missionary should have, not only classroom instruction on the nature of the Christian community and of the roles of clergy and laity, but also practical experience in group techniques. Such a training will make him more effective in direct missionary work as well as in forming leaders for socio-economic development. Indeed, Catholic life must be manifested as a community of love as clearly in socio-economic activities as in the direct apostolate. I know from experience in China that otherwise our socio-economic activities will appear as merely philanthropic work, quite as if they were carried out by a secular agency.

"I would say that the missionary in an urban parish should proceed on two fronts. First, he should make his flock aware of the social implications in Catholic life through liturgical functions and pulpit instructions. Secondly, he should organize Catholic Action as the social expression of the Christian community. Pope Pius XI enunciated two basic principles for Catholic Action: 1) a program of leadership training; 2) a program of mass action."

Leadership Training for the Christian Community.   Father Meyer stressed again that he is not interested in pointless organizing for organization's sake. The times require specific action.

"Leadership training movements," he explained, "which represent a new departure in Catholic lay organizations, are the Legion of Mary, the Young Christian Workers and the Christian Family Movement. Instead of limiting themselves to the mutual support of the members, as do a number of parish societies, they are outgoing and apostolic. The aim of the Legion of Mary is to manifest the love of Christ for the individual through personal contacts. The Young Christian Workers aim to make working youth aware of their dignity as members of Christ, to show forth Christ at work and in leisure hours, to give life the meaning of which urban industrialism tends to rob it. The Christian Family Movement seeks to manifest Christ in and through the family by neighborhood and community relationships.

"Y.C.W. leadership operates through Service Committees. It may organize a Service Committee of non-members in a factory to deal with working conditions or union activity. It employs Service Committees for youth work, vocational guidance, adult education, employment service, housing service, welfare service.

"The Christian Family Movement sets up Action Groups of married couples as more or less the equivalent of the Y.C.W. Service Committees. They are concerned in action at the family or neighborhood levels.

"These movements have brought a new vitality into lay action. They were the first to approach, in a practical way, man's isolation and depersonalization by urban industrialism. They apply the small group method to training leaders. They give the individual a new sense of belonging. They have effected great transformations, making apostles out of men who found little meaning to being Catholic laymen.

"Men need a sense of social status. A Detroit businessman said to me, 'Father, I know that my religion is the most important thing in my life, but it is the least interesting." That man will, I think, remain faithful from conviction. But the mass of workers are swayed more by their feelings. For them, any relationship, in this case that of being a Catholic, which lacks a direction and a sense of personal participation seems dull and fails to hold them against the other pulls around them."

Mass Action for the Christian Community. The weakness

in Catholic urban activities, Father Meyer asserted, is the too frequent absence of mass action for the building of Christian community.

"Even under favorable conditions," Father Meyer said, "the movements in the category of those we have mentioned will not embrace more than 5 percent of a parish. How are the other 95 percent to be brought to a sense of personal participation in a Christian community? None of these movements has fully solved the problem of how their trained elite will bring about mass action through personal participation in Christian urban problems. The Christian Family Movement has very few card-carrying union members. The Legion of Mary depends mostly on the personal contacts of a few members, instead of aiming rather to leaven other organizations by working with them as its own handbook suggests.

"One obstacle seems to be the tendency of elite movements to keep groups which they set up among the masses as appendages of their own movements. For a true sense of participation, the masses must have their own organization, run by themselves.

"In certain parts of the world mass organizations have been successful in the form of neighborhood associations, block committees or area societies with activities such as welcoming newcomers, providing recreation, organizing religious instruction, promoting religious devotions, conducting clean-up campaigns, providing family services, voicing social wrongs and so forth. This is the procedure of the Neighborhood Associations of Japan, the Barangay of the Virgin in the Philippines, as well as the Free Christian Workers and the Free Christian Farmers, found also in the Philippines.

"In all of these organizations, for strength the social and spiritual vitality must be planted within the hearts of the participants. Wise old Lao-tse voiced this principle thousands of years ago when he observed that it was the test of true leadership that, when a community had been inspired by its ministering angel to accomplish a good deed, the people all said, 'We have done it ourselves!' The urban missionary will have fulfilled most perfectly his role of catalyst when, with the words of the Chinese philosopher, the people cry out at the good accomplished, 'We have done it ourselves!' "

For recommended reading, see Bibliography Nos. 12 and 13, pages 279 and 281.

COOPERATIVES TO BUILD
CHARACTER AND THE ECONOMY

Am I My Brother's Banker? It falls within the normal thought processes of every missionary to be solicitous about the needy in terms of food, raiment and rooftop. But keeping the small farmer or the city householder out of the claws of the loanshark is quite another thing. Many feel no prompting to regard this as a normal part of the day's duties.

Yet, throughout the underdeveloped countries of the world, non-institutional credit, which is the dignified title that applies principally to the professional money-lender, is at least three times as costly, and sometimes as much as ten times as costly, as properly organized forms of credit.

The situation regarding rural indebtedness in general and the problems connected with the small farmer's credit has not changed to any substantial degree in recent years, despite all the cries to do something about it and despite the many modest projects launched. The world problem of family credit is unbelievably huge. According to the All-India Credit Survey, early in the 1950's 93 percent of the total rural borrowings among India's little people came from private persons, of whom almost 45 percent were professional money-lenders and 25 percent big landowners. Non-institutional credit represents 54 percent in Celyon, 51 percent in Japan, 84 percent in Thailand.[1]

In many areas of the earth well-functioning credit facilities simply do not exist. Even when they do exist, farmers who cannot provide land or cattle as collateral cannot obtain a low-priced loan for seed grain in the spring against their harvest in the fall.

Obstacles to a properly functioning credit system are the following:

1 an excess or insufficiency of legal protection for either the borrower or the lender;
2 cumbersome or costly legal procedures;
3 difficulties in legal recovery of amounts due;
4 illiteracy of small operators that makes it difficult to apply for loans;
5 lack of communications that limits the scope of operation of existing credit institutions;
6 complicated and often unnecessary paper work, delays in handling applications or in disbursement;
7 the tempting ease with which the professional money-lender offers credit, even for social expenses such as weddings and funerals. Many a missionary in India and elsewhere stands helplessly by as a young husbandman incurs his first debt for some such event and thus shoulders money burdens which are to dog his life to the day of his death.

The new missionary, unprepared for this problem of family credit, will find himself quoting some such easy aphorism as "Neither a borrower nor a lender be," in indicating to his parishioners that under no circumstances should they incur debt involvements. But, practically speaking, few of the poorer rural or urban families can hope to make capital improvements, to increase their production or their income or to meet the crises

of family life without at least occasional resort to the seeking
of credit.

Hence the reasonableness of our consideration of this socio-
economic problem. "In our day, the economic question has a
particular religious significance," explained Monsignor Coady,
the late distinguished Director of Extension at St. Francis
Xavier University of Nova Scotia, seat of the celebrated Antigonish Movement. "As a matter of fact, it is the great modern
religious question, for, if it is not solved, freedom, culture and
religion may easily be seriously endangered. . . . It is more
than a question of supply and demand, more than a matter of
food, clothing and shelter. It is basic to the life of man. Economic action is intimately linked up with spiritual activities. It
influences all man's actions, and when his economic life is
deficient there is grave danger of his spiritual life being likewise deficient. Poverty is not always holy. It may frequently
be a proximate occasion of sin." [2]

Cooperatives and Their Basic Principles.   The missionary
will do well to maintain through life a passing acquaintance
with the economy that guides the country in which he labors
and in which his people must earn their livelihood. He can
hardly encourage any specific form of economic assistance for
his people if he is totally uninformed about the economic institutions around him. With this elementary precaution, he can
wisely undertake to assist his people by such aids as the cooperative.

Cooperative activities fall into five general classes:

1   *Credit unions.* Systematic weekly or monthly deposits by en-
    rolled members build a fund from which members may make
    borrowings according to accepted rules, to meet their family
    or business needs. Credit unions have assets in some countries
    that run to millions and have successful loan records which
    likewise run to millions.
2   *Processing and market cooperatives.* Farmers and fishermen,
    through cooperatives, have secured a greater share of the con-
    sumer's dollar and have thus improved their living condition.

The lobster fishermen, organized from Antigonish, today are among the biggest marketers of lobsters in the world, with an annual business of more than $1,500,000.

3 *Service cooperatives.* Housing projects and family health and hospitalization enterprises have been successfully organized along cooperative lines.

4 *Consumers' cooperatives.* Cooperative stores handling merchandise are another form of this group activity. Most are modest efforts, but some retail organizations have built considerable networks with cooperative wholesale centers that, all together, gross millions.

5 *Multi-purpose cooperatives.* Some cooperatives represent several types of activity. Fishermen may possess a credit union as well as a marketing co-op for their fish and a cooperative store for consumer merchandise.

A cooperative, to obtain success in underdeveloped countries, must give attention to much more than the purely economic. Six principles advocated by the Antigonish Movement embody the philosophy on which the cooperative is built:

1 *The primacy of the individual:* The cooperative, while a group action, is based on both religious and democratic teaching which primarily respects the rights of the individual.

2 *Social reform must come through education:* Social progress can come only if there is an improvement in the quality of the people themselves.

3 *Education must begin with the economic:* It is good technique to suit the educational effort to the most intimate interests of the individual or group. Economic reform is generally the most immediate necessity, because the economic problems are usually the most pressing.

4 *Education must be through group action:* Man's problems are commonly group problems; an effective adult education program should, therefore, fit into the basic group organization of society.

5 *Effective social reform involves fundamental changes in social and economic institutions:* Real reform will necessitate strong measures of change which are likely to prove unpopu-

lar. Most often the local group has the greatest likelihood of achieving changes.

6   *The ultimate objective of the movement is a full and abundant life for everybody in the community:* Economic cooperation is only a first step toward a society which will permit every individual to develop to the limit of his capacities.

Properly operated cooperatives are more than a business. They represent an organization through which men gain without taking any toll from their confreres. They are organizations of society that permit charity and mercy to have full play.

The Missionary and Cooperatives. Modern cooperatives had their origin among a group of weavers in Rochdale, England, in the 1840's. The Rochdale operating principles which this group evolved remain fundamentally unchanged from what they were when the shutters were first removed from the window of their little shop in Toad Lane. These principles were: 1) A modest annual interest to members on their investment share; 2) A sum set aside annually to continue unceasingly the education of the members; 3) Distribution of the consumer cooperative's net profits in proportion to each member's purchases; 4) Trading for cash, and at current market rates; 5) An open membership list known to all other members; 6) Each man one vote, regardless of his investment share.

This technique, originated at Rochdale, pioneered an idea that is world-wide today and represents hundreds of millions of dollars in cooperative activities. Such movements as Antigonish seek to continue the Rochdale practices. Representing the Extension Department at St. Francis Xavier University today is Father George E. Topshee, whose counsels to missionaries are invaluable.

"If the missionary is to do any enduring work with cooperatives and credit unions," stated Father Topshee, "he must have a strong conviction of the great importance of the role of the economic side of life in the establishment and *in the maintenance* of Christianity. Without this conviction, the missionary will be regarded with a certain amount of suspicion by his people. They will readily sense any lack of conviction and dismiss his efforts as superficial dabbling.

"The day is coming, I believe, when the Pope will make it mandatory for Church leaders to take a more realistic view of the role of economics in the establishment and maintenance of Christianity.

"In the meantime, how is the missionary to obtain this deep conviction of the importance of the material side of life for the salvation of souls?

"A brief consideration of history, the experience of his contemporaries, reflection on his own experience and the use of reason should lead him to this conviction. Throughout history large numbers of people have left the Church because they were crushed economically and they felt that the Church was on the side of the vested interests, was helping to maintain a terrible system of land distribution. In Latin America and in Eastern Europe Christianity has lost ground largely because of the economic system which builds pyramids of gold for a favored few.

"Cooperatives and credit unions are one important part of the formula for an economic society that will develop and distribute the natural resources of the earth for the good of all human beings. The missionary who goes out with a program that strives for justice and charity in the economic order, wins the confidence of his people and makes great gains for the Church.

"The people reason thus: The Church that is on the side of the suffering masses, that represents the Good Samaritan in our day, must be the true Church.

"Direct and immediate relief must be given at times of emergency. But the real scientific, long-term program is one of self-help and mutual assistance and self-development through cooperatives and credit unions. It is a matter of developing people."

Men Who Have Made Cooperatives Work. Father Topshee cited successful use of cooperatives by missionaries in the Dominican Republic and in Ghana.

"It is not necessary that every missionary have an extended course of training to begin work in this field," noted Father Topshee. "It would be well, however, if there were one man in each mission territory who has acquainted himself thoroughly with the subject. Many missionaries are doing excellent work without formal training. With a sincere interest in the whole man, they have won the confidence of their people and led them in development of body and soul.

"Father John McIver of the Scarboro Foreign Missions was sent to Yamasa, Santo Domingo, something over a dozen years ago. Yamasa at that time was considered the most backward mission on the island, the epitome of stupidity and backwardness. After getting to know his people and their needs, he called together fourteen of the best men in the village.

"He barely mentioned the credit union at this first meeting. Instead, he posed the question as to how they could obtain legal title to the land they were farming. This he knew was their main concern. He told them that there was information on this subject at government headquarters and this they voted to secure. At the second and third meetings, he helped them digest the four typewritten pages from the government on their land titles and in passing made reference to the credit union. 'Let's better ourselves,' the men agreed. 'Let's start a credit union.'

"Father McIver obtained copies of a pamphlet by Joseph MacIsaac of Antigonish containing a simple question and answer presentation of credit unions. At its own request, the group began a serious study of this credit union catechism. Each week for a year they met, read aloud a lesson and then discussed it. By the end of the year the group had grown from 14 to 140.

"Father McIver explains that he learned by experience not to get too far ahead of his people in announcing his plans. He prompted them to think and waited for them to express their thoughts, in order that the initiative would be on record as coming from them.

"At the end of two and a half years, with a very successful credit union in operation, some of the members began to ask questions about cooperative marketing and cooperative retailing. Father McIver sent for the necessary literature.

"Over a five-year period of regular meetings, leaders with civic pride and a sense of responsibility for the common good were developed. The total product in Yamasa was not only a credit union, a cooperative marketing association and a cooperative retail society, but as well a new village church, a new school and a convent for teaching Sisters from Canada.

"Father McIver did not have an extensive course of training for this venture in cooperatives but he learned by doing. He learned with his people and thereby developed in them a strong sense of loyalty to himself and to the Church. He trained leaders who have already assisted and will continue to assist the Church and the community."

Example from Northern Ghana. Father Topshee's second example of successful development of cooperatives by a non-professional leader is the work of Father John McNulty of the White Fathers, whose station is Jirapa Mission in Ghana, West Africa.

"Father McNulty has been an African missionary for twenty years," Father Topshee explained. "Jirapa, when he arrived, was a backward agricultural community with critical problems of poverty and illiteracy as well as exploitation by Moslem traders.

"Father McNulty heard about credit unions while on leave in Scotland, and on his return to Jirapa he began corresponding with Monsignor MacKinnon, the Director of Extension at St. Francis Xavier in Antigonish. He organized study groups using material sent by the University. The credit union was actually formed in September, 1955. In July, 1956, a cooperative corn mill came out of the discussions of the study group. This freed the families from exorbitant charges for grinding corn when this service was secured outside the farm and from burdensome work by the women when it had to be done at home.

"An outstanding feature in these Ghana co-ops is the active participation of women, who are thus given status and training.

"Father McNulty's effort resulted in credit unions at Jirapa, Nandam and Ko, in two corn mills at Jirapa, in a hammer mill in Nandam. Members have improved their homes by substituting sheet aluminum roofs for straw thatch and have tried a health insurance cooperative to pay ambulance fees. Through Father McNulty's urging, a Ghanaian diocesan priest was sent for training to Antigonish. He himself continues to get advice from Monsignor MacKinnon."

Seven Steps to Successful Cooperatives.   If cooperatives are everything that is claimed for them, why do cooperatives fail? The proportion of failures in cooperative enterprise is lower than in private business. When failure does come, it is because amateurs choose to ignore the safeguarding principles. Father Topshee offered the missionary seven protective steps to avoid failure.

1 *Acquire a sound philosophy.* By resort to literature, such as is listed for this chapter at the end of this book, the missionary removes his misconceptions before he launches forth. If the missionary is to be successful, he has to raise his sights above the idea that he is merely organizing a casual savings club. "He must be convinced," said Father Topshee, "that he is: i) developing man as an individual and men as groups to realize their possibilities for good; ii) teaching a deep sense of responsibility toward others; iii) cultivating self-denial and self-sacrifice essential for the common good; iv) educating people to have motives of justice and charity toward one another; v) building a society based on these virtues of justice and charity."

2 *Start with the credit union.* The credit union comes first because it is easiest to operate and because the little people of most countries suffer greatly from the money-lender. This

should be only the start. Occasionally some other cooperative form should be first because of a greater need locally.

3 *Prepare a group of leaders.* About a dozen well-trained laymen are needed as treasurer, board of directors, credit committee, supervisory committee. All the discussion group techniques for this training are obtainable; they should not be improvised. "Village people tend to be suspicious and pessimistic," noted Father Topshee. "It is absolutely necessary to create confidence by having it known that you have a well-trained group who will defend the aims and objectives of the movement."

4 *Educate the community.* Depending on circumstances, leaflets, pamphlets, papers, films, slides, radio and television should be used. "Variety is very important," declared Father Topshee, "especially with illiterate people." Meetings should include leadership courses, children's programs, study groups for women, week-end institutes and conferences. However, best of all is the discussion circle or study club.

5 *Enlist the membership.* There must be a potential credit union membership of at least 100 people. If the credit union remains too small, it will not give the service that it is intended to give, since the saving capacity of only a few people is too limited.

6 *Create a community bond through membership.* A cooperative should not be a divisory element in the community. "Ordinarily it becomes a good contact with various people in the community," said Father Topshee. "When the parish is the only common bond, let the cooperative be a parish organization. In some Latin American parish credit unions, the board of directors (advised by the missionary) equates the 'good character' requirement for membership with fulfillment of Easter duties. This interpretation is not for general application but, rather, should be used with care only in particular circumstances."

7 *Keep the rules; don't go too fast.* "The over-all techniques and procedure in bringing adult education and ownership to people," noted Father Topshee, "is the same in every area though they vary in application according to the needs. The same techniques may be used for an electrical cooperative in

Guatemala or a kerosene retailing cooperative in Ghana. The missionary should proceed only as fast as he can educate his leaders and his people. But let him move with courage, conviction, hard work and the grace of God."

Strong Social Fiber for Cooperatives. It is evident, from Father Topshee's portrayal, that the Antigonish Movement places great stress on building into the people clear principles and strong convictions, in order that the factor of high character will contribute quality to the employment of the cooperative idea.

"What possibilities do you see, Father Topshee," asked Monsignor Ligutti, "in the use of the buying club, let's say in some village in Africa, as a first step in training people for a consumers' cooperative?"

"The buying club can be used very effectively under just such circumstances," answered Father Topshee. "The buying club is very temporary by its nature. It is merely a group of people who, under guidance, contribute each a share for buying something jointly. If you have a group that is starting, you can give them a feeling of accomplishment if through a buying club they purchase something they could not have without getting together. But, of course, for consumer problems over an indefinite period of time such people need constant training through the educational program of a purchasers' cooperative."

"In some sections of Latin America," stated Doctor Goncalves, "rural communities have been developing the mixed cooperative that saves, buys, sells and carries on other operations. It has created great interest."

"In Canada, Doctor," commented Father Topshee, "we operate this type. In eastern Nova Scotia farmers, fishermen, miners and steelworkers have 43 retail cooperative stores in their organization and the same organization markets produce for the farmers."

"How difficult do you find it to establish your cooperatives, in view of the middlemen?" asked Doctor Goncalves.

"There has been a lot of opposition and there always will be. In the case of consumers' cooperatives, particularly, you have to oppose the vested interests. It often takes a great deal of fortitude on the part of the missionary."

The Capacity to Inspire Village People. A notable example of the type of grassroots missionary worker who possesses that indefinable magic which inspires simple people of the back country to answer confidently the admonition of the stranger to better their lives, is embodied in the person of Father Marion Ganey of the St. Louis Jesuits. Father Ganey worked first in British Honduras. His unusual success in organizing cooperatives caught the attention of the Governor of British Honduras who, when in later years he was transferred to the Fiji Islands, arranged with Father Ganey's superiors to use his services for organizing cooperatives in the Pacific, first in the Fijis and later in Samoa.

"Since the facts I relate are all the result of personal experience," Father Ganey told us, "I believe a few words of introduction are necessary. In 1937 I went to British Honduras as a missionary and was stationed in Belize, the capital city, for four years. The social problems and the consequent trouble they made were quite apparent to me, and I tried to do something about them but I did not succeed to any extent. I had no training whatsoever. I had never read a book about a credit union.

"In 1942 I was assigned to Puntagorda, a Carib village of the interior near the Guatemala border, inhabited by some 700 souls who lived in mud-floor houses with thatched roofs. The social problems became even more apparent among these people. In 1943 I saw my first credit union take shape. Those who knew the people said it was very rash to start such a thing among such an unbusinesslike group as the Caribs. However, the union succeeded and the people, witnessing its success, went on to other successes in similar simple forms of cooperation.

"After two years, the Bishop came to Puntagorda and, when he saw what these people had done, he decided that I should leave the parish and preach the new social doctrine to all the colony. This I did until 1953 when the Governor of the Fiji Islands, who knew of the successes among the Caribs, thought that his people, who were having a bad time of it, should be told the story. He asked Bishop Foley of the Marists of Fiji to get hold of me.

"I reached Fiji in November of 1953. I was to have stayed six months, but the Fijians took so well to the idea that my term there stretched to forty-two months. Then Bishop Pearce invited me to work in Western Samoa."

The Fruits of a Career.   "I met a Mother Superior in Fiji," said Father Ganey, "who had just come out from Scotland for a visitation of her community. She asked me what I was doing, and I rehearsed briefly the story of the cooperatives. She listened politely and then said, 'I suppose, Father, while you're going about on this job you find time also to do some good on the side, don't you?' Without flicking an eye, I replied quite solemnly that I hoped I did.

"We mustn't blame Mother Superior; other people are likewise not too sure that there's any fruit in what I do. For whatever it's worth, the record for Fiji reads as follows: At the end of 1957 there were 231 cooperatives on the islands, most of them in villages, with 24,000 members in all, a little better than 100 people per cooperative. These folk, who had never saved before, had put away $425,640 in those first three and a half years. Their cooperatives had made 31,000 loans to a total of $876,360, with an outstanding net balance from the loans of $300,000. Thus they had met their obligations very well.

"Then there's the record for British Honduras as told in a clipping from the local newspaper, *The British Honduran,* which goes like this: 'Today there are 34 credit unions scattered all over British Honduras. In 1956 7,522 people belonged to credit unions. From a beginning in 1943 at Puntagorda, these people up to today have saved in small sums a total of $325,-746, an impressive figure. This means that each member has averaged $43 a year. Last year members borrowed $252,303 and paid interest of $24,110 on their loans.'

"Finally, there's the little record from Samoa. In the first six months nine credit unions were founded with 986 members. These people have saved $5,642 that, loaned out in short-term borrowings, has represented $90,000 in 862 loans."

Teaching Men How to Save. "On the eve of my departure from Samoa," Father Ganey continued, "the credit union in one of the Samoan villages wished to offer me a going-away party. I beheld the dances, expressed my delight at the gifts of eleven roast pigs and many fine meats and I drank some of their kava. While they made merry, I reflected that, had I come to that village four months previously and made them a gift of a couple of thousand dollars, by then the $2,000 would have been dissipated and I would have been quite forgotten. Instead, I had come to them and said, 'I am a poor man. Give me a cup of tea and a mat to sleep on tonight and I will teach you this thing, I will teach you how to save.' I had taught them and now they gave me roast pigs because they had learned how to put two thousand dollars of their own money into the bank.

"During my four years in the Pacific, my constant statement to the people was, 'It is your business and you must run it, you must manage it. I can only teach it. There are people who tell me you cannot do it. But you must do it.'

"The big question from the beginning was, could these bare-foot island people, wearing only their sulus, living a communal life and plagued by the lack of any strong incentives, could they rise to the problems of management of even such a simple thing as a credit union. They did rise to it, as the financial statements you've seen prove.

"As time passed, I was received like a paramount chief in hundreds of Fijian villages and I listened to many variations of the same speech: 'We are now better citizens. We are now better able to manage our own money affairs. We ourselves and our children have and always will have a better life. You have crossed racial and religious barriers and have brought us this thing. We thank you.'

"That theme has been woven by the village poets into ancient tribal chants and dances. While the by-laws of the co-operatives follow our U. S. model, this did not prevent the villagers from enhancing all their credit union activities with the cultural ways of Fiji. And though only 10 percent of the Fijians are Catholic, this did not prevent the 90 percent from accepting me and the credit union idea. There are some completely Catholic villages, and when I visited them the burden of their speeches was, 'We are proud that one of ours brought this way of life to free the whole Fijian people.' "

What Fijians Do with Credit Unions. What do Pacific islanders do with their credit union savings? Father Ganey had some interesting answers.

"If there is an easy way to start credit unions in Fiji," Father Ganey remarked, "I do not know it. But once they are sparked they certainly understand how to make them work. To start a union in one village, I was poled along a stream in a leaky old punt for three hours. It was the only way they had to get to their village. A year later I waited at the same spot as a delegation in white sulus and dark jackets and neckties stepped out from a new white boat, which was powered by an Evinrude, and the Chief made a speech: 'A year ago you came and planted a seed in our village. Today'—and he pointed to the boat and the Evinrude—'you behold the fruit.' It was his word.

"What do people buy with their loans? I will list for you what a village with 230 members in its credit union bought over a period of four months:

"Most numerous were household needs: 1 loan for a chest and a safe, 1 loan for a pressure lamp, 7 loans for suitcases, 2 loans for furniture, 4 loans for beds, 1 loan for house property, 6 loans for clothing, 1 loan for a sewing machine, 4 loans for kitchen utensils, 1 loan for flour, 1 loan for a camera, 1 loan for tobacco, 2 loans for bicycles, 1 loan for a blanket, 3 loans for mosquito nets, 3 loans for school clothes and school fees.

"A number of loans were for farming needs: 8 loans for oxen, 1 loan for a barn for a bull, 1 loan for a wire fencing tool, 1 loan for a plough, 1 loan for an axe and file, 1 loan for carpenter tools.

"In connection with fishing, there were a couple of requests: 10 loans by 10 different members who jointly were buying a fishing net; 2 loans for fishing boats.

"Then there were several loans for social expenses: 1 loan for the bride-price for a marriage, 1 loan for a funeral, 2 loans to pay court summonses.

"Altogether this village credit union loaned $2,422 to their village members in four months and substantially all was repaid without incident.

"Of particular interest are the half dozen urban credit unions in the capital city of Suva in the Fijis. The Cathedral Parish Credit Union in Suva is the largest in Fiji, with 1,300 members and $25,000 in assets. You are all aware of the outrageous rates of city usurers and the pitiful stories of debt entanglement. The Cathedral Credit Union and the others in the city relieve this onerous burden somewhat. Catholic native urban migrants are absorbed immediately into these unions and thus many are saved from falling prey to debts through ignorance of city ways.

"To young missionaries who get into this work, I would say that they'll never do very much in this field until they realize that they are not doing the people the favor by going to them; it is the people who do us missionaries the favor by opening the door of their village to us. We are not the people's boss; we are their servant. We cannot make the credit union, the cooperative, the new social way of life work; we can only point the way. We can only reap the harvest of consolation when they, God's people, succeed in bettering their lives.

"The best advice I ever got was not from a spiritual book nor a spiritual exhortation. It was from a Mason in Wisconsin one evening who had drunk a little too much. He buttonholed me and said, 'You know, you fellows, you priests, who get into this social work for others had better be careful. You get so interested, so bothered about things, so anxious, that you forget the spiritual sources from which you draw your strength.' That Mason had my number."

For recommended reading, see Bibliography No. 14, page 282.

CHAPTER 12

Rural Vitality Through
Community Small Industries

New Income for the Rural World. Rural families almost everywhere in the world are too exclusively dependent on agriculture for their livelihood. The problem has been solved in much of Western Europe and North America, where agriculture engages only a small minority and government support aims to stabilize farm income at a fairly high level. But even these areas possess regions in which people must search out non-agricultural income to make ends meet.

In the mission lands of Asia, Africa and Latin America low farm incomes make trouble. The problems are grave because national economics are usually undiversified and gainful employment outside agriculture is severely limited.

Accent, therefore, rests on creating employment. Three types of frontal attack on the problem, which means solving it in the rural areas themselves, are: 1) intensification and diversification of agricultural production by introduction of new money crops; 2) the introduction of new industries into rural areas; 3) the expansion of traditional rural crafts and industries.

Most one-crop and two-crop countries in Asia, Africa and
Latin America are keenly aware that they are highly vulnerable;
in the unstable world market, a price drop in coffee brings disaster to Brazil, in cocoa impoverishes Ghana, in rubber ruins
Malaya. Some of these countries today are financially strong
enough to try intensifying production of their specialty in order
to get capital to improve their other cash crops, such as rice,
sugar, tobacco, thus creating diversity and spreading their risk.
Most, however, must limit themselves to marginal efforts, such
as encouraging an increase in the growth of vegetables in kitchen
gardens, the promotion of family fish ponds, small farm animal
husbandry, small stands of lumber-producing trees or of orchards.

We are concerned here, rather, with the second and third
categories of means of creating employment, namely, community small industries and village crafts. Rural industrialization,
as it involves national governments, has dealt to a major degree
with agricultural processing industries. The current Five-Year
Plan of the Philippines emphasizes the processing of foods,
textiles, leather goods and pulp in order to reduce the dependence of the nation on foreign sources of supply. In countries of
Latin America and Africa to cotton growing has been added
ginneries in rural areas as well as textile mills in the cities. All
these activities, while touching rural life, are usually operations
of national rather than local scale. These likewise we pass by
to consider the smaller but immensely important initiatives at
town and village level.

The Pattern of Community Small Industries. Minor though
they be, community small industries today represent an investment of hundreds of millions of dollars. Terms are used loosely
but in the interest of clarity the following descriptions are worth
noting:

1 *Cottage industry.* Production under this term is carried on in
   the home on a handicraft basis, that is, without power-driven
   machinery, although various implements and hand-tools are

used in production (hand-looms, oil ghannies, potters' wheels and the like). Cottage industries fall into two main categories:

  i *those engaged in the processing of locally grown agricultural products: rice hulling, oil expressing, sugar cane crushing, fur manufacture, peanut shelling and so forth;*

 ii *those engaged in handicraft manufacture: hand-loom weaving, mat-weaving, spinning, basket making, gold and silver work, carving of traditional art objects and so forth.*

2 *Small workshops.* Such shops engage typically in carpentry or blacksmith work, repair of machinery such as oil engines, electric motors, rice hullers, sugar crushers. They may manufacture such small articles as utensils, fountain pens, small machinery parts. Production may be for immediate neighbors or nearby markets or, less often, for a wider market. Equipment may consist of small power-driven machines such as lathes or drills. Personnel will be a few hired workers.

3 *Small factory industry.* The work done, the production, the equipment and the personnel are on a larger scale than in the workshop but yet are under minimum factory specifications.

A working definition suggested by the International Labor Organization says a small factory employs 20 or less persons if it uses power-driven machinery, or 50 or less when it does not. Definitions vary according to country.

The workshop or small factory can be organized in one of three ways: 1) as a family-owned enterprise, or single proprietorship; 2) as a partnership; 3) as an industrial cooperative. Thus in this third form the missionary interested in serving his people can resort to an organization such as is described in the previous chapter.

What are the goals envisioned for community small industries by governments and by non-governmental organizations such as the Church? The general purposes are two-fold:

1 *Relief of the needy.* Small industries in many cases aim at alleviating seasonal or chronic unemployment or underemployment, particularly in rural areas, thus augmenting the slender income of poor families;

2 *Strengthening the rural economy.* Small industries are likewise employed as a constructive force:
    i   *to help mobilize and utilize whatever capital there is in*
       rural areas;
    ii *to maintain the traditional social fabric;*
    iii *to prevent an over-rapid flow of population to urban*
       areas;
    iv *to contribute to production and income.*

Failure of such industries, on the other hand, magnifies the
problem of population pressure on the land and aggravates rural
unemployment. The alert missionary, accordingly, views the
promotion of small industries as an important contribution to
the country's common good. He is encouraged to give the matter
his attention through papal interest in it. Pius XII, in an address
of September 1, 1944, declared, "Small and medium holdings
in agriculture, in the arts and trades, in commerce and industry
should be guaranteed and promoted; cooperative unions should
ensure for them the advantages of big business."

The Missionary and Community Small Industries. Again
we find ourselves inquiring into the role which the missionary
should fill in the betterment of his people by the promotion of
a major socio-economic instrument for good in mission countries. To this end we turn to Father James J. Berna, S.J., holder
of a degree in economics from Georgetown University and now
at work as an economics specialist in Jamshedpur, India.

"When the missionary tackles the task of community small
industries," explained Father Berna, "he usually faces a situation of urgent distress affecting his people. Possibly too much
pressure on the land is prompting the younger men to migrate
into the cities, with many undesirable consequences. Or it may
be the continuing hardships of dire poverty such as I saw in one
village in Kerala on the southwest coast of India.

"The village of Savaripalayam is populated by 600 souls, almost all Catholics. Most of the land is owned by Hindu landlords who live about 20 miles away. A few of the villagers own
land and some are tenants, but about two-thirds are landless

laborers. They are paid by the day. The area produces rice and cotton. The men receive one rupee, which is about 20 cents, for eight to ten hours work in the fields, and even in India one rupee doesn't buy enough to support a family of six to eight children that some of these men possess.

"The women also work in the fields. They are likewise paid by the day but receive half a rupee for a day's work. If it rains so hard on a given day that tending the fields is impossible, these people don't work and don't get paid. In certain seasons each year, when the fields are being prepared, only half the people are earning their wage.

"Thus the state of normalcy of these people is poverty, but during certain periods it is desperation. Then they are reduced to one meal every two days, with rice water to dull their hunger in the interval.

"Hence the Indian priest in Savaripalayam has instituted a community small industry to gain additional income for his people. He has set up hand-looms in the homes and during every spare hour someone in the family is at the loom. Details of production and market contacts must be carefully watched if proper returns are to be insured. Whatever the weaknesses, here is an example of the world problem of inadequate family income being solved by a community small industry.

"Sometimes the village problem of inadequacy is a seasonal one. I have had some experience in another village on the other side of India, on the shores of the Bay of Bengal. This village of Covelong has sandy, arid land which forbids farming. Hence one of the village castes lives from fishing. The other caste works in the government salt pans, an outdoor salt manufacturing establishment constructed on the beach. The workers maintain a series of dykes that constitute the pans. These are flooded from the sea, the water evaporates under the torrid sun and the salt remains ready to be gathered.

"But during the monsoon rains the salt operation comes to an end; you can't get evaporation during the six weeks or so of the rains. And for six weeks or so after the monsoon only a small core of men have work, rebuilding the dykes destroyed by the downpour. Thus for about three months these people are out of work, and they almost starve.

"Here again a Catholic missionary has resorted to community small industries. He has organized an industrial cooperative that engages in various cottage industries which, when all is properly managed, provide these humble folk with money for food."

The Frame in Which the Missionary Should Work. The very fact that Father Berna has been able to enter India from abroad has a bearing on the next point which he makes for us. He is a specialist in community small industries. The Government of India, which sees fit at present to refuse visas to Christian missionaries, gladly accepts technical experts, whether clerical or lay, who can contribute to the solving of India's socio-economic problems. Father Berna makes the point that the missionary, wherever he works, should inform himself, at least by taking guidance from his superiors and from properly informed specialists, on how the solutions which he feels are needed for the socio-economic problems of his flock fit into any general governmental plans in course of execution for the betterment of the people among whom he works.

"The question of the missionary's activity in starting small industries where they are needed," noted Father Berna, "is intimately related to a much broader question, the general problem of the industrialization of the underdeveloped areas. In many of these areas, strenuous efforts at development are presently being made by their governments and this development usually takes the form of industrialization. The two concepts of economic development and industrialization are theoretically distinct but, in practice, governments are attempting to stimulate the growth of industries as an aid to economic development.

"In these plans, which are in existence in many countries of the world, the emphasis on industrialization is rather great. So is the emphasis on the growth of small factory industries. There are sound social reasons for this; one of the ambitions of these countries is to avoid some of the mistakes which were made in the West. At least, the advisers of these countries consider them to be mistakes. They wish to avoid the huge organizations which have grown up, the concentration of industry, in particular the concentration of economic power. Consequently their ideal is to attempt to create an industrial society but on a decentralized base. They would like to have small factories dotting the countryside and turning out the products they need.

"In some of these plans and projects, cottage industries also play an important role, though the term industrialization is used to mean the growth of factory industry as distinct from cottage industries. In India, for instance, the Second Five-Year Plan involves important programs for the development of cottage industries, even though it is not clear yet whether or not they will be able to remain as permanent parts of the economy."

The Missionary's Concern for Industrialization. Father Berna, with his knowledge of missionaries, senses the uneasiness that his discussion of industrialization will awaken in many of his confreres.

"In a sense," he reflected, "industrialization does not directly concern the missionary. He is working in an underdeveloped area, but he is not an agent of industrialization. It is not his problem to industrialize the country. However, there are serious reasons why he should give the subject his attention.

"In the first place, he wants to be in tune with the aspirations, the hopes, the ambitions of the country which he has adopted. He should know something about the plans and the general trends of economic development. Many of the people are pinning all their hopes for the future on these plans. The press and the radio make constant reference to the economic program.

"Secondly, the missionary wants to know the general over-all picture in his country because, as much as possible, his actions should fit into the local context. Again we are back to that notion of the socio-economic whole. If he is going to do anything at all about starting industries for his people, his plan must have relation to the over-all picture.

"The general economic program will affect his area eventually, possibly much sooner than he thinks. The rate of change in these countries is sometimes terrific, and as time passes it will accelerate rather than slow down. He doesn't want his actions to be haphazard or out of relation with events in the country at large, or in his region or community.

"A practical reason why the missionary should know the economic picture is its practical effect on his plans if he proposes to his people a community small industry. The type he suggests should fit the trends. If the country's program includes heavy accent on a textile spinning industry, it would be foolish to spend time and money developing a local hand-spinning unit.

"A further reason for knowledge is that the country's plans may include important assistance to small industries. A prime example is India. Cottage industries and small factory industries are receiving great attention, and programs are in force to give assistance. There is provision for the training of artisans and handicraft workers, for equipment under hire-purchase and installment buying plans, direct financial aid in the form of loans, various forms of extension service to cottage and small factory industries.

"However, all this is background. As I have said, it is not the missionary's direct problem to promote the industrialization of the country. But the true, spiritual, cultural, physical welfare of his people is his concern, and industrialization may well serve this end."

The Employment of Small Industries. Father Berna then approached directly the role which the missionary may fill in employing community small industries to better his people.

"Granted the missionary judges that there is a need for starting some small industry to help his people, what should his role be? Well, we are all of the same mind, I think, as to what the most important factor is. In general, it is education. If the principle of the felt need applies anywhere, it is here. Industries must ultimately be run by the people. The people must supply the enterprise and the initiative.

"The people have to be convinced, first, of the need of this project to improve their social and economic status. Then they must see the relationship between a higher economic and social status and this particular industry. They may agree that they should be better off, but they may not agree that they should work in their cottages seven or eight hours a day pounding rice by hand, especially when the women and children will have to do much of the pounding. The women may prefer to be down by the river all afternoon, gossiping with their neighbors as they launder the clothes. Don't overlook the need to convince them of the relationship between industry and their well-being. But take pains to proceed very, very carefully.

"The second contribution of the missionary after providing for the education of his group is the role Doctor Arceneaux described so well in the general relations of the missionary with country people, namely, that of mediator between the people and the technicians. Contact must be made with the persons in the area, or in the capital of the country, who can advise on the technical aspects involved in launching a small industry. It has to be a workable business proposition. It may be a cooperative, which involves as well a way of life, but it should be viable commercially.

"True, the project may be merely a little operation oriented to aiding the subsistence economy of the village. But if it is to be a commercial venture, precautions must be taken that it proves a paying proposition. This may involve some analysis of markets, of sources of raw materials, of sources of capital, whether for launching the operation or working capital for a continuing flow of supplies.

"The missionary will hardly possess the technical knowledge or the time to apply himself personally to directional details of a small industry. If possible, he must put his people in touch with competent extension services such as we possess in various parts of India. He must likewise search out the leaders, those with potential business aptitude who can provide managerial capacity and who will contribute enthusiasm to the project."

The Proper Selection of a Small Industry. Father Berna made reference to his first-hand contact with small industries in India, when the authorities engaged him to survey the patterns, sound or unsound, which characterize this newly developing Indian institution.

"My recent assignment in India," he explained, "had to do with the origins of small workshops and small factory industries in rural South India. I made a sampling of the small factories, all now employing more than 50 people each. Many of them started as little shops for repairs and odd jobs, employing two, three, four, five people. Some were blacksmiths or factory workers who set themselves up as artisans. I would like to make the point for missionaries that if they get four or five of these started in a little community, after ten years these enterprises can well represent decentralized little factories turning out important industrial products for the district, which will provide employment for several hundred families and will constitute a very durable part of the economy.

"Too often missionaries think only along lines of traditional industries for their people. In favor of the traditional is the fact that they are comparatively easy to start. One draws on skills already possessed; indeed, often very little skill is required. They have the advantage of affording immediate relief to a considerable number of people.

"But they have limitations. Often the supplementary income they yield, though real, is very small. The life of such industries is precarious in an economy that is industrializing. If a rice mill comes to the area, it will quickly put all the hand-pounders out of business. If a spinning mill opens, we must say goodbye to the hand-looms. A utensils factory ruins any cottage industries along this line.

"A longer-range view would look to other possibilities, which do not rule out the traditional forms, but represent an additional dividend for a community by harnessing the skills and the enterprise of certain of the hardier and more intelligent elements. A

missionary might think of developing a few social-minded entrepreneurs, who could start small industrial workshops, which
might eventuate into small factories creating permanent employment in the area. A couple of these could mean work for
the heads of a hundred families.

"This policy requires careful appraisal of the possibilities.
Are there any central factories looking for ancillary producers?
Has the government any plans to favor small factory development to meet local needs? Do irrigation or power projects give
prospects for the use of small power-driven pumps or equivalent machinery that would call for processing or repair shops?

"The discovery and training of potential entrepreneurs could
well become the marginal concern of an alert missionary interested in the betterment of his people. Sometimes traders will
team up with workmen to the advantage of both. Facilities not
too far away may be available for industrial school training of
capable young men. Scholarships for engineering courses may
possibly be secured. Training as apprentices in nearby factories
is a consideration.

"But let the missionary not forget that, if he is concerned
with the good of the community, he must innoculate his young
men with this same concern. True, he will not always succeed;
many will take advantage of opportunities and quickly become
wrapped up only in personal gain of a selfish sort. But many
will see the wisdom of serving their community as well as
themselves. Young men should be imbued with the ideal of contributing to the common good.

"Let the missionary likewise reflect that small industries *will*
be started in his neighborhood sooner or later, however backward it may seem. It is according to the way of doing these
days. Why not aid his young people to be in the vanguard,
stirring them to interest in broad social motives as well as personal profit?"

Check-List for Organizing Industry. Father Berna offered
the following check-list for the interested missionary:

1 *General survey of conditions*
   a   general trend of economic planning;
   b   government planning;
   c   business planning;
   d   regional and local plans touching small industry;
   e   sources of information (government, business, United Nations, voluntary agencies).

2 *Purpose of foundation*
   a   temporary stop-gap relief measure to alleviate urgent distress;
   b   long-term betterment of enlisted members;
   c   long-term betterment of socio-economic life of the community.

3 *Government regulations regarding industry*
   a   licenses required if any;
   b   registration, taxation requirements;
   c   factory regulations; will often determine whether work should be done in houses or in common work-place.

4 *Government-aid programs for small industry*
   a   general form of programs—what aid is rendered; who is eligible; cooperatives only?
   b   forms of aid:
       i   *financial—loans, purchase of equipment on installment plan;*
       ii   *technical—training of artisans, extension schemes; service units for assisting small industries;*
       iii *marketing.*

5 *Determinants of the choice of an industry*
   a   skills of the people;
   b   raw materials;
   c   markets;
   d   finance;
   e   viability.

6 *Skills of the people*
   a   skills possessed;
   b   traditional industries among them—
       i   *which perhaps are languishing and could be rejuvenated;*
       ii   *which have died out and could be rejuvenated;*

    c occupations or activities opposed on social or religious grounds (e.g., caste-assigned occupations in India; tanning taboo among Hindus);

    d potentialities of training:

       i *government training programs;*

      ii *industrial schools;*

     iii *factories accepting apprentices.*

7 *Raw materials*

    a raw materials needed;

    b source; cost of transport; degree of availability;

    c government provision (e.g., yarn to the hand-loom industry in South India).

8 *Marketing arrangements*

    a markets aimed at:

       i *local surrounding villages, nearby city;*

      ii *regional or export;*

    b precise forms of marketing:

       i *by individual producers to individual dealers;*

      ii *jointly by the cooperative;*

     iii *cost of transportation and source of payment;*

     iv *sale at factory to middlemen;*

      v *government marketing agency;*

     vi *safeguards on fair price, correct weights and measures, time of payments; hidden price reductions in form of required "samples";*

    c custody of goods before sale:

       i *storage;*

      ii *safeguards against theft, wastage, damage.*

9 *Financing: fixed and working capital*

    a fixed capital requirements:

       i *common work-place;*

      ii *equipment;*

    b working capital requirements:

       i *purchase of raw materials;*

      ii *storage;*

     iii *operational costs (wages, etc.);*

     iv *transportation to market;*

      v *reserves and contingencies;*

    c sources of capital:

      i   *government loans or subsidies;*
      ii *banks;*
      iii *private money lenders;*
      iv *credit union.*

10 *Viability of the industry (favorable and unfavorable factors for survival)*

    a social conformity of project with local traditions, tastes, etc.;

    b economic soundness, in light of national planning for small industries;

    c economic soundness, in light of local area factors.

11 *Form of organization*

    a cooperative (favored form for rural processing industries, for social benefits; most apt for government subsidies, but nevertheless a difficult form of organization for industry because there is not enough incentive of personal gain for the directing officers);

    b individual proprietorships (suitable for developing decentralized industry and social-minded entrepreneurs of small industries);

    c individual proprietorships bound together in marketing cooperative (Japanese plan).

12 *Follow-up after establishment*

    a continuing supervision:

        i   *continuing training;*
        ii *expansion plans;*
        iii *unforeseen problems;*

    b development of lay leadership;

    c use of government extension services.

Economic Guidance of Mission Peoples.   Consideration of community small industries draws attention to the general subject of the economic guidance of mission peoples.

"One of the finest points in Father Berna's presentation," observed Monsignor Ligutti, "is his recommendation that the missionary exercise active solicitude for the entry of the young men of his mission into worth-while life careers, particularly into the new field of industry developing in mission lands. I believe that our mission schools can do much to stir in their students a greater pride in and appreciation of their economic careers.

"While journeying with a missionary through the countryside in a land of Central Africa, I discovered every once in a while along the road a particularly good-looking farm. On three different occasions I asked my missionary friend to stop, and on all three occasions the African farmer whom we greeted told us he was an Adventist. 'How is it you are doing so well?' I asked. Believe it or not, on each of the three different occasions the African Adventist replied, 'We help each other; our religion teaches us to work for our fellows.'

" 'How is it,' I asked the missionary after our third experience, 'that these Adventists take such pride in having good farms and make it a religious duty to help each other build up first-rate farms?' 'I can only suppose,' my companion replied quite humbly, 'that there's something the Adventist missionaries teach these people that we don't teach them.' "

"Our Catholic school teachers do quite well," replied Father Berna, "but I think there are two important things our schools should do for our mission people. First of all, I think it is obvious that they should supply industrial training of some sort. Secondly and more important, I think we should give our children the ideal of taking great pride in their business career, whether it is farming or an industrial occupation. They should see private enterprise, or entrepreneurship, as a profession. And of course they should be social-minded entrepreneurs, aiming to accomplish a great deal of social good in their communities."

"I am wondering, Father Berna," commented Mr. Miniclier, "if as an economist you do not think there should be a much more careful appraisal of the handicrafts that are taught to various peoples both by missionaries and by government people. I recall an experience in the Philippines where we found a village of fishermen who had been painstakingly taught as a cottage industry the handicraft of making pottery utensils. Very shortly their community development program moved their fishing activities up the scale to a money economy, and over-night they and their neighbors were buying aluminum pots and pans that didn't break. Their pottery business became all lost effort.

"Recently in Sardinia I saw a similar mistaken effort. A weaving cooperative had been organized for the production of very beautiful but very expensive Sardinian fabrics. Decorators in Europe bought them avidly for a season but then European mills tooled up the designs and the Sardinian weavers were out of a market. I saw a similar loss of market hit villagers in Peru who put hand-woven Peruvian fabrics on the market for two years until the mills stole the business away."

"Certainly," replied Father Berna, "the capacity to be competitive in the market is essential if we are going to be of real help to the people to whom we bring small industries. Rural artisans need to be equipped with better tools and equipment, as is done in countries like Japan. When electricity is available, these people can employ electric looms and drills. The matter of proper tools and proper working conditions to insure humane living conditions and proper financial return for a reasonable day's work in village industries, is quite as essential as are the regulations imposed by law on urban industry."

"In Puerto Rico," observed Monsignor Illich, "our celebrated Operation Bootstrap placed considerable importance on the role of community small industries. In 1950 one-third of Puerto Rico's gross product was industrial; in 1955 one half; by 1960 more than two-thirds. So we have there a shift from agriculture to industry such as could not possibly be accomplished in India within a decade. Some of the lessons we have learned are worth noting.

"For one thing, the employers generally insist that in industry, even if it concerns only a craft, as soon as you need machines you should employ school graduates, because country folk who have not been disciplined to sit at a desk for hours are unsuitable for the job.

"Secondly, industrialization in Puerto Rico, at its present

development, has created fewer jobs than it has destroyed. The home needlework, which is our type of cottage industry, has been totally wiped out. We produce today many more needlecraft products but fewer people produce them.

"Light industry is not, unfortunately, the solution for every part of the country without exception. There is a particular section of Puerto Rico that I know well, because I work among the people there on Sundays and in all my free time from the university. I recall one village in particular where people scrounge out a living by four months' work in the sugar-cane fields, and during eight months have no source of income whatsoever except government subsidies and insurances.

"Now no industrial entrepreneur will build a factory in that village. Why? Because as soon as small industries opened their doors, the women would start to work and money would come into the community, but the community, as has happened in nearby communities, would completely break up. People would secure enough money to migrate and only the old and lazy would be left.

"How explain this? Primarily it is because the people don't own any land. The men are merely hands on the sugar-cane plantations. And on this south side of Puerto Rico it is impossible, for practical reasons, to have individual holdings of land or even cooperative ownership of land, unless financing can be had for irrigation, since there is too little rain to grow things without irrigation.

"Thus the people live in my section because they haven't enough money to migrate to New York. The men remain because they have nothing else to do, and know nothing else except to cut sugar. One thing might catch them, namely, heavy industry factories, but there is no hope of heavy industry for at least another decade."

"Puerto Rico teaches us the lesson," added Father Fitzpatrick, "that we need not only an economic program; we need a social program as well that can convince people that, in addition to a job, rural life will provide the compensations that men dream of and without which they will run away to the city as soon as they get enough money.

"Puerto Rico has profited as a whole from its industrialization, but nevertheless many of the small factories in rural areas are closed for want of manpower because people got money enough to move away. The Puerto Rican government trains the technicians for the decentralized factories, but as soon as a man learns enough to be a machinist and earns the price of a ticket he answers the lure of living in a hovel in New York where, incidentally, he can make three times more as a machinist than at home. Unless the rural home acquires more meaning, the march to the city will go on. But we're still doing the right thing in promoting rural industrialism."

For recommended reading, see Bibliography No. 15, page 284.

THE MISSIONARY AND
THE WORKER

Greater Concern for the Worker. Monsignor George Higgins, Director of the Department of Social Action of the National Catholic Welfare Conference, reminded the missionary, as well as all other clergy, of the larger place in our thinking which the worker around the world is due to occupy.

"With the rapid growth of industrialization," noted the Monsignor, "ten years from now missionaries will be faced with the organized labor problem in much more substantial fashion than most of them are today. To my knowledge, there are very few missionaries who are currently active in the trade union field. There are some notable examples, as Father Walter Hogan and his group in the Philippines, Father Enright and his associates in India and a scattering of others. Relatively few, even in the mission countries that are already industrialized, as in Japan, have come to grips with the problem. Hence I fear that it is due to steal up on the missionary forces at a rather dangerously rapid pace in the coming few years.

"Work by the missionary or by the homeland priest in the

field of labor is going to be much more difficult than the missionary task in the agricultural field or in the development of cooperatives. The type of direct personal initiative, which the missionary in many cases may take in these other fields, cannot be taken in the labor field without jeopardizing his work.

"The role of the priest in the labor field, it seems to me, is much more delicate. The trade union movement very properly, in my opinion, is extremely sensitive, almost instinctively so, to any kind of interference from outside its own ranks. That is certainly true in the United States, and if the clergy in the United States have had any measure of success in their dealings with the labor movement I think it is because they have kept that fact foremost in their minds.

"With very few exceptions, the priests in this country who have entered this field have been extremely careful to draw a sharp line between their legitimate role and the role of the trade union leader. The union leader is sensitive, and I believe properly so, about the autonomy of his organization. At times, when the union happens to be in the wrong hands, this can be embarrassing or troublesome to those concerned with general justice for all. Nevertheless this autonomy is a healthy instinct that needs to be encouraged for the common good.

"If we can have a trade union movement which will control its own affairs while being properly responsible to the public and to government, I think we are likely to have a much stronger and better labor movement."

Contributing to the Trade Union Movement. Monsignor Higgins, genuinely dedicated as he is to trade unionism throughout the world, reveals his keen insight into the state of mind necessary in the missionary if he is to contribute to this phase of the socio-economic problem.

"Any priest," stated the Monsignor, "who wants to do an effective service job in the trade union movement has to lean over backwards, lest he give even the slightest impression of interfering in the internal affairs of the organization or that his purpose in taking an interest in the labor problem is clouded with any motive other than the genuine good of the men.

"A trade unionist, whether he be a Christian or a pagan, will detect instinctively any wrongly directed motive in our actions. He will be particularly offended if he thinks that our primary interest in the trade union movement is not really concern for justice to the workers or for the stability and integrity of the organization. Falling under such suspicion would present a very difficult psychological as well as spiritual problem for a priest.

"The chances are that the majority of effective trade union leaders in underdeveloped countries are going to continue to be either socialists or some variety of secularist, unreligious or anti-religious persons. We in the United States are not faced with this situation. We possess a kind of secularism in our culture, but it is not too strongly opposed to religion and not sharply tinged with anticlericalism.

"The spirit in the labor circles of many mission countries presents an extremely difficult problem for the priest to approach. How can he encourage a union which is controlled substantially by people of that ilk without seeming to compromise some of his own principles? Yet the attempt has to be made, I think, even at the risk of making occasional mistakes. We can't wait to become active in the trade union movement until all of its leaders are people whose basic philosophy is the same as ours, or whose basic philosophy is at least a natural law philosophy that we can accept. If we wait that long, I am afraid it will be too late."

The Command to the Priest to Participate. Monsignor Higgins established the clear mandate of the missionary to recognize trade union work as within his field of duty, however difficult to carry out, should his superiors give him such an assignment. The labor movement is among the most delicate of all forms of social activity within the missionary's orbit. Hence the young missionary will be particularly careful to be guided in its regard by the local Church's experienced leaders in this field.

"We need waste no time discussing the importance of our doing the work in the labor field," the Monsignor said. "The official Church view on the task is briefly stated by Father Edward Murphy, S.J., in his excellent paper in the proceedings of the Fordham Conference of Mission Specialists of 1955 entitled, *Social Action in Mission Lands* (p. 11). Noting the march of industrialization in mission lands, Father Murphy says, 'It is the easiest thing to make a proletariat out of the less developed masses, and I imagine the temptation to do so will be very great. We know too that no corner of the world, where there are disorganized masses, will be left unexplored by the communist world-revolution. Thus we have two cogent reasons for encouraging the organization of working masses.

" 'The Canadian Bishops in a pastoral on the problem of workers wrote, "If there are still men so poorly informed as to contest the right and the duty of the clergy to enter into the economic and social field so that the doctrine of the Church be applied, we could repeat to them the words which Benedict XV used in a letter to the Bishop of Bergamo in 1920, 'Let no member of the clery imagine that such activity (to deal with unions) is outside his priestly ministry on the ground that it lies in the economic sphere, for it is precisely in that sphere that the salvation of souls is in peril.' "

" 'And the Canadian Bishops say of the priest in this apostolate, "He is neither leader, director, propagandist or business agent. He is the educator: develop among all members and especially among leaders, the supernatural life, the virtues of justice and charity; the social spirit, the virtues of fortitude, temperance and prudence; fill minds with the wonderful social doctrine of the Church."

" 'We must, then,' Father Murphy concludes, 'look upon the organization of workers as part of our missionary apostolate where it is required.' "

The Missionary's Labor Program. Monsignor Higgins

added his own conclusions as to the specific role of the missionary in the labor field.

"First, I would say that in mission lands missionaries should recognize that, in order to secure any standing at all for the Church among the workers, they should go beyond the role of spiritual adviser prescribed by the Canadian Bishops and place emphasis on the role of general educator in the social doctrine of the Church, a role likewise recommended by these Bishops. The missionaries should, in a certain sense, be propagandists for the trade union movement by insisting, publicly where this is advisable, on the right of labor to organize. The missionaries should be ready to stand up and be counted in defense of this right.

"Secondly, in some situations I think missionaries should follow the example of Father Walter Hogan and his Jesuit confreres in Manila in undertaking the formal instruction of both labor and management in the Church's teachings as applied to labor-management relations."

Monsignor Higgins here made reference to the efforts in the Philippines by the New York Province of the Society of Jesus, which was part of the post-war world-wide program of the Jesuits to advance the Church's social apostolate. Father Walter Hogan was sent to Manila to deal with Filipino management and with the workers.

Father Hogan began on the docks, which are among the toughest in all East Asia. After years of intimate contact, he has acquired shrewd understanding and deep sympathy for the longshoremen and the factory and farm hands in the islands.

"A man, when he gets his paycheck," he wrote, in *Jesuit Missions,* "should be full of joy. He should be able to buy some candy for his children on the way home; he should be able to look forward to a clean home, a fair and happy wife, and children on the floor with their books.

"But what is the situation that exists on the Manila waterfront? On the Manila docks, a man for years got mighty few pesos to take home. There has been no money for candy. His home is a six-foot-square shack, often with a dirt floor, built within inches of other shacks. Some families even live in the packing cases the Cadillacs come in. His wife is aged before her time, wearied with the filth and poverty. The youngsters are uneducated and unfed. The man himself is beaten down in despair. He may buy some cheap drink to forget his worries for the evening. Perhaps he visits a house of prostitution, so unattractive are his home surroundings.

"Shall we merely be shocked or shall we get rid of his worst occasions of sin?"

Father Hogan, when he first took up his task, saw as his logical approach a review of Catholic social principles with the big businessmen and politicians of Manila. These men welcomed him when they thought that "labor priest" meant a catechist to teach the workers respect for the bosses. But many became deeply resentful when he began teaching the workers the principles of social justice and the techniques of labor organization. He fought through their opposition, and the workers, under his guidance, built themselves an honest union of over 30,000 members.

Perhaps of still more enduring importance is the systematic teaching in labor-management relations which Father Hogan's companion Jesuits established at the celebrated College of the Ateneo in Manila. This took the form of an Institute of Social Order. A summer course was organized for priests and seminarians which aimed at familiarizing the clergy with the philosophy of trade unionism. A much more pragmatic approach to labor principles was offered in the course for union leaders. Soon A.B. graduates of the Ateneo, well prepared in Catholic social principles, teamed up with working elements in labor circles, who likewise were well coached, and there resulted the foundation of the Federation of Free Workers, the anti-Communist union just referred to.

The Ateneo labor school currently provides a one-year course in training under a staff of four Jesuit specialists in social teachings. The course has prepared many of the hard-core social action leaders now active in Filipino public affairs.

Concern for General Worker Betterment. Trade unionism may be described as the most dramatic factor in the betterment of the worker and as the principal key to this betterment, but the missionary does well to remember that trade unionism is the great instrument and not the end itself. The end product sought is the worker and his family everywhere on earth properly possessed of good living conditions. How much nearer to this goal have the world's workers moved? What are the goals striven for currently by governmental agencies, the labor forces themselves, enlightened management and the general public?

Many of these goals are the practical concern of field missionaries in many parts of the world. Developments at present receiving wide consideration are: 1) measures to promote better employment machinery in backward areas; 2) measures to increase productivity without injury to the worker's interests; 3) improved conditions under which to do the day's work; 4) more constructive labor-management relations; 5) improved conditions for special categories of workers; 6) the protection against improper labor exploitation of the tribal populations of the globe.

It should be kept in mind that while we speak mainly of industrial workers, agricultural workers have an equal right to consideration. Indeed, non-manual workers figure on the same footing with factory and farm labor. The power exercised in leftist ranks, in certain areas of the globe, by large numbers of the educated unemployed have awakened the world generally to the realization that labor ranks are a heterogeneous whole of the educated and uneducated, of the highly intelligent as well as the more modestly endowed, of the comfortably fixed along with the needy and desperate. The missionary's concern is not mere minimal relief or the righting of gross wrong but the task of building in the worker's world a full Christian society.

Guides on Conditions for Work. When a young missionary goes to the Amazon jungle, should he call for a 35-hour week?

Should he shrug his shoulders with indifference if he finds a 60-hour week? He will do best if he takes prudent advice before pronouncing on local conditions of work, yet takes pains lest in the name of prudence he ignore his duty to have Christian concern for the essential good of his fellow man.

There are ten basic areas touching the conditions of work which the modern world has come to accept as criteria. A word on each:

1   *Wage standards.* We look for justice and fairness in the distribution of income between wage-earners and the rest of the population and between different groups of wage-earners. Advanced countries have minimum wage regulations. Although similar laws exist in some low-income countries, especially in Latin America, the actual application is difficult when so many people are desperate. The desire for minimum wage regulations is widespread, however, in Asia and Africa as well as in Western lands.

2   *Hours of work.* In Europe, where 48 hours a week was standard between the two world wars, it is now between 44 and 46. The 40-hour week is standard in France, the United States, Australia and New Zealand. In Asia, Africa and interior Latin America plans to reduce the work hours must reckon with the risk to the national economy, through loss of production in the face of backward methods, the effects of the reduction on gross weekly pay, and the influences of work change on local customs. In short, change must be introduced in terms of local standards, not Western World concepts. Yet the fact must be recognized that excessive physical exertion and brain-fagging labors should in the end be judged wrong no matter how sanctioned by local custom.

3   *Child labor.* Viewing the matter at the world level, we cannot say that child labor has been abolished. Nevertheless steady progress, however unspectacular, is being made.

In the more highly developed countries, there is increasing support for setting the minimum age both for leaving school and admission to employment at 16 years. Ceylon recently raised the minimum age for employment to 14 years; in France's overseas community the minimum is now

14; in the Netherlands the minimum for girls is now 15 years.

The attack on child labor is made difficult by several factors: 1) family poverty in newly industrialized countries; 2) early school-leaving; 3) lack of enforcement of attendance at school; 4) simple lack of educational facilities. When there is a gap between the school-leaving age and the minimum age of employment, there is the seed of grave social problems. Youth forced into idleness get into illegal activities on the streets. On the other side of the picture, a substantial family budget is needed to keep teenagers properly fed, clothed and free from economic responsibilities until they are 16 years old. The missionary should be keenly aware of the family burden created by the 16-year-old minimum age for employment. Part-time employment of some sort is often requisite.

Until child labor is abolished, laws must minimize abuses. A six-hour day for youths under 16 is prescribed in some countries. The wide gap between pay to the young and to adults is being narrowed. Protective measures in working conditions are requisite.

4 *Working conditions for women.* There is a world shift of women from agriculture to industry and to services. We have already spoken of this but note it again here for completeness. Equal pay for equal value is the current goal. Some 30 countries have ratified the Equal Pay Convention, with only a few of these countries in Asia, Africa or Latin America.

Accepting the concept of the woman as a wage-earner, proper conditions of work include:

i *maximum facilities to minimize the handicaps of home-making while fulfilling work responsibilities;*

ii *reasonable work security according to her responsibilities in family support (if she is a family bread-winner she should not be in the "last-hired-first-fired" category);*

iii *recognition of woman's production efficiency to remove any stigma on her as a second-class worker.*

5 *Weekly rest.* There is now an international minimum standard of 24 consecutive hours of rest per week accepted al-

most everywhere. In Moslem countries this is Friday; in
Israel it is Saturday; in most of the rest of the world it is
Sunday, though not necessarily out of respect for the Chris-
tian significance of that day.

6   *Paid public holidays.* Wide acceptance of the principle that
workers are paid for holiday closure is becoming more the
rule. Compensational provision for time-workers and piece-
workers in respect to public holidays is likewise gaining
headway. Some countries provide higher than normal rate
of pay for workers kept on the job on holidays.

7   *Paid annual vacation.* In general, the shortest period of paid
annual leave in most countries of the world is one week.
However, two weeks of paid holidays is gaining ground. In
Mexico the majority of union workers get two weeks and
the legal minimum is six days. In France the minimum paid
holiday is 18 days. The concept of paid holidays has much
ground to gain in Asia, Africa and interior Latin America.

8   *Industrial welfare facilities.* Reasons of self-interest in the
way of increased productivity prompt management as well
as labor to be interested in workers' welfare. Among the
improvements in many countries are:

   i   *better medical services at work;*
   ii   *subsidized meals in the shop canteens;*
   iii   *subsidized housing;*
   iv   *free recreational facilities;*
   v   *accident-prevention measures in the shops;*
   vi   *organization of occupational health services for work-
     ers in industry.*

9   *Working conditions of non-manual employees.* In almost
every country of the world there is a steady increase in the
salaried and professional class, the so-called white-collar
workers. Ironically, so far as concerns the factors of betterment, the working conditions of these categories have not
kept pace with the improvements obtained by the manual
workers who a generation ago were regarded as far less for-
tunate in their employment. This, to a certain extent, is due
to the successful battle waged by trade unionism for the
betterment of the laboring classes.

The teaching profession suffers from shortages in every

country while the supply of scientists, engineers and tech-nicians is likewise insufficient. On the other hand, there is an over-supply in such occupations as law, economics, po-litical science, the arts, and of clerical and sales personnel. The remuneration of all of these groups is frequently low by current scales. There has been a consequent decline in the prestige status of many of these occupations.

10   *Working conditions of seafarers.* Missionaries, because they are found in so many ports of the world, have been inter-ested in the Apostolate of the Sea, which concerns itself with the spiritual needs of seafarers. Too frequently, however, missionaries have been uninformed and unconcerned with the socio-economic problems of seafarers.

Working and living conditions aboard ship have greatly improved. Outstanding advances have been registered in crew accommodation. Progress has been made in securing the 8-hour day for all categories of the crew. A few coun-tries have adopted the 40-hour week for seafarers. Welfare services in port and recreation aboard get attention. The missionary might likewise concern himself with insuring best possible relations between seamen and their families at home.

Fishermen have been neglected so far as betterment of working conditions is concerned. Three items receiving cur-rent attention are:

i   *minimum age for hiring aboard fishing vessels;*
ii *antecedent medical examinations and care aboard;*
iii *content of the articles of agreement when signing aboard.*

A World Christian Work Creed.   Governments, non-gov-ernmental social and economic organizations, business interests, the academic world, religious bodies, all have a lively concern for the worker. The missionary, however, as the bearer of the Christian worship and way of life into new lands, needs to be keenly aware that his Church has something more than a mere clutter of opinions on work. It has, rather, a clear-cut philos-ophy which can be summarized into what may be called a

Christian creed of work for all men. This Christian creed of work needs to be preached among all men over the globe as a counter-attack against all who declare that Christianity does not concern itself with the living needs of mankind.

The articles of such a creed are found in any standard manual of Christian social principles [1] but are worth presenting here as a *vade mecum* of the apostolic man who must concern himself with socio-economic guidance.

A World Christian Work Creed

A. Basic Principles

1 Work is a duty for mankind. Most people, it is true, can only thus secure their livelihood. But even those not faced with economic need require this form of activity to avoid physical, mental and spiritual harm.

2 Man has the right to secure work. It is not a right to a specific job but certainly a moral claim against economic society.

3 Man cannot be discriminated against in obtaining a job because of race, religion, national origin or rightful social affiliation (for instance, union affiliation). The employer willfully so acting is guilty of grave moral offense and at least a violation of charity.

4 The worker, once hired, does not acquire a right in strict justice to his job but cannot without good cause have his security placed in jeopardy by the threat of arbitrary dismissal. The assumption should be that he may retain his job so long as his work remains satisfactory and conditions do not change.

5 All workers are moral equals one to another and to all non-workers. This is born of man's equal dignity as man in relation to all other men. The man who happens to occupy the most subordinate position is the moral equal of his highest placed employer.

6 The worker recognizes the essential necessity of authority in orderly society. Authority, to be rightly used, must respect the person of the subordinate and must be employed for the common good.

7 The key to the dignity of the worker is respect for his person. This element of respect enters from the very beginning of the employee relationship. He is immediately treated as an individual, not as a name or a number. An effort is made to place him right, explain his duties, overcome his mistakes, make him a welcome partner in production.

8 Personal attitudes of employer and employee rather than techniques determine their relations. While kindness is important, consistent justice and equity are much more essential. A warm human relationship based on good principles, aided by good techniques, is the Christian pattern.

B. *The Worker and His Union*

9 Workers organize in trade unions to remove themselves from a depersonalized proletariat and to obtain the status of a recognized, influential group in society, capable of effective dealings with their employers and with society at large, with consequent economic, social, cultural and spiritual advantages for themselves and their families.

Workers need unions: i) because the average worker lacks the ability, experience and knowledge to deal with his employer and with society; ii) because the average worker himself lacks economic power to back up his arguments with management; iii) because the union can supply him with economic information and leadership, legal aid, a degree of guidance to economic, social and cultural improvement.

10 Workers have a moral right to form a labor union by man's natural right of association. In most countries of the world they are accorded the legal right to form unions.

11 Under normal circumstances, so long as other moral reasons do not intervene, the worker has the duty, based on social justice and charity, to join a union even if he individually does not need aid.

12 Since workers have the right to form unions, employers have the correlative duty to recognize such unions and deal with them in collective bargaining. Naturally, both employers and workers are justified in fighting a proven corrupt union or a hostile Communist-dominated union which

by its ulterior political objectives has ceased to be a true labor union.

C. *Collective Bargaining*

13   Union-management negotiations in collective bargaining aim to procure to the satisfaction of both workers and employers their equitable claims in matters of wages, hours and working conditions. Workers have a right to a just wage and hours and working conditions consonant with their human dignity.

14   The employer has a right to a fair profit and responsible performance of work by his employees.

15   The worker may properly make equitable claim to higher standards of living than the minimum requisite in strict justice. Among items recognized by employers as subjects for union contracts are: i) seniority in promotion where abilities are equal; ii) paid vacations and holidays; iii) pensions; iv) medical insurance.

16   Employers recognize the right of the workers to proper grievance machinery which assures the workers a system of appeals consonant with human dignity.

17   Workers recognize themselves as bound by social justice to care for company property, to exercise concern for quality in performance of their work, to display proper interest in the welfare of the company and to cooperate with management toward efficiency in production.

18   The public may properly expect to share, through increased productivity, in the gains achieved through collective bargaining. It has the right to expect conscientious dealings on both sides and thus be spared unjust inconvenience or hardship through unnecessary strikes or lockouts. The public must expect to pay its just share in higher prices for higher living standards for the workers. It should not overlook society's socio-economic gains through these higher living standards.

19   Catholic social teaching calls for full cooperation between management and the workers, beyond all minimal regulatory requirements, to achieve excellence of product and moderateness of costs in order that the public may be served

to the maximum. Collusion by management and the workers against the public interest is immoral.

20 Every worker recognizes, as a loyal union member, his duties toward his union: i) to insist that his union maintains just principles and practices; ii) to exercise his responsibility by attendance at meetings, conscientious voting and courageous participation in union activities; iii) to avoid improper pressure on union officers for improperly selfish ends.

Money Invades Asia's Economy. The full force of the preceding World Christian Work Creed is measured, not by any consideration of its practical use in the United States, but rather by its application to the problems facing the missionary at work in underdeveloped countries. To this end, we are provided with a striking example of a new Asian program by Father Johannes J. Dijkstra, S.J., a veteran of social action work in Java and a specialist in industrial relations, who recently made studies at Loyola University in Chicago.

"In a tropical climate where the soil is very fertile," noted Father Dijkstra, "the people live easily. The day's necessities are ready at hand. It is quite common to have three harvests a year. People do what has been done for ages and live nicely. For special needs, they go to the village market and buy by bartering a little of their extra food. A man does not calculate in terms of money the cost of his work in the rice fields or in the building of his house. Villagers live by mutual cooperation. This gives us an idea of yesterday's traditional Eastern economy, which in its essentials is that of a pre-capitalistic society.

"When such a society, however, comes into contact with a money economy, mishaps easily occur. Rice, houses, all things in the village are cheap when calculated without taking labor into account. Thus when a man alien to the village comes along and buys a house, he gets it very cheaply because the villager calculates that it cost him little aside from his time which he values at nothing.

"But then comes the intruder, the new money economy. Taxes must now be paid in money, and new commodities that catch men's fancy at the market now call for money. It is hard to believe how much work a villager is at first prepared to do to get the little sums of money needed for taxes or novelties and at what improperly low prices in money men sell their possessions—rice, livestock, houses. Thus the quondam easy-living villager suddenly finds himself poverty-striken and forced to become a laborer.

"At this point in Java, the Communists appeared. They had all the answers, all the solutions for the newly felt poverty, and many simple people believed them. They *are* the people, the Communists say, and they are *for* the people and hence the workers are compelled to become members of the Red authoritarian worker and farmer unions."

Catholic Responsibility to Asian Workers. Few though they are, Asia's Catholics are forced by the times to undertake to offer to Asians the Christian work creed if they are to possess a true counter-philosophy to the Communist promises which can only lead to enslavement.

"Our Catholics have a special task in the social and economic development of Asia," declared Father Dijkstra. "Usually the Catholics are better educated than other groups. Hence it is of great importance that our Catholics be trained in their social duties and in the possibilities for good in this field. Much advice needs to be given, much needs to be put right, much knowledge needs to be imparted, much character needs to be formed. If we can teach our Catholics to lead others according to Christian social and economic principles, they will become a great influence on them.

"In the economic field, Catholics are as yet weak because of lack of organization. To unite our forces, that is the heart of the matter. We have two immediate goals:

"1   Our Catholics must work among the farmers along our various cooperative lines;
"2   Our Catholics must work in good neutral trade unions, mostly along industrial union lines, attentive to the principles of the papal encyclicals."

The Labor Aid Plan of the Indonesian Bishops. Father Dijkstra possesses an immense advantage in being able to offer for consideration a labor aid organization, already in active being in Indonesia, that is achieving encouraging results.

"In Indonesia," explained Father Dijkstra, "the joint assembly of the Bishops erected a social action committee headed by one Bishop and composed of priests and laymen. Each Bishop called upon the laity in his diocese to enter the socio-economic field. The Bishops were not satisfied with general terms; in most specific fashion they stated that the needs of the farmers, workers and the huge mass of unemployed must be met. They declared that there must be cooperatives for the farmers, unions for the workers and relief employment for the unemployed.

"Very important, the Bishops recognized that this socio-economic movement could not be an exclusively Catholic movement since the good to be accomplished needed to be community-wide. The Catholics, few though they were in number, should unite all good elements in the community. In this they took their cue from the Antigonish Movement, which recommends action that embraces the entire community on the basis of natural law. The practice of the Church in the United States, of encouraging all right action by the neutral unions of the nation, was also recognized.

"However, the special problem in Indonesia presented by the superior power of Communism was taken into consideration. Previous to this latest episcopal plan, Catholic leaders had organized neutral unions on the Island of Java, but these were infiltrated by the Reds who then took over the leadership and destroyed the original Catholic spirit. The biggest union today in Indonesia, the SOBSI, now violently Communist, was originally the foundation of Indonesian Catholics. Our laymen refused to risk a repetition of this misfortune.

"Thus the Ikatan Buruh-Tani Pantjasilla (The Pantjasilla Workers and Farmers Movement), though declaredly neutral in membership, community-wide in aims and democratic in general procedure, made the provision this time that, in order to keep its organization from being stolen by leftist infiltrators, each local should possess a moral adviser with right of legislative veto, who should be a Catholic priest named by his Bishop. This was the guarantee provided by the moderate-minded laymen that their work would not be frustrated.

"The Pantjasilla movement, to which reference is made in the title, is a distinctly Indonesian idea originated by Indonesia's great leader, Soekarno himself. Pantjasilla means the five pillars or principles which are the foundation of the state: 1) belief in one God; 2) respect for all humanity; 3) love of country; 4) dedication to democracy; 5) social justice. It is clear that this word, though non-Christian in origin, is quite in harmony with Catholic ideals and made an excellent title for a general moderate-front movement."

Pantjasilla Leadership Education.   Indonesia's missionaries, most of them natives of the Netherlands, were familiar enough with the labor movement in Europe to understand that its basic structure must be lay if it is to function effectively. Nevertheless, they likewise recognized that it was they and to all practical purposes they alone who possessed the vision to be achieved. They were keenly aware that there was *periculum in mora*—danger in delay. Hence, as Father Dijkstra explained, they made themselves the first heralds of the idea in every parish.

"The solid core of the Pantjasilla movement in each community," stated Father Dijkstra, "was a carefully selected group of men who were to be the union leaders. Our task was to inspire these men, to challenge them to make this movement theirs. They were to go out to the homes, factories and offices of both Catholics and non-Catholics and enlist followers.

"Training these men was to be no hot-house affair, no ivory tower theorizing. We carried it on in genuinely Asian fashion, in the homes of the people, where there is much easy talk, and much long talking around, before any project becomes a reality. We aimed at both young men and old so that the movement would not suffer from the conservatism of the old or the radicalism of youth. Basically we followed the Young Christian Workers' technique of 'observe-judge-act.' As soon as possible, our guidelines-for-leaders course was placed in the hands of capable laymen. We were astonished and proud to note how quickly these men, often unlettered workmen, learned to conduct the union meetings, to solve their problems and assume initiative in enlisting recruits.

"The role of the missionary was an unobtrusive one. He kept on the side-line. Perhaps before the end of the meeting he would ask quietly how some matter voted at a previous meeting had been executed. Our people talk much and often forget to provide the action for their words. The missionary's task in the early stages is to prompt the keener leaders to fight slipshodness and mediocrity, to supply the sword of the spirit for the battle in which these worthy laymen, Christian and non-Christian, are very ready to engage."

National Headquarters and Paid Organizers. The organizational factor in the Pantjasilla trade union movement in Indonesia is worthy of study for the ideas it may offer to other mission areas of the globe.

"Once the foundations of the Pantjasilla movement were sufficiently well laid to indicate its general prospects for success," explained Father Dijkstra, "the social committee of the Indonesian Bishops presented recommendations in August, 1957. These recommendations emphasized two points, namely, the advisability of a strong national organizational network and, secondly, heavy enough financial outlays to permit the engagement of a salaried staff of first quality full-time organizers. It is to the credit of the Indonesian Bishops that they placed themselves on record as being probably the first Catholic hierarchy, in any country on the globe, to decide to finance the initial support of a national trade union organization. It is to be noted that, while we speak of a union of Catholic inspiration, it is not a Catholic union. The Bishops acted primarily to assist in the establishment in Indonesia of a labor force of moderate spirit to offset the heavy leftist tendency in Indonesian labor.

"The Bishops determined, in the first place, to set up decent national headquarters for the Pantjasilla movement in Djakarta, capital of Indonesia. Secondly, they voted to provide the salary for the Indonesian layman who would be the full-time national director of the union with residence in Djakarta. Several full-time travelling organizers, it was decided, would be engaged to work out of the national office. Thirdly, it was decided, that each Bishop would provide a local union office for the union and that for the first three years the Catholics of the diocese would pay the salary for this provincial director of the union. After three years it was foreseen that the union would be strong enough financially to meet these costs from its own budget."

It may be noted that this program has to a substantial degree already become a reality and that many thousands of Indonesian workers are enrolled in the Pantjasilla movement.

"Of utmost importance," continued Father Dijkstra, "is the policy of *positive* action that characterizes the movement. First of all, it is basic that every union leader must make every member under him appreciate that any labor problem he has is the earnest concern of the union. This demands time, training and charity, but it explains the fine spirit in the movement.

"Secondly, our union gives careful attention to securing first-rate contracts from its collective bargaining efforts, providing better wages, pensions and other social services. This represents good technical training in our officers.

"Thirdly, the Pantjasilla movement cooperates generously with all non-Communist unions. These unions are different from ours; many are infiltrated with Communists and often are 'used' by political parties. But we place primary importance not on judging them but on helping them obtain better socio-economic life for their men. We don't mind if they copy our methods and are happy when they ask for our labor philosophy. We understand that, as Nationalist unions or Mohammedan unions, they have goals different from ours but we aid them to become aware of the evils of Communism.

"Fourthly, we maintain positive and friendly liaison with government and international social agencies. They admire our keen concern for all forms of socio-economic betterment.

"Fifthly, we envision the Pantjasilla movement as integrating its ideals of social justice into Indonesian society generally and into the changing society of many countries of Asia. Men are hungry for ideas. In default of anything better, they are now taking Communist ideas. They would be happy to accept Christian social ideas if we would but apprise them effectively of their soundness and of their beauty."

The Christian's Responsibility for the World Community. Pope Pius XII, in speaking to the Assembly of the International Movement of Catholic Intellectuals on April 25, 1957, gave us the following thought which is a fitting one on which to close:

"A Christian cannot remain unmoved by international developments. As he sees the pressure of events give rise to a more and more strictly defined world community, he knows that this divinely willed unification should result in a union of hearts and minds in a single faith and love.

"He not only may but must work for the accomplishment of this growing community, because he has at hand an incomparable light and strength, the example and command of the Divine Master. All men are his brothers, not merely because of their common origin and participation in the same nature, but in a way which is yet more striking in their common vocation to the supernatural life."

For recommended reading, see Bibliography No. 16, page 285.

REFERENCES

Chapter 2

1. Civardi, Luigi, *A Manual of Catholic Action* (Martindale translation), Sheed and Ward, 1943, p. 235.
2. *Op. cit.,* p. 245.
3. A reference covering this subject and recommended by Father Dijkstra is: George M. Foster, "Guidelines to Community Development Programs," *Public Health Reports,* Vol. 70, No. 1, January, 1955.

Chapter 3

1. Batten, T. R., *Communities and Their Development,* Oxford University Press, 1957, p. 43.
2. Taylor, Carl C., "Making a Community Development Program Work," *Community Development Review* (I.C.A.), December, 1958, p. 40.
3. *Op. cit.*

4. *Study Kit on Training for Community Development,* UN Pub·
    lications, No. 57. IV. 6, United Nations, New York, 1956.

Chapter 4

1. "Instruction for the Guidance of Vicars Apostolic Leaving for
    the Chinese Kingdoms of Tonkin and Cochinchina," *La Siège
    Apostolique et les Missions,* Propagation of the Faith, Paris 19,
    pp. 9–20. See article by A. Retif, "La Charte des Missions Mod-
    ernes," *Etudes,* January, 1959, p. 49.
2. Royal Anthropological Institute of Great Britain and Ireland,
    Notes and Queries on Anthropology, 6th ed., London, 1951.
3. Murdock, George P., et al., *Outline of Cultural Materials,*
    Human Relations Area Files, Inc., New Haven, 1950.
4. Tylor, Edward B., *Primitive Culture,* Boston, 1871.
5. Redfield, Robert, *The Folk Culture of Yucatan,* Chicago, 1941,
    p. 132.
6. Kluckhohn, Clyde, and Kelly, William J., "The Concept of
    Culture," in *The Science of Man in the World Crisis,* R. Linton,
    ed., New York, 1945.
7. These basic characteristics are derived from the following
    sources: Aberle, D., et al., "The Functional Pre-requisites of
    a Society," *Ethics.* And Levy, M., *The Structure of Society,*
    Princeton, 1952, Chapter 4, "The Functional Pre-requisites of
    Any Society."
8. Singh, Rudra Datt, "An Introduction of Green Manuring in
    Rural India," in *Human Problems in Technological Change,*
    New York, 1952, pp. 55–68.
9. Adair, John, and Vogt, Evon Z., "Navaho and Zuni Veterans:
    A Study of Contrasting Modes of Culture Change," *American
    Anthropologist,* Vol. 51, 1949, pp. 547–61.
10. Vogt, Evon Z., *Modern Homesteaders,* Cambridge, 1955, p. 5.
11. Wright, Arthur F., "The Chinese Language and Foreign Ideas,"
    in *Studies in Chinese Thought,* A. F. Wright, ed., Chicago,
    1953, pp. 300–301.
12. But Vogt makes the useful distinction between "values" as at-
    tached to everything that is desirable and "value-orientations"

which are patterned arrangements of associated values around important foci in the life situation of a community.

13. Sharp, Lauriston, "Steel Axes for Stone Age Australians," in *Human Problems in Technological Change,* E. H. Spicer, ed., New York, 1952, pp. 69–90.

14. Tannous, Afif I., "Extension Work among the Arab Fellahin," in *Farmers of the World,* E. de S. Brumer, et al., eds., New York, 1945, pp. 78–100.

15. This process is variously called enculturation or socialization. If the former term is used, the emphasis is on the cultural values which are transmitted to the young. When the latter term is used, the emphasis is on the social relationships in the process of transmitting cultural values.

16. See Bruner, Edward M., "Primary Group Experience and the Process of Acculturation," *American Anthropologist,* Vol. 58, 1956, pp. 605–623.

Chapter 5

1. See Chapter III, p. 48, of this volume for Carl Taylor's four stages.

2. Vogt, Evon Z., and O'Dea, Thomas F., "A Comparative Study of the Role of Values in Social Action in Two Southwestern Communities," *American Sociological Review,* December, 1953, pp. 645–654.

3. *Ibid.,* pp. 648–649.

4. *Ibid.,* p. 650.

5. *Ibid.,* p. 649.

6. *Ibid.,* p. 650.

7. *Ibid.,* p. 649.

8. *Ibid.,* pp. 650–651.

9. *Ibid.,* p. 649.

10. *Ibid.,* p. 650.

11. Collier, John and Mary, "An Experiment in Applied Anthropology," *Scientific American,* January, 1957, p. 39.

12. *Ibid.,* p. 41.

13. *Ibid.,* p. 41.

14. Dobyns, Henry F., "Blunders with Bolsas." Adapted from *Human Organization,* Vol. X, No. 3, Fall 1951, pp. 25–32. Quoted from Lyle W. Shannon, ed., *Underdeveloped Areas,* New York, 1957, pp. 434–444.

Chapter 6

1. Keesing, Felix M., *Cultural Anthropology,* Rinehart, New York, 1958, p. 268.
2. *Op. cit.,* p. 267.
3. Catholic International Outlook No. 192, *Human Rights,* Sword of the Spirit, London, p. 11.

Chapter 8

1. See *International Survey of Programmes of Social Development,* United Nations, New York, 1959, p. 136.
2. Vizzard, James L., *Who Shall Own the Land?* National Catholic Rural Life Conference, Des Moines, Iowa, 1959, 12 pp.

Chapter 9

1. Informe de la Comision Nacional de la Vivienda, Junio, 1957, Buenos Aires.
2. Informe de la Comision para la Reforma Agraria y la Vivienda, 1957, Lima.

Chapter 10

1. *International Survey of Programmes of Social Development,* United Nations, New York, 1959, p. 170.
2. Aronov, Edward, "European Approaches to 'Problem Families,' Reviewed, Analysed," *Journal of Housing,* April, 1957.

Chapter 11

1. *International Survey of Programmes of Social Development,* United Nations, New York, 1959, p. 140.
2. Coady, M. M., *Masters of Their Own Destiny,* Harper, New York, 1939, p. 144.

Chapter 13

1. See Cronin, S.S., John F., *Social Principles and Economic Life,* Bruce, Milwaukee, 1959, pp. 174–196.

TOPICAL BIBLIOGRAPHIES

Bibliography No. 1   General Socio-Economic Reference Material

(Readings for Chapter 1)

The Aging of Populations and Its Economic and Social Implications, UN Publications, No. 56.XIII.6, United Nations, New York, 1956.

Asher, R. E., Kotschnig, W. M., Brown, W. A., Jr., and associates, *The United Nations and Economic and Social Cooperation,* Washington: Brookings Institution, 1957.

Bauer, P. T., *Economic Analysis and Policy in Underdeveloped Countries,* Durham, N.C.: Duke University Press, 1957.

Brown, S.J., L. C., et al., *Social Orientations,* Chicago: Loyola University Press, 1954.

Bruehl, C., *The Pope's Plan for Social Reconstruction,* New York: Devin-Adair, 1939.

Burke, S.J., Thomas J. M., *Catholic Missions: Four Great Encyclicals,* New York: Fordham University Press, 1958.

Cronin, S.S., John F., "The International Common Good," *Social Order,* June, 1959.

Cronin, S.S., John F., *Social Principles and Economic Life*, Milwaukee: Bruce, 1959.

Drinkwater, Francis H., *Money and Social Justice*, London: Burns Oates, 1934.

Drinkwater, Francis H., *Why Not End Poverty?* London: Burns Oates, 1935.

Drummond, S.J., W. F., *Social Justice*, Milwaukee: Bruce, 1955.

Duff, S.J., E., *The Social Thought of the World Council of Churches*, New York: Association Press, 1956.

Economic Developments in Africa 1956–57, UN Publications, No. 58.II.C.3, United Nations, New York, 1958.

Economic Developments in the Middle East 1956–57, UN Publications, No. 58.II.C.2, United Nations, New York, 1958.

Economic Survey of Asia and the Far East 1957, UN Publications, No. 58.II.F.1, United Nations, New York, 1958.

Economic Survey of Latin America 1957, UN Publications, No. 58.II.G.1, United Nations, New York, 1958.

Evans, J. W., and Ward, L. R., eds., *The Social and Political Philosophy of Maritain*, New York: Scribner's, 1955.

Everyman's United Nations, published by United Nations, Department of Public Information.

Ewing, J. F., *Social Action in Mission Lands*, New York: Fordham University Press, 1955.

Ferree, S.M., William, *The Act of Social Justice*, Dayton, Ohio: Marianist Publications, 1951.

Ferree, S.M., William, "Social Justice and Social Order," *Social Order*, May, 1956.

The Future Growth of World Population, UN Publications, No. 58.XIII.2, United Nations, New York, 1958.

Galbraith, J. K., *The Affluent Society*, Boston: Houghton Mifflin, 1958.

Haas, F. J., *Man and Society*, New York: Appleton-Century-Crofts, 1952.

Harte, C.Ss.R., Thomas J., *Papal Social Principles: A Guide and Digest*, Milwaukee: Bruce, 1956.

Hobhouse, L. T., *The Elements of Social Justice*, London: Allen and Unwin, 1958.

International Union of Social Studies, *A Code of Social Principles*, Oxford, England: Catholic Social Guild, 1952.

Kerby, William J., *The Social Mission of the Church*, Washington: Catholic University Press, 1944.

Lombardi, S.J., Riccardo, *Towards a Better World*, New York: Philosophical Library, 1958.

McKevitt, Peter, *The Plan of Society*, Dublin: Catholic Truth Service, 1944.

Messner, J., *Social Ethics*, St. Louis: Herder, 1949.

Mihanovich, Clement S., *Current Social Problems*, Milwaukee: Bruce, 1950.

Murray, Raymond W., *Sociology for a Democratic Society*, New York: Appleton, 1950.

Pollock, Robert C., *The Mind of Pius XII*, New York: Crown, 1955.

Proceedings of the Lima Methods Conference of the Maryknoll Fathers, Maryknoll P.O., New York, 1954.

Report on the World Social Situation, UN Publications, No. 57.IV.3, United Nations, New York, 1957.

Sheed, F. J., *Society and Sanity*, New York: Sheed and Ward, 1953.

Social Order, Vol. 1, No. 1, 1951, et seqq., St. Louis: Institute of Social Order.

Sturzo, Luigi, *Inner Laws of Society, A New Sociology*, New York: Kenedy, 1944.

Vessels, S.J., John L., "The Movement for a Better World," *Social Order*, February, 1957.

World Economic Survey, 1957, UN Publications, No. 58.II.C.1, United Nations, New York, 1958.

Yearbook of the United Nations, New York: United Nations, 1958.

Bibliography No. 2   Missionary's Role in Socio-Economic Betterment

(Readings for Chapter 2)

Anderl, S., and Ruth, Sr. M., *The Religious and Catholic Action*, La Crosse, Wis.: St. Rose Convent, 1947.

Chinigo, M., *The Pope Speaks: The Teachings of Pope Pius XII*, New York: Pantheon, 1957.

De La Bedoyere, M., *Christianity in the Market Place*, London: Dakers, 1943.

Donovan, J. D., "The Sociologist Looks at the Parish," *American Catholic Sociological Review*, June, 1950.

Giordano, Igino, *The Social Message of the Early Church Fathers*, Paterson: St. Anthony Guild, 1944.

Giordano, Igino, *The Social Message of Jesus*, Paterson: St. Anthony Guild, 1943.

Harte, C.Ss.R., Thomas J., "Sociology of the Parish," *Conference Bulletin of the Archdiocese of New York*, XXXV, No. 6, New York: St. Joseph's Seminary and College, February, 1958.

Harte, C.Ss.R., Thomas J., *Papal Social Principles*, Milwaukee: Bruce, 1956.

Hyde, D., *One Front Across the World*, Westminster, Md.: Newman, 1956.

Michonneau, *Revolution in a City Parish*, Westminster, Md.: Newman, 1949.

Montcheuil, Y. De, *A Guide for Social Action*, Chicago: Fides, 1954.

Nuesse, C. J., and Harte, T. J., C.Ss.R., *The Sociology of the Parish*, Milwaukee: Bruce, 1951.

Philips, G., *The Role of the Laity in the Church*, Chicago: Fides, 1956.

Putz, C.S.C., L. J., *The Modern Apostle*, Chicago: Fides, 1957.

Ross, M. G., and Hendry, C. E., *New Understanding of Leadership*, New York: Association Press, 1957.

Saliege, Jules Cardinal, *Who Shall Bear the Flame?* Chicago: Fides, 1949.

Suhard, E., *The Church Today*, Chicago: Fides, 1953.

Tead, O., *The Art of Leadership*, New York: McGraw-Hill, 1935.

Walsh, M. E., and Furfey, P. H., *Social Problems and Social Action*, Englewood Cliffs, N. J.: Prentice-Hall, 1958.

Ward, C.S.C., L. R., ed., *The American Apostolate*, Westminster, Md.: Newman, 1952.

Bibliography No. 3   Community Development

(Readings for Chapter 3)

Batten, T. R., *Communities and Their Development*, London: Oxford University Press, 1957.

Burke, L., and McCreanor, J., *Training Missionaries for Commu-*

nity Development. A report on experiences in Ghana. National Conference of Catholic Charities, Washington, 1960.

Community Development, *Rural Sociology,* March, 1958 (Special Number).

Community Education, Principles and Practices from World-Wide Experience, 58th Yearbook, National Society for the Study of Education, Part I, University of Chicago Press, 1959.

Du Sautoy, Peter, *Community Development in Ghana,* London: Oxford University Press, 1959.

Education for Better Living: The Role of the School in Community Improvement, Washington: Government Printing Office, 1957.

Foster, George F., "Guidelines to Community Development Programs," *Public Health Reports,* Vol. 70, No. 1, January, 1955.

A Guide to Community Development, Ministry of Community Development, Government of India, 1957.

I Saw Technical Assistance Change Lives, UN Publications, No. 57.I.10, United Nations, New York, 1957.

Maddox, J. C., *Technical Assistance by Religious Agencies in Latin America,* Chicago: University of Chicago Press, 1956.

Mial, H. Curtis, "Community Development—A Democratic Social Process," *Adult Leadership,* April, 1958.

Randhwa, M. S., ed., *Developing Village India,* Bombay: Longmans Ltd., 1951.

Smith, M. G., "Community Organization in Rural Jamaica," *Social Economic Studies,* September, 1956.

Study Kit on Training for Community Development, UN Publications, No. 57.IV.6, United Nations, New York, 1957.

Taylor, Carl C., *A Critical Analysis of India's Community Development Programme,* The Community Projects Administration, Government of India, 1956.

Technical Assistance, the Role of UNESCO, UNESCO, United Nations, New York, 1959.

Technical Assistance: What? How? Why? United Nations Office of Information, No. 58.I.9, 1958.

Bibliography No. 4   Social Anthropology, General

Acknowledgment is made to William A. Smalley: "Selected and Annotated Bibliography of Anthropology for Missionaries," *Occasional Bulletin,* January 29, 1960, Missionary Research Library, New York.

(Readings for Chapter 4)

Bennett, J. W., "The Study of Cultures: A Survey of Technique and Methodology in Field Work," *American Sociological Review*, 13, pp. 672–689, 1948.

Bennett, W. C., and Bird, J. B., *Andean Cultural History*, American Museum of Natural History Handbook Series, 15, New York, 1949.

Berndt, Catherine H., "Socio-cultural Change in the Eastern Central Highlands of New Guinea," *Southwestern Journal of Anthropology*, Vol. 9, No. 1, pp. 112–138, 1953.

Bouma, Donald H., *Anthropology and Missions*, Grand Rapids: International Publications, 1957.

Capell, A., "Interpreting Christianity to Australian Aborigines," *International Review of Missions*, Vol. 48, No. 190, pp. 145–156, April, 1959.

Casagrande, Joseph B., and Gladwin, Thomas, eds., *Some Uses of Anthropology: Theoretical and Applied*, Washington, Anthropological Society of Washington, 1956.

Duignan, Peter, "Early Jesuit Missionaries: A Suggestion for Further Study," *American Anthropologist*, Vol. 60, No. 4, pp. 725–732, 1958.

Evans-Pritchard, E. E., *Social Anthropology*, London: Cohen and West, 1951.

Firth, Raymond, *Human Types: An Introduction to Social Anthropology*, New York: New American Library, 1958.

Foster, G. M., "Relationships between Theoretical and Applied Anthropology: A Public Health Program Analysis," *Human Organization*, Vol. 11, No. 3, pp. 5–16, 1952.

Goldschmidt, Walter, *Man's Way, A Preface to the Understanding of Human Society*, New York: World Publishing Company, 1959.

Herskovits, Melville J., *Cultural Anthropology*, New York: Knopf, 1955. A revision and abridgement of *Man and His Works*.

Hoebel, Edward Adamson, *Man in the Primitive World*, 2d ed., New York: McGraw-Hill, 1958.

Hutchinson, Bertram, "Some Social Consequences of Missionary Activity among South African Bantu," *Africa: Journal of the*

International African Institute, Vol. 27, No. 2, pp. 160–177, April, 1957.

Junod, Henri Philippe, "Anthropology and Missionary Education," *International Review of Missions,* Vol. 24, No. 94, pp. 213–228, April, 1935.

Keesing, Felix M., *Cultural Anthropology, The Science of Custom,* New York: Rinehart, 1958.

Kluckhohn, Clyde, *Mirror for Man,* New York: McGraw-Hill, 1949.

Linton, Ralph, ed., *Most of the World,* New York: Columbia University Press, 1949.

Linton, Ralph, ed., *The Science of Man in the World Crisis,* New York: Columbia University Press, 1945.

Mead, Margaret, ed., *Cultural Patterns and Technical Change,* New York: New American Library of World Literature, 1955.

Minnich, R. Herbert, Jr., *A Manual of Social Science Material for Missionaries,* Elkhart: Mennonite Board of Missions and Charities, 1958. (Multilith.)

The Missionary and the Cultures of Man: The Second Annual Conference with Mission Board Secretaries to Consider the Question: How Shall We Prepare the Missionary to Relate Himself Constructively to the Social Complexities He Must Encounter Abroad? Hartford, Conn.: The Kennedy School of Missions, Hartford Seminary Foundation, 1955. (Mimeo.)

Murdock, George P., et al., *Outline of Cultural Materials,* Human Relations Area Files Inc., New Haven, 1950.

Newell, W. H., " 'Functional' Social Anthropology and the Christian Missionary Method," *International Review of Missions,* Vol. 36, No. 142, pp. 253–257, 1947.

Nida, Eugene A., *Customs and Cultures: Anthropology for Christian Missions,* New York: Harper, 1954.

Nida, Eugene A., "The Role of Cultural Anthropology in Christian Missions," *Practical Anthropology,* Vol. 6, No. 3, pp. 110–116, May–June, 1959.

Nida, Eugene A., "The Roman Catholic, Communist, and Protestant Approach to Social Structure," *Practical Anthropology,* Vol. 4, No. 6, pp. 209–219, November–December, 1957.

Paul, B. D., "Interview Techniques and Field Relationships," in Kroeber, A. L., ed., *Anthropology Today,* Chicago: University of Chicago Press, 1953.

Rainey, F., "Culture Changes on the Arctic Coast," *Transactions, New York Academy of Sciences,* Vol. 2, No. 3, pp. 172–176, 1941.

Redfield, R., *Peasant Society and Culture,* Chicago: University of Chicago Press, 1956.

Royal Anthropological Institute of Great Britain and Ireland, *Notes and Queries on Anthropology,* 6th ed., London, 1951.

Schmidt, Wilhelm, *The Origin and Growth of Religion,* London: Methuen, 1931.

Smalley, William A., and Fetzer, Marie, "A Christian View of Anthropology," *Modern Service and Christian Faith,* 2d ed., pp. 98–195, Wheaton, Ill.: Van Kempen Press, 1950.

Smalley, William A., "Cultural Implications of an Indigenous Church," *Practical Anthropology,* Vol. 5, No. 2, pp. 61–65, March–April, 1958.

Smalley, William A., "The Moral Implications of Social Structure," *Practical Anthropology,* Vol. 6, No. 3, pp. 140–144, May–June, 1959.

Smith, Edwin W., "Anthropology and the Practical Man," *Journal of the Royal Anthropological Institute,* Vol. 64, Part 1, pp. xiii–xxxvii, January–June, 1934.

Smith, Edwin W., "Social Anthropology and Missionary Work," *The International Review of Missions,* Vol. 13, pp. 518–531, 1924.

Social Science Research Center, University of Puerto Rico, *The People of Puerto Rico: A Study in Social Anthropology,* 1956.

Tax, S., "Selective Culture Change," *American Economic Review,* Papers and Proceedings, 41, pp. 315–320, 1951.

Thompson, Laura, *Culture in Crisis,* New York: Harper, 1950.

The University Teaching of Social Sciences: Sociology, Social Psychology and Anthropology, UNESCO, United Nations, New York, 1954.

Wallis, Wilson D., *Religion in Primitive Society,* New York: Crofts, 1939.

Periodicals

Africa: Journal of the International African Institute, London: Oxford University Press. Quarterly. One of the major journals on

Africa. Missionaries have contributed heavily to the contents of the journal as well as to the leadership of the Institute. Articles are often slanted to practical considerations.

American Anthropologist, Lancaster, Pa.: American Anthropological Association. Quarterly. The most important professional journal of American anthropology.

Anthropological Quarterly (formerly *Primitive Man*), Washington: Catholic University of America Press. Quarterly. Publishes the research of professional anthropologists and Roman Catholic missionaries. Many articles on the problems of applied anthropology in relation to Roman Catholic missionary work.

Anthropos, International Review of Ethnology and Linguistics. A multilingual journal published three times a year in Fribourg, Switzerland (address: Imprimerie St. Paul). A major international journal, edited by Roman Catholic scholars.

Human Organization, Ithaca, New York: The Society for Applied Anthropology. Quarterly. A journal specializing in the practical applications of anthropology to industry, administration, etc. Articles are often of value to missionaries.

Journal of the Royal Anthropological Institute, published semi-annually, 21 Bedford Square, London W. C. 1. The leading anthropological journal on the use of the Social Sciences.

Bibliography No. 5   Culture Change

Acknowledgment is made to William A. Smalley: "Selected and Annotated Bibliography for Missionaries," Occasional Bulletin, January 20, 1960, Missionary Research Library, New York.

(Readings for Chapter 5)

Barnett, Homer G., *Innovation: The Basis of Cultural Change,* New York: McGraw-Hill, 1953.

Bascom, William R., and Herskovits, Melville J., eds., *Continuity and Change in African Cultures,* Chicago: University of Chicago Press, 1959.

Collier, John, Jr., and Buitron, Anibal, *The Awakening Valley,* Chicago: University of Chicago Press, 1949.

Foster, George M., *Problems in Intercultural Health Programs,* New York, Social Science Research Council Pamphlet No. 12, 1958.

Geertz, C., "Ritual and Social Change: A Javanese Example," *American Anthropologist,* Vol. 59, pp. 32–54, 1957.

Goodfriend, A., *Rice Roots,* New York: Simon and Schuster, 1958.

Hayden, Howard, *Moturiki. A Pilot Project in Community Development,* New York: Oxford University Press, 1954.

Herskovits, Melville J., *Acculturation, The Study of Culture Contact,* Gloucester, Mass.: Peter Smith, 1938.

Herskovits, Melville J., *The Myth of the Negro Past,* New York: Harper, 1941.

Hogbin, Herbert Ian, *Experiments in Civilization. The Effects of European Culture in the Solomon Islands,* London: George Routledge & Sons, 1939.

Hogbin, Herbert Ian, *Social Change: Josiah Mason Lectures Delivered at the University of Birmingham,* London: C. A. Watts, 1958.

Hogbin, Herbert Ian, *Transformation Scene. The Changing Culture of a New Guinea Village,* London: ILSR, 1951.

Jeffreys, M. D. W., "Some Rules of Directed Culture Change under Roman Catholicism," *American Anthropologist,* Vol. 58, No. 4, pp. 721–731, 1956.

Keesing, F. M., *Culture Change: An Analysis and Bibliography of Anthropological Sources to 1952,* Stanford, Calif.: Stanford University Press, 1953.

Kietzman, Dale W., "Conversion and Culture Change," *Practical Anthropology,* Vol. 5, Nos. 5 & 6, pp. 203–210, September–December, 1958.

Leighton, A. H., *Human Relations in a Changing World,* New York: Dutton, 1949.

Leighton, A. H., and Smith, R. J., "A Comparative Study of Social and Cultural Change," *Proceedings, American Philosophical Society,* 99, pp. 79–88.

Lewis, Oscar, *Life in a Mexican Village: Tepoztlan Restudied,* Urbana, Ill.: University of Illinois Press, 1951.

Linton, Ralph, ed., *Acculturation in Seven American Indian Tribes,* New York: Appleton-Century-Crofts, 1940.

Lowie, R. H., *Social Organization,* New York: Rinehart, 1948.

Mead, M., "The Implications of Culture Change for Personality Development," *American Journal of Orthopsychiatry,* Vol. 17, pp. 633–646, 1947.

Paul, Benjamin D., *Health, Culture and Community, Case Studies of Public Reactions to Health Programs,* New York: Russell Sage Foundation, 1955.

Rapoport, Robert N., "Changing Navaho Religious Values: A Study of Christian Missions to the Rimrock Navahos," Cambridge, Mass.: Peabody Museum, 1954.

Redfield, Robert, *The Primitive World and Its Transformation,* Ithaca, N.Y.: Cornell University Press, 1953.

Redfield, Robert, *A Village That Chose Progress: Chan Kom Revisited,* Chicago: University of Chicago Press, 1950.

Sharp, Lauriston, "Steel Axes for Stone Age Australians," *Human Organization,* Vol. 11, No. 2, Summer 1952.

Spicer, Edward Holland, ed., *Human Problems in Technological Change: A Casebook,* New York: Russell Sage Foundation, 1952.

Thompson, Laura, *Culture in Crisis: A Study of the Hopi Indians,* New York: Harper, 1950.

Wagley, C., *Economics of a Guatemalan Village,* American Anthropological Association Memoirs, 58, Nenasha, Wis., 1941.

Watson, James Bennett, *Cayua Culture Change: A Study in Acculturation and Methodology,* Nenasha, Wis.: American Anthropological Association, 1952.

Wilson, Godfrey, and Wilson, Monica, *The Analysis of Social Change, Based on Observations in Central Africa,* Cambridge, England: Cambridge University Press, 1954.

Bibliography No. 6   Socio-Economic Problems of the Family

(Readings for Chapter 6)

American Hierarchy, "The Christian Family," *The Catholic Mind,* Vol. 43, February, 1950.

Bertram, B. F., *The Cooperative Challenge,* Boston: Little, Brown, 1948.

Book, Dorothy L., *Family Budget Counselling,* New York: Family Welfare Association of America, 1944.

Brown, Leo C., "Making a Living," *Social Orientations,* Chicago: Loyola University Press, 1954.

Callaghan, S.J., Hubert C., *The Family Allowance Procedure,* Washington: Catholic University Press, 1947.

Cissell, R., and Cissell, H., *Stretching the Family Income,* New York: Wagner, 1953.

Clemens, A. H., *The Cana Movement in the United States,* Washington: Catholic University Press, 1953.

Clemens, A. H., *Marriage and the Family: An Integrated Approach for Catholics,* Englewood Cliffs, N. J.: Prentice-Hall, 1957.

Clemens, Alphonse, "Values in Family Living," *Social Order,* March, 1953.

Corley, S.J., Francis J., *Family Allowances,* St. Louis: The Queen's Work, 1947.

Elmer, M. C., *The Sociology of the Family,* Boston: Ginn, 1945.

Epstein, Abraham, *Insecurity: A Challenge to America,* New York: Random House, 1938.

Faherty, W. B., *The Destiny of Modern Woman,* Westminster, Md.: Newman, 1950.

Galdston, Iago, ed., *The Family in Contemporary Society,* New York, International Universities Press, 1958.

Goode, William J., "Economic Factors and Marital Stability," *American Sociological Review,* December, 1951.

Harwood, E. C., and Fowle, H., *How to Make Your Budget Balance,* Great Barrington, Mass.: American Institute of Economic Research, 1947.

Hill, Reuben, *Families Under Stress,* New York: Harper, 1949.

Institute of Social Order Study, "American Low-Income Families," *Social Order,* February, 1952.

International Labor Office, *Indigenous Peoples, Living and Working Conditions of Aboriginal Populations in Independent Countries,* Geneva, 1953.

Kamarovsky, Mirra, *The Unemployed Man and His Family,* New York: Dryden, 1940.

Koos, E. L., *Families in Trouble,* New York: King's Crown Press, 1946.

Leclercq, J., *Marriage and the Family, A Study in Social Philosophy,* New York: Pustet, 1947.

Legal Status of Married Women, UN Publications, No. 57.IV.8, United Nations, New York, 1957.

Linton, Ralph, "The Natural History of the Family" in Ruth Anshen (ed.), *The Family,* New York: Harper, 1949.

Locke, Harvey J., and Mackeprang, Muriel, "Marital Adjustment and the Employed Wife," *American Journal of Sociology,* May, 1949.

Lord, S.J., Daniel J., *Money Runs or Ruins the Home,* St. Louis: The Queen's Work, 1942.

McGuire, C., "Family Life in Lower and Middle Class Homes," *Marriage and Family Living,* February, 1952.

Marie-André, Soeur, "Women's Indignity in Africa," *Worldmission,* Fall 1953.

Mihanovich, C. S., et al., *Marriage and the Family,* Milwaukee: Bruce, 1952.

Nickell, Paulena, and Dorsey, J. M., *Management in Family Living,* New York: Wiley, 1945.

Ogburn, W. F., "Education, Income and Family Unity," *American Journal of Sociology,* May, 1948.

Ogburn, W. F., "Marital Separations," *American Journal of Sociology,* February, 1944.

Ogburn, W. F., and Tibbits, C., "The Family and Its Functions," *American Sociological Review,* August, 1941.

Redfield, M. P., "The American Family: Consensus and Freedom," *American Journal of Sociology,* November, 1946.

Report on a Coordinated Policy Regarding Family Levels of Living, UN Publications, No. 57.IV.7, United Nations, New York, 1957.

Schmiedeler, O.S.B., E., *Marriage and the Family,* New York: McGraw-Hill, 1946.

Thomas, S.J., J. L., *The American Catholic Family,* Englewood Cliffs, N. J.: Prentice-Hall, 1956.

Thomas, S.J., J. L., "The Catholic Family in a Complex Society," *Social Order,* December, 1954.

Thomas, S.J., J. L., "The Changing Family," *Social Order,* February, 1952.

Thomas, S.J., J. L., *The Family Clinic: A Book of Questions and Answers,* Westminster, Md.: Newman, 1958.

Werth, Alvin, and Mihanovich, Clement A., *Papal Pronouncements on Marriage and the Family from Leo XIII to Pius XII (1878–1954)*, Milwaukee: Bruce, 1955.

Bibliography No. 7   Farm Problems

(Readings for Chapter 7)

Agriculture Yearbooks of the U.S. Government Printing Office, Washington 25, D. C.:
   1959 Yearbook: Food and Nutrition. Catalog No. A. 1.10:959.
   1958 Yearbook: Land. Catalog No. A. 1.10:958.
   1957 Yearbook: Soil. Catalog No. A. 1.10:957.
   1956 Yearbook: Animal Diseases. Catalog No. A. 1.10:956.
   1955 Yearbook: Water. Catalog No. A. 1.10:955.
   1954 Yearbook: Marketing. Catalog No. A. 1.10:954.
   1953 Yearbook: Plant Disesases. Catalog No. A. 1.10:953.
   1951 Yearbook: Crops in Peace and War. Catalog No. A. 1.10:950–51.
   1949 Yearbook: Trees. Catalog No. A. 1.10:949.
   1948 Yearbook: Grass. Catalog No. A. 1.10:948.
   1947 Yearbook: Science in Farming. Catalog No. A. 1.10: 943–47.
Baer, U. J., *Letters to an American Farmer*, Des Moines, Iowa: National Catholic Rural Life Conference, 1956.
Benedict, M. R., *Can We Solve the Farm Problem?* New York: Twentieth Century Fund, 1955.
Binnis, Sir B., *Agricultural Credit for Small Farmers*, FAO, United Nations, New York, 1952.
Food and Agricultural Organization, *FAO's Role in Rural Welfare*, UN Publications, United Nations, New York, 1958.
Hambidge, G., *The Story of FAO*, New York: Van Nostrand, 1955.
Howard, T. E., *Agricultural Handbook for Rural Pastors and Laymen: Religious, Economic, Social and Cultural Implications of Rural Life*, Des Moines, Iowa: National Catholic Rural Life Conference, 1947.
Lee, D. H. K., *Climate and Economic Development in the Tropics*, New York: Harper, 1957.

Moomaw, I. W., *Deep Furrows,* New York: Agricultural Missions, 1957.

Mosher, Arthur T., *Technical Cooperation in Latin American Agriculture,* Chicago: University of Chicago Press, 1957.

Schultz, T. W., *Economic Organization of Agriculture,* New York: McGraw-Hill, 1953.

The Selective Expansion of Agricultural Production in Latin America, UN Publications, No. 57.II.G.4, United Nations, New York, 1957.

Shepherd, G. W., *They Wait in Darkness,* New York: John Day, 1955.

The Social Sciences in Relation to Extension Work. Extracts from Conference Reports on *Extension Experiences around the World,* Washington: U.S. Dept. Agric., Extension Service and Office of Foreign Agricultural Relations, 1951.

Spencer, J. E., *Land and People in the Philippines: Geographic Problems in Rural Economy,* Berkeley, Calif.: University of California Press, 1953.

Wilson, Charles M., *New Crops for the New World,* New York: Macmillan, 1945.

Bibliography No. 8   Land Reform

(Readings for Chapter 8)

Crofts, A. M., *Property and Poverty,* Dublin: Irish Rosary Office, 1948.

Davis, Jim E., "New Hope in Italy: Land of the Noonday Sun," *Land Economics,* February, 1959.

Fathallael Khatib, "Agrarian Reform in the Arab World," *Arab World,* July, 1959.

Ford, Thomas R., *Man and Land in Peru,* Gainesville, Fla.: University of Florida Press, 1955.

Harbrecht, S.J., Paul P., "Property in Transition," *Social Order,* February, 1958.

Heath, Dwight B., "Commercial Agriculture and Land Reform in the Bolivian Oriente," *Inter-American Economic Affairs,* Autumn 1959.

International Labour Office, *The Landless Farmer in Latin America*, Studies and Reports #47, 1957.

Ladejinski, Wolf, "Agrarian Reform in Japan," *Foreign Affairs*, October, 1959.

Land Reform: Defects in Agrarian Structure as Obstacles to Economic Development, UN Publications, No. 51.II.B.3, United Nations, New York, 1951.

Margold, Stella, "Agrarian Land Reform in Egypt," *American Journal of Economic Sociology*, October, 1957.

Mark, Max, "Land Reform and the Revolution in Asia," *American Journal of Economic Sociology*, October, 1957.

Niaz, Shafi, "Land Reforms in Pakistan," *Pakistan Quarterly*, Spring 1959.

Oluwasammi, H. A., "Land Tenure and Agricultural Improvement in Tropical Africa," *Journal of Farm Economics*, August, 1957.

Parsons, Kenneth H., "Land Reform in the Postwar Era," *Land Economics*, August, 1957.

Progress in Land Reform, UN Publications, No. 56.II.B.3, and No. 54.II.B.3, United Nations, New York, 1956 and 1954.

Rao, C. R. M., "The Failure of Bhoodan: India's Land-Gift Movement," *New Leader*, June, 1958.

"Syrian Agriculture: Agricultural Structure and Land Reform in Syria," *Egyptian Economic and Political Review*, May–September, 1959.

Thapar, P. N., "Land Reform in India," *Eastern World*, July, 1957.

Bibliography No. 9 Rural Problems, General

(Readings for Chapter 9)

Allen, H. B., *Rural Reconstruction in Action*, Ithaca, N.Y.: Cornell University Press, 1953.

Boeke, J. H., *Economics and Economic Policy for Dual Societies*, New York: Institute of Pacific Relations, 1953.

Educational Approaches to Rural Welfare, FAO, UN Publications, 1949.

Essentials of Rural Welfare, FAO, UN Publications, 1949.

Lindstrom, D. E., *American Rural Life*, New York: Ronald Press, 1948.

Reports and Publications of the National Catholic Rural Life Conference, 3801 Grand Avenue, Des Moines 12, Iowa. The following are relatively recent and of special value in the fields indicated.

"Policy Statement, June 18, 1958." For statements on agricultural revolution, vertical integration, and efficiency of family farms.

"Policy Statement, January, 1958." Vertical integration, large versus small farms, low-income problems, migratory labor.

"A Program for the Rural Community," 1957 Policy Statement. Wide range of issues.

"Start Where You Are" (1957). Jocist-type brochure for young people.

"A Program for the Family Farm" (1956). Defines the family farm.

"Our Thirty-Fourth Year" (1956). Organization and work of the Conference.

"A Program for Shared Abundance." Abundance for the farmer and for the world.

"Conclusiones de Panama" (1955) and "Conclusiones de Manizales" (1953). Primarily Latin-American problems, with principles that apply more widely to world problems of population and food.

"The Land: God's Gift to Man" (1952). Broad statement on farm problems, with suitable reference material.

"Christianity and the Land" (1951). Primer on Catholic rural philosophy, statements on international food problems, papal address on farming, July 2, 1951.

"Rural Life Prayer Book" (1956). Contains prayers for the country family, liturgical devotions for country living, selected psalms.

"The Farm Problem," *Social Order,* October, 1958.

Shannon, L. W., ed., *Underdeveloped Areas: A Book of Readings and Research,* New York: Harper, 1957.

Water and the World Today, UN Publications, No. 57.I.9.E., United Nations, New York, 1957.

Bibliography No. 10   Housing

(Readings for Chapter 9)

Asia and Far East Seminar on Housing through Non-Profit Organizations, UN Publications, No. 58.II.H.3 United Nations, New York, 1958.

Attacking the Housing Problem, United Nations Department of Public Information, *United Nations Review,* November, 1954, Vol. 1, No. 5, pp. 25–29, illus. In English, French and Spanish editions.

Beyer, C. H., *Housing, A Factual Analysis,* New York: Macmillan, 1958.

Decent Housing at Low Cost: New Delhi's International Exhibition Gives a Glimpse of Future Trends, United Nations Department of Public Information, *United Nations Bulletin,* March 1, 1954, Vol. 16, No. 5, pp. 186–191, illus. In English, French and Spanish editions.

Drew, Fry and Ford, *Village Housing in the Tropics,* London: Lund Humphries, 1947. Special reference to West Africa.

Economic and Social Aspects of Workers' Housing in Non-Metropolitan Territories, with Special Reference to Responsibilities for Its Provision, 1953, document CNT/3/II. In English, French and Spanish editions.

First Report on the Current Activities of the United Nations, Its Regional Economic Commissions and the Specialized Agencies in the Fields of Housing, Building and Planning, May 15, 1957, no document symbol. English edition.

Guiding Principles for Housing Standards and Building Codes in Countries of the ECAFE Region: Preliminary Report, May 10, 1955, limited document I and T/HBWP. 3/1. In English, United Nations, New York.

Housing, Building, Planning: International Film Catalog, UN Publications, No. 56.IV.8, United Nations, New York, 1956.

Housing and Community Improvement Programmes. Chapter 4 in the *International Survey of Programmes of Social Development,* 1955, document E/CN.5/301/Rev. 1—ST/SOA/21. (UN Publ. Sales No. 1955.IV.8). In English, French and Spanish editions.

Housing and Employment, 1948, printed document (Studies and reports, new series, 8). International Labour Office, Geneva. In English.

Housing and Town and Country Planning Bulletin, United Nations, New York:

No. 3. (49.IV.8).
No. 6. *Housing in the Tropics* (52.IV.2).
No. 7. *Urban Land: Problems and Policies* (53.IV.22).
No. 9. *International Action in Asia and the Far East* (55.IV.19).
No. 10. *Housing through Non-Profit Organization.*
No. 11. *Training for Town and Country Planning* (57.IV.11).

Housing in Ghana, UN Publications, No. 57.II.H.3, United Nations, New York, 1957.

Manual on Stabilized Soil Construction for Housing, UN Publications, No. 58.II.H.4, United Nations, New York, 1958.

The Organization and Administration of Housing and Building Societies, 1949, mimeographed document, 33 pp. ILO(02)068. In English.

Report on Housing in the Gold Coast, April 26, 1956, document TAA/GOC/1. In English; November 5, 1956, document TAA/GOC/1, Add. 1. United Nations, New York.

Report of the Seminar on Housing through Non-Profit Organizations in Latin America (Copenhagen 1954), June 5, 1956, document TAA/LAT/6. United Nations, New York.

Survey of Housing and Building Materials in Asia and the Far East, 1956, November, 1956, document E/CN.11/432. (U.N. Publ. Sales No. 1956.II.F.9). In English.

United Nations Seminar on Housing and Community Improvement in Asia and the Far East, New Delhi, India, 21 January–17 February, 1954. 1 December, 1954, document TAA/NS/AFE/1. In English.

Workers' Housing in Asia: Statement by the Representative of the International Labour Office at the Inter-Secretariat Working Party on Housing and Building Materials in Asia and the Far East Concerning Workers' Housing. 1953, document E/CN.-11/I and T/HBWP/L.7. In English and French editions.

Bibliography No. 11   Public Health

(Readings for Chapter 9)

Davis, M. M., *Medical Care for Tomorrow,* New York: Harper, 1955.

Environmental Sanitation, WHO (Bulletin of WHO, 1954, Vol. 10, No. 2), United Nations, New York.

First Report on the World Health Situation, WHO (WHOOR No. 94), United Nations, New York.

Keeny, S. M., *Half the World's Children,* New York: Association Press, 1957.

Leimana, J., *Public Health in Indonesia: Problems and Planning,* Nieuwstraat 21, The Hague: Van Dorp, 1956.

McDermott, Walsh, Kurt Deuschle, John Adair, Hugh Fulmer and Bernice Loughlin, "Introducing Modern Medicine in a Navajo Community," *Science,* Vol. 131, 1960, pp. 197–205, 280–287.

Means, M.D., J. H., *Doctors, People and Government,* Boston: Little, Brown, 1953.

Millions Go Hungry, FAO, UN Publications, United Nations, New York, 1957.

Morgan, M., *Doctors to the World,* New York: Viking, 1958.

Ritchie, Jean A. S., *Teaching Better Nutrition,* FAO, UN Publications, United Nations, New York, 1950.

World Food Problems, FAO, *Nutrition and Society,* 1956; *Man and Hunger,* 1957; United Nations, New York.

Bibliography No. 12   Urban Problems, General

(Readings for Chapter 10)

Bergel, E. C., *Urban Sociology,* New York: McGraw-Hill, 1955.

Comhair, Jean, *Urban Conditions in Africa,* 2d ed., London: Oxford University Press, 1952.

Comhair, Jean, and Cahnman, Werner J., *How Cities Grew,* Madison, N. J.: Florham Park Press, 1959.

Corley, S.J., Francis J., "Leisure and Work," *Social Order,* April, 1952.

Dollard, John, *Caste and Class in a Southern Town,* 2nd ed., New York: Harper, 1949.

Ferree, William, Fitzpatrick, Joseph P., and Illich, John D., *Report on the First Conference on the Spiritual Care of Puerto Rican Migrants Held in San Juan, Puerto Rico, April 11 to 16, 1955,* New York, 1955.

Fichter, S.J., Joseph H., *Social Relations in the Urban Parish,* Chicago: University of Chicago Press, 1954.

Fichter, S.J., Joseph H., *Southern Parish: Volume One. The Dynamics of a City Church,* Chicago: University of Chicago Press, 1951.

Fosselman, David H., *Transitions in the Development of a Downtown Parish,* Washington: Catholic University Press, 1952.

Geaney, O.S.A., D. J., *You Are Not Your Own,* London: Chapman, 1958.

Gist, N. P., and Halbert, L. A., *Urban Society,* New York: Crowell, 1956.

Hatt, P. K., and Reiss, A. J., *Cities and Society: The Revised Reader in Urban Sociology,* Chicago: Free Press, 1957.

Keller, M.M., J., *Government Is Your Business,* Garden City, N. Y.: Doubleday, 1951.

Lee, R. H., *The City,* Philadelphia: Lippincott, 1955.

Lewis, Oscar, *Five Families,* New York: Basic Books, 1959.

Marx, P. B., *Virgil Michel and the Liturgical Movement,* Collegeville, Minn.: The Liturgical Press, 1957.

Mayo, E., *The Social Problems of an Industrial Civilization,* Boston: Harvard Graduate School of Business Administration, 1945.

Miller, Walter B., "Implications of Urban Lower-Class Culture for Social Work," *The Social Service Review,* Vol. 33, 1959, pp. 219–236.

Monographs on Fundamental Education: *Haiti Pilot Project, Progress of Literacy in Various Countries, Use of Vernacular Languages in Education, World Illiteracy at Mid-Century,* UNESCO.

Neumeyer, Martin H. and Esther S., *Leisure and Recreation: A Study of Leisure and Recreation in Their Sociological Aspects,* New York: Ronald Press, 1958.

Nuesse, C. J., and Harte, T. J., *The Sociology of the Parish,* Milwaukee: Bruce, 1951.

Owen, W., *Cities in the Motor Age,* New York: Viking, 1959.

Pieper, J., *Leisure: The Basis of Culture,* New York: Pantheon, 1952.

Quinn, J. A., *Urban Sociology,* New York: American Book, 1955.

Redfield, R., *From Primitive Life to Civilization,* Chicago: University of Chicago Press, 1955.

Riesman, D., *The Lonely Crowd,* New Haven: Yale University Press, 1950.

Scheuer, J. F., and Santopolo, F. A., "Why Not an Adequate Parish Census," *The Priest,* March, 1960, pp. 280–284.

Smith, Thomas L., and McMahan, C. A., *The Sociology of Urban Life, A Text-Book with Readings,* New York, Dryden, 1951.

Social Implication of Industrialization and Urbanization in Africa South of the Sahara, UNESCO, 1956.

Urbanization in Asia and the Far East, UNESCO, 1957.

Whyte, W. F., *Street Corner Society,* Chicago: University of Chicago Press, 1943.

Wirth, Louis, "Urbanism as a Way of Life," *American Journal of Sociology,* July, 1938.

Bibliography No. 13   Group Leadership Techniques

(Readings for Chapter 10)

Bonner, Hubert, *Group Dynamics: Principles and Applications,* New York: Ronald Press, 1959.

Brown, A. C., and Geis, S. B., *Handbook for Group Leaders,* New York: Woman's Press, 1952.

Cardijn, Joseph, *Challenge to Action,* Chicago: Fides, 1955.

Cartwright, Dorwin, and Zander, Alvin, eds., *Group Dynamics: Research and Theory,* Evanston, Ill.: Row, Peterson, 1953.

Dimock, Hedley S., and Trecker, Harleigh B., *Supervision of Group Work and Recreation,* New York: Association Press, 1949.

Guitton, Jean, *Make Your Mind Work for You,* New York: Macmillan, 1953.

Harris, Henry, *The Group Approach to Leadership Testing,* London: Routledge and Paul, 1949.

Hemphill, John Knox, *Situation Factors in Leadership,* College Park, Md.: University of Maryland Press, 1947.

Hendry, Charles E., *The Role of Groups in World Reconstruction,* New York: Woman's Press, 1952.

Klein, Alan F., *Role Playing in Leadership Training,* New York: Association Press, 1956.

LaFarge, S.J., John, "Psychologists Study Group Relations," *Social Order,* March, 1951.

Maher, S.J., Trafford, P., "Human Relations Workshops," *Social Order,* March, 1953.

Meyer, M.M., B. F., *Lend Me Your Hands,* Chicago: Fides, 1955.

Miller, Paul M., *Group Dynamics in Evangelism,* Scottsdale, Pa.: Herrald Press, 1958.

O'Connor, John J., "Industrial-Age Apostles," *Social Order,* November, 1952.

Ritchie, M. A. F., ed., *Toward Better Intergroup Education: A Report of the Workshop in Intergroup Education,* Coral Gables, Florida; University of Miami Press, 1951, 1952, pp. 1–26.

Trecker, Audrey and Harleigh, *How to Work with Groups,* New York: Woman's Press, 1952.

Utterback, William E., *Group Thinking and Conference Leadership,* New York: Rinehart, 1950.

Bibliography No. 14   Credit Unions and Cooperatives

(Readings for Chapter 11)

Bergengren, Roy F., *Crusade, The Fight for Economic Democracy,* New York: Exposition Press, 1952.

Bowen, E. R., *The Cooperative Road to Abundance,* New York: Abelard, 1953.

Boyle, George, *Democracy's Second Chance: Land, Work and Cooperation,* New York: Sheed and Ward, 1941.

Boyle, George, *The Poor Man's Prayer,* New York: Harper, 1951.

Casselman, Paul H., *The Cooperative Movement and Some of Its Problems,* New York: Philosophical Library, 1952.

Coady, M. M., *Masters of Their Own Destiny,* New York: Harper, 1939.

Coady, M. M., *The Social Significance of the Cooperative Movement,* Antigonish, N.S.: St. Francis Xavier University, 1958.

Credit Problems of Small Farmers in Asia and the Far East, UN Publications, No. 57.II.F.2, United Nations, New York, 1957.

Credit Union Yearbook 1959 (et seq.), Credit Union National Association, Filene House, Madison, Wis.

Croteau, John T., *The Federal Credit Union—Policy and Practice,* New York: Harper, 1956.

Digby, M., and Gretton, R., *Cooperative Marketing for Agricultural Producers,* FAO, UN Publications, United Nations, New York.

Doig, Thomas W., "The Credit Union's Proper Place in History," *The Bridge* (official publication of CUNA), Madison, Wis., January, 1947.

Giles, Richard Y., *Credit for the Millions,* New York: Harper, 1951.

Hall, Cameron P., *Economic Life: A Christian Responsibility,* New York: Department of the Church and Economic Life, The Federal Council of the Churches of Christ in America, 1947.

Laidlow, Alexander F., *A Factual Outline of the Antigonish Movement,* Antigonish, Nova Scotia: Extension Dept., St. Francis Xavier University, 1955.

Landis, Benson Y., *Bethlehem and Rochdale,* New York: The Cooperative League of the U.S.A., 1944.

Landis, Benson Y., *Manual on the Church and Cooperatives,* New York: The Committee on the Church and Cooperatives, Department of the Church and Economic Life, The Federal Council of the Churches of Christ in America, 1947.

Morris, S.J., John J., "Bishops, Priests and Credit Unions," *Social Order,* November, 1957.

Myers, James, *Labor and Co-ops,* New York: The Cooperative League of the U.S.A., 1948.

Smith, Erdis W., "Federal Credit Unions: Origin and Development," *Social Security Bulletin,* November, 1955, U.S. Dept. of Health, Education and Welfare, Social Security Administration, Washington, D. C.

Stewart, Maxwell S., *Credit Unions—Self-Help Family Finance,* Public Affairs Pamphlet No. 50 A, Public Affairs Committee, Inc., 22 East 38th Street, New York, 1955.

Voorhis, Jerry, *Credit Unions—Basic Cooperatives* (Booklet), Chicago: The Cooperative League of the U.S.A., 1949.

Bibliography No. 15   Community Small Industries

(Readings for Chapter 12)

Asia Kyokai, *The Smaller Industry in Japan,* Tokyo, 1957.

Begum Ikramullah, "Pakistan's Cottage Industries," *Asian Review,* January, 1957.

Burki, H. K., "Developing Pakistan's Cottage Industries," *New Commonwealth,* December 23, 1957.

Cottage and Small Industries in Indonesia, U.S. International Cooperation Administration, Office of Industrial Resources, 1958.

Ford Foundation, *Report on Small Industries in India,* New Delhi Ministry of Commerce and Industry, Government of India, 1954.

Hemranjan Bose, "Economics of Small Scale and Cottage Industries in India," *Indian Journal of Economics,* October 1954, January, 1955.

Herman, Theodore, "The Role of Cottage and Small-Scale Industries in Asian Economic Development," *Economic Development Cultural Change,* July, 1956.

Leighton, Fred, *Report on Handicrafts and Cottage Industries in the British West Indies,* Kingston, Jamaica, 1951.

Malhotra, D. K., "Why Small Industries?" *March of India,* August, 1958.

Management of Industrial Enterprises in Under-developed Countries, UN Publications, No. 58.II.B.5, United Nations, New York, 1958.

Navin, C. Joshi, *Cottage and Small Scale Industries in India: A Study,* New Delhi, India: Suneja Book Center.

Rao, R. V., "Cottage Industries and Their Planning in Andhra Pradesh," *Indian Journal of Economics,* October, 1958.

Report of the Study Group of Small-Scale Industry Experts on Their Visit to Japan, April–May, 1954. UN Economic Commission for Asia and Far East, UN, 1955, E/CN. 11/I & I/108.

Shah, D. A., *A Manual for Industrial Cooperatives and Village Industries in the Bombay State,* Bombay Government Central Press, 1952.

Sushil, Dey, *Industrial Development, A New Approach,* Calcutta: Thacker Spink, 1955.

Tokutaro, Yamanaka, *The History and Structure of Japan's Small and Medium Industries,* Japan Science Council, Division of Economics and Commerce, Econ. Series #15, March, 1957.

Bibliography No. 16 Social Questions Touching Labor

(Readings for Chapter 13)

Alexander, R. J., *Communism in Latin America,* New Brunswick, N.J.: Rutgers University Press, 1957.

Black, J. M., and Piccoli, J. G., *Successful Labor Relations for Small Business,* New York: McGraw-Hill, 1953.

Budenz, L. F., *The Techniques of Communism,* Chicago: Regnery, 1954.

Bursk, E. C., ed., *Human Relations for Management, The Newer Perspective,* New York: Harper, 1956.

Ginzberg, E., *The Labor Leader,* New York: Macmillan, 1948.

Heron, A. R., *Beyond Collective Bargaining,* Stanford, Calif.: Stanford University Press, 1948.

Horrell, M., *Racialism and the Trade Unions,* Johannesburg, S.A.: Institute of Race Relations, 1959.

Jarlot, S.J., Georges, "Christian Trade Unions," *Social Order,* February and March, 1959.

Knox, J. B., *The Sociology of Industrial Relations,* New York: Random House, 1956.

Labor's Library, Washington: Workers Education Bueau, A.F. of L., 1952.

LeRoy, A., *The Dignity of Labor,* Westminster, Md.: Newman, 1957.

Liveright, A. A., *Union Leadership Training: A Handbook of Tools and Techniques,* New York: Harper, 1951.

Lorwin, L. L., *The International Labor Movement,* New York: Harper, 1953.

Moore, W. E., *Industrial Relations and the Social Order,* New York: Macmillan, 1951.

Myers, J., and Laidler, H. W., *What Do You Know about Labor?* New York: John Day, 1956.

National and International Measures for Full Employment, UN Publications, No. 49.11.A.3, United Nations, New York, 1949.

Newman, Jeremiah, *Co-responsibility in Industry, Social Justice in Labor-Management Relations,* Westminster, Md.: Newman, 1956.

Planty, E. G., et al., *Training Employees and Managers for Production and Teamwork,* New York: Ronald Press, 1948.

Publications of the International Labour Office 1944–1957, Geneva, Switzerland, 1958. (New York Office: 345 East 46th Street, New York 17, N. Y.)

Reder, M. W., *Labor in a Growing Economy,* New York: Wiley, 1957.

Reynolds, L. G., *Labor Economics and Labor Relations,* Englewood Cliffs, N. J.: Prentice-Hall, 1954.

Roberts, M., *Labour in the Farm Economy,* Johannesburg, S.A.: Institute of Race Relations, 1959.

Smith, S.J., W. J., *Spotlight on Social Order,* Rochester, N. Y.: Christopher Press, 1954.

Tannenbaum, F., *A Phlilosophy of Labor,* New York: Knopf, 1950.

Vanistendael, August, "The Neutrality of American Trade Unions," *Social Order,* March, 1959.

Bibliography No. 17   General Bibliographies

(By Eugene F. Higgins, M.M.)

Food and Agriculture Organization, *Bibliography on Land and Water Utilization and Conservation in Europe,* United Nations, New York, 1955, $1.50.

Food and Agriculture Organization, *Bibliography on Land Tenure,* United Nations, New York, 1955, $3.50; 1959 Supplement, $2.50.

Food and Agriculture Organization, *Select Bibliography on Cooperation,* United Nations, New York, 1957, $0.50.

International Documents Service Catalogue 1959–60, Columbia University Press, 2960 Broadway, New York 27, New York.

    Catalogue, distributed free of charge, presents an integrated listing by category of the publications of the United Nations, Food and Agriculture Organization, General Agreements on Tariffs and Trade, International Court of Justice, United Nations Educational, Scientific, and Cultural Organization (UNESCO) and the World Organization. Columbia University Press handles sales originating in the United States.

The following is a listing of the catalogue's subject headings and a partial listing of sub-headings:

Agriculture: General, Animal Health and Disease, Agronomy, Commodities, Land Development, Livestock, Marketing, Processing.

Art and Literature.

Bibliography.

Communications: Film, Press, Television and Radio, Miscellaneous.

Demography.

Economics: World, Africa, Asia and the Far East, Europe, Latin America, Middle East, Miscellaneous, Regional Studies, Technical Assistance.

Education: Teaching, Training, Miscellaneous and Regional Studies.

Fiscal and Taxation Studies.

Health and Medicine: Communicable Diseases, Dental Health, Drugs and Addiction, Education and Training, Epidemiology, Vital and Health Statistics, Nutrition and Nutritional Diseases, Miscellaneous.

Industry and Industrial Development.

International Organizations.

Law.

Libraries.

Natural and Physical Sciences: General, Cartography.

Natural Resources: Fisheries, Forestry, Water, Miscellaneous.

Non-Self-Governing Territories.

Publications of General Interest.

Social Welfare: Child, Family, Community Welfare, Immigration, Race Question, Social and Cultural Studies, Social Problems, Miscellaneous.

Statistics.

Trade and Commerce.

The International Reporter. Folder announces new publications of the United Nations and its related agencies. Published by and issued free of charge by International Documents Service, Columbia University Press, 2960 Broadway, New York 27, New York.

UNESCO Bibliographical Services throughout the World. First and Second Annual Report, $2.75, C1 $3.50; Third Annual Report, Free. United Nations, Department of Public Information, Sales and Circulation Section, New York; Sales Section, United Nations Office, Palais des Nations, Geneva, Switzerland.

UNESCO Education for Community Development: Selected Bibliography, United Nations, New York.

UNESCO International Bibliography of Economics, United Nations, New York. Vol. 1, 1955, $7.50; Vol. 2, 1955, $7.50; Vol. 3, 1956, $8.00; Vol. 4, 1957, $10.00; Vol. 5, 1958, $8.00; Vol. 6, 1959, $9.50.

UNESCO International Bibliography of Sociology, United Nations, New York. Vol. 5, 1957, $6.00; Vol. 6, 1958, $6.00; Vol. 7, 1959, $5.00.

UNESCO International Bibliography of Technical and Vocational Education, United Nations, New York, 1959, $1.00.

UNESCO International Bibliography of Social and Cultural Anthropology, United Nations, New York. Vol. 1, 1957, $5.50; Vol. 2, 1958, $6.50; Vol. 3, 1959, $7.00.

UNESCO National Bibliographical Services, United Nations, 1954, $1.75.

United Nations and related agencies publications:
There are sales agents of these publications in most of the member nations of the United Nations, usually in the capital cities. Periodicals of the United Nations and its related agencies usually carry the addresses of their sales agents on the back cover.

Orders and inquiries from countries where sales agents have not been appointed may be sent to: United Nations, Department of Public Information Sales and Circulation Section, New York, New York; or Sales Section, United Nations Office, Palais des Nations, Geneva, Switzerland.

United Nations Bibliography of Recent Official Demographic Statistics, United Nations, New York, No. 53.XIII.14, $0.80.

United Nations Bibliography on Industrialization in Under-Developed Countries, United Nations, New York, $2.00.

United Nations International Bibliography of Public Administration, United Nations, New York. No. 53.II.H.1, $0.30; No. 57.II.H.2, $1.00

United States Government Publications:

Order from: U.S. Government Printing Office, Washington 25, D. C.

Price Lists of U.S. Government publications may be obtained free of charge. The Price Lists describe the books, pamphlets, periodicals and posters that are on sale at the U.S. Printing Office.

A partial list of Price Lists follows:

PL 11: *Home Economics.* Food and Cooking.

PL 15: *Geology.*

PL 21: *Fish and Wildlife Service.*

PL 31: *Education.*

PL 33: *Labor.* Personnel management and work simplification. Women's Bureau.

PL 36: *Government Periodicals,* for which subscriptions are taken.

PL 38: *Animal Industry.* Farm animals, poultry, dairying.

PL 41: *Insects.* Worms, and insects harmful to man, animals and plants.

PL 42: *Irrigation.* Drainage, Water Power.

PL 43: *Forestry.* Lumber and timber, ranges and grazing.

PL 44: *Plants.* Culture, grading, marketing, and storage of fruits, vegetables, grasses and grain.

PL 46: *Soils and Fertilizers.* Soil surveys, erosion, and soil conservation.

PL 48: *Weather, Astronomy, and Meteorology.* Climate, precipitation and flood control.

PL 51: *Health.* Hygiene, drugs and sanitation.

PL 51A: *Diseases.* Contagious and infectious diseases, sickness and vital statistics.

PL 53: *Maps, Engineering, Surveying.*

PL 58: *Mines.*

PL 62: *Commerce.*

PL 64: *Scientific Tests, Standards.* Mathematics, physics.

PL 68: *Farm Management.* Rural electrification, foreign agriculture.

PL 71: *Children's Bureau,* and publications relating to children and youth.

PL 72: *Homes.* Construction, masonry, maintenance, furnishings.

PL 78: *Industrial Workers.* Health, hygiene, safety, compensation.

PL 81: *Posters and Charts.*

PL 82: *Radio and Communications.*

USEFUL ORGANIZATIONAL DATA

(By Eugene F. Higgins, M.M.)

AGRICULTURE

Food and Agriculture Organization of the United Nations (FAO),
Viale delle Terme di Caracalla, Rome, Italy.

The publications of the FAO are primarily tools for the attainment of its objective, which is to increase agricultural production and raise the standard of living. The publications cover agriculture, economics, fisheries, forestry, nutrition and legislation. Catalogues of publications, films and filmstrips available on request. Missionaries desiring information on the FAO should write to: The Permanent Observers of the Holy See to the Food and Agricultural Organization of the U.N., Palazzo S. Carlo, Vatican City.

4-H Clubs, Federal Extension Service, U.S. Department of Agriculture, Washington 20, D. C.

For boys and girls between 10 and 21 years of age, chiefly in rural areas. Gives national leadership to program on a wide variety of farming, home-making, community service and other projects. The 4-H program is part of the national educational system of cooperative extension work. State extension services give state leadership to the program.

Publication: *4-H News,* monthly. Other 4-H Club publications listed in Price List 68 issued by Government Printing Office, Washington 25, D. C.

National 4-H Club Foundation of America, 7100 Connecticut Avenue, Chevy Chase, Maryland.

Sponsors: National 4-H Center, International Farm Youth Exchange, Human Development-Human Relations Training.

Publication: *National 4-H Foundation Journal.*

Heifer Projects, Inc., 45 Ashby Road, Upper Darby, Pennsylvania.

Interfaith group to supply livestock to people of underdeveloped areas.

Interstate Publishing Company, 19-27 North Jackson Street, Danville, Illinois.

Text books for vocational agriculture.

Meals for Millions Foundation, 115 West 7th Street, Los Angeles 14, California.

Multi-purpose food for the relief and prevention of malnutrition and starvation.

United States Department of Agriculture, Washington 25, D. C.

Publications are listed in Price Lists available gratis from the Government Printing Office, Washington, D. C.

COOPERATIVES AND CREDIT UNIONS

Bureau of Federal Credit Union, Social Security Administration, U.S. Department of Health, Education and Welfare, Washington 25, D. C.

Cooperative League of the U.S.A., 343 South Dearborn Street, Chicago 4, Illinois.

Credit Union National Association, Inc. (CUNA), World Extension Department, 1617 Sherman Avenue, P. O. Box 431, Madison 1, Wisconsin.

Catalogue of literature, office supplies and equipment. CUNA invites inquiries from all responsible organizations dedicated to a higher standard of living for peoples overseas.

CUNA Latin American Office, Dr. Jose Arroyo Riestra, Representative, Jiron Quilea 306, Lima, Peru.

Farmer Cooperative Service, U.S. Department of Agriculture, Washington 25, D. C.

Publications listed in Price List No. 68, *Farm Management,* issued free of charge by the Government Printing Office, Washington 25, D. C.

Oficina Central de Cooperativas de Credito Parroquiales, Pasaje Santiago Acuna 127—Oficina 210, Apartado 4474, Lima, Peru.

Director: Rev. Daniel McLellan, M.M.

Pan American Union, Division of Regional Development, Department of Economic and Social Affairs, Washington 6, D. C.

Provides information on the cooperative movement in the Americas, including bibliographies and the addresses of institutions serving cooperatives.

St. Francis Xavier University, Extension Service, Antigonish, Nova Scotia.

Conducts the following courses in Cooperatives and Credit Unions: Social Leadership Diploma Course, twelve months; Practical Course of training in adult education for group economic action, using, as basic economic instruments, the credit union, consumer and producer cooperatives, six weeks; Short Course for Seminarians and Priests, about ten days starting in mid-August.

FAMILY LIFE

Cana Conference of Chicago, 720 North Rush Street, Chicago 11, Illinois.

Publishes: *The New Cana Manual,* 1957, Edited by Rev. Walter Imbiorski, Delaney Publications, 206 South Grove Street, Oak

Park, Illinois. This was prepared in order to have all the better material on the Cana Conference in one compact unit. A five-page bibliography lists the ten titles that a group of experienced Cana conductors selected as books that have been most helpful in preparing Cana and Pre-Cana presentations. It lists also many titles under the following subject headings: Documentation; Married Love; Secular Works; Parents and Children; Sociological; Spiritual Life; Philosophical-Psychological; Doctrinal; Lay Apostolate.

Christian Family Movement, 100 West Monroe Street, Chicago 3, Illinois.

Periodical: *Act,* published monthly, annual subscription $1.00.

Marriage Preparation Service, The Catholic Center, University of Ottawa, 1 Stewart Street, Ottawa, Canada.

Economic preparation is one subject treated in the series of fifteen lessons prepared by the Marriage Preparation Service.

HEALTH

American Public Health Association, 1790 Broadway, New York 19, New York.

Pan American Sanitary Bureau, Regional Office of the World Health Organization, 2001 Connecticut Avenue, Washington 6, D. C.

Catalogue of publications free on request.

United States Department of Health, Education and Welfare, Washington 25, D. C.

Publications are listed in the Price Lists available gratis from the Government Printing Office, Washington, D. C.

United States Public Health Service, Washington 25, D. C.

World Health Organization (WHO), Palais des Nations, Geneva, Switzerland.

Catalogue of publications free on request. WHO is a specialized agency of the United Nations, with several regional offices. WHO conducts programs relating to public health, such as: public health administration, environmental sanitation, health education for the public, professional education and training, malaria, tuberculosis, communicable diseases, nutrition, nursing, maternal and child care, mental health, social and occupational health.

Publications of the World Health Organization, 1947–57, Bibliography, World Health Organization, 1958, $3.25.

HOUSING

Catholic Building and Maintenance, Joseph F. Wagner, Inc., 53 Park Place, New York 7, New York.
Published six times a year. Subscription, $3.00.

Catholic Management Journal, Bruce Publishing Company, 400 North Broadway, Milwaukee 1, Wisconsin.
Published five times a year. Subscription, $4.00.

Centro Interamericano de Vivienda (Inter-American Housing and Planning Center), Ciudad Universitaria, Apartado Aereo 6209, Bogota, Colombia.
The fundamental objective of CINVA is to serve as a catalyst for the many agencies that are striving to improve the physical environment of many Latin American families. CINVA is assisting the various national housing programs in the following ways:
by training housing technicians;
by carrying out research projects in the many aspects of housing, especially in the application of local materials to low-cost housing construction;
by means of its publications program;
through its Scientific Exchange and Consulting Service making its findings available to all concerned with the complex field of housing.
CINVA developed the CINVA-RAM, a machine for making block and tile from soil stabilized with cement or lime. The CINVA-RAM is designed to give low-income families in rural areas a manual tool to help build walls and floors of their houses. Not designed for mass production.
CINVA publishes *Cartilla de la Vivienda,* an illustrated "How-to-Do-It" book giving instruction on all phases of construction and installation of services for a rural home (200 pp. 9" x 13", 1956, $3.00). Available at CINVA in Bogota, Colombia, and at the Pan American Union, Washington 6, D. C.

Church Property Administration, The Administrative Publishing Company, Inc., 20 West Putnam Avenue, Greenwich, Connecticut.
A magazine for planning, construction, equipping and operation of Catholic institutions. Bi-monthly. One year, $2.00; foreign, $5.00.

Directorio de Instituciones de Vivienda y Planeamiento, Division de Vivienda y Planeamiento, Departamento de Asuntos Economicos y Sociales, Pan American Union, Washington, D. C., 1953.

LABOR

American Federation of Labor and Congress of International Organizations, 815 Sixteenth Street, N.W., Washington 6, D. C.
Has a section of Religious Relations.
The following publications of the Industrial Union Dept., AFL-CIO, are sent free on request: *I.U.D. Digest,* quarterly; *I.U.D. Bulletin,* monthly; *I.U.D. Fact Sheet,* monthly.

Association of Catholic Trade Unionists (ACTU), 327 Lexington Avenue, New York 16, New York.
Publication: *The Labor Leader.* Labor News in the Light of Catholic Social Thought. A 4-page monthly newspaper. Annual subscription, $2.00.

Catholic Council on Working Life, 21 West Superior Street, Chicago 10, Illinois.
Publication: *Work,* an 8-page monthly newspaper. One section covers YCW news. Annual subscription, $2.00.

Catholic Employers, Managers and Technologists Study Groups, 51 East 42nd Street, Room 622, New York 17, New York.
Publication: *Newsletter.*

International Labor Advisory Service, 1026 Seventeenth Street, N.W., Washington 6, D. C.

International Labor Organization, Sales Section, Geneva, Switzerland.

Catalogue of publications available on request.

U.S.A. Branch Office, International Labor Organization, 917 Fifteenth Street, N.W., Washington, D. C.

International Secretariate Apostolatus Maris, Apollinaris Palace, Via della Scrofa, 70, Rome, Italy.

The Apostleship of the Sea is a worldwide movement and organization for the spiritual, moral and social welfare of seafarers. It provides valued services for seamen, and supervises and cares for ships' altars as part of its general religious program.

Centers and Clubs of the Apostleship of the Sea may be found in all chief ports of the world. In U.S.A.: National Office, National Conference of the Apostleship of the Sea, 711 Camp Street, New Orleans 12, Louisiana.

United States Department of Labor, Washington 25, D. C.

Publications are listed in Price List 33 available gratis from the Government Printing Office, Washington 25, D. C.

Xavier Institute of Industrial Relations, College of St. Francis Xavier, 30 West 16th Street, New York 11, New York.

Labor Courses on Wednesday night.

Young Christian Worker International, 78, Bd. Poincaré, Brussels, Belgium.

Publishes a catalogue, *Y.C.W. Publications in the Different Countries throughout the World.* Lists Y.C.W. publications currently available and some titles on spirituality, youth problems and teenage workers, of interest to all Y.C.W's. Lists addresses of many regional offices.

Periodical: *International Y.C.W.* Annual subscription (U.S.), $1.25 for six issues. Published in English, French, Spanish and German.

U.S.A. headquarters: Young Christian Workers, 1700 Jackson Boulevard, Chicago 12, Illinois.

SOCIAL INSTITUTIONS

Better World Movement, Centro Internationale Pio XII, Via dei Laghi Km 3, Rocca di Papa, Rome, Italy.

Foundations with Social Science Activities: International Catalogue, UNESCO, 1957, $1.00.

International Organizations in the Social Sciences, UNESCO, $0.50.

National Catholic Social Action Conference, 1312 Massachusetts Avenue, N.W., Washington 5, D. C.
Regular membership, annual dues, $3.00. Publication: *NCSAC Newsletter.*

National Recreation Association, 8 West Eighth Street, New York 11, New York.
Periodical: *Recreation.* Published monthly, except July and August. Subscription, $4.00.
Publishes: *A Guide to Books on Recreation.* Lists titles of books under the following subject headings: Activities for Special Groups; Arts & Crafts; Camping; Community Recreation; Dancing; Drama; Facilities, Layout, Equipment; Games & Puzzles; Hobbies; Holidays & Special Days; Leadership; Music; Nature; Organization & Administration; Parties & Entertainment; Pets; Philosophy of Recreation; Program Planning; Safety; Sports; Storytelling.

World Justice Review, 100 Avenue des Allies, Louvain, Belgium.
A Catholic quarterly on international social justice. Annual subscription, $6.00. (Special subscription rate for missionaries who are actually on the missions, $3.00 a year.)

TECHNICAL ASSISTANCE, VOLUNTARY GROUPS FOR

Bureau for Technical Assistance for the Missions (BUTAM), Oude Delft 57, Delft, Holland.
The bureau is managed by students of the High School of Delft, who are assisted by the professors and by engineers, most of whom are former members of the group.

Christian Union of Architects for the Missions, Mr. Albert Wider, Technical Leader, Barenstrasse 1001, Widnau/SG, Switzerland.
The members of this voluntary association of architects give advice in their field to missionaries.

Center for International Social and Cultural Assistance (KAROSI), Hague, Holland.
A Dutch Catholic non-profit agency for fostering better relations among nations through voluntary cultural, social and technical assistance.

UNESCO

UNESCO, 19, Avenue Kleber, Paris 16, France.
UNESCO Publications Check List. Free. 1958 Supplement, Free.

International Catholic Coordinating Center for UNESCO, 98 rue de l'Université, Paris 7e, France.
Publication: *The Month at UNESCO.* Annual subscription, $3.00. Printed in English, French and Spanish.

United States National Commission for UNESCO, Department of State, Washington 25, D. C.
Publishes: *Newsletter.*

YOUTH

Boy Scouts of America, New Brunswick, New Jersey.
Publications: For adult leaders, *Scouting,* a monthly. For boys, *Boys' Life,* monthly.

Catholic Committee on Scouting (Boy Scouts), New Brunswick, New Jersey.
To provide for the integration of Catholic teachings and practices in the program of scouting for Catholic boys.

National Council of Catholic Youth, 1312 Massachusetts Avenue, N.W., Washington 5, D. C.
Periodical: *Youth.* Published monthly, except June, July, August. Annual subscription, $3.00.
Bi-monthly Kit: *Program Service for Youth Groups.* Contains suggestions for spiritual, cultural, social and physical programs for youth.

Young Christian Students, International Office, Rue de La Fédération, Paris 15, France.
Coordinates work of National YCS groups on the secondary and university levels.

MISCELLANEOUS

Carnegie Endowment for International Peace, United Nations Plaza at 46th Street, New York 17, New York.
European Center, 172 route de Ferney, Grand-Saconnex, Geneva, Switzerland.
Catalogue lists publications under following subject headings: International Organization; International Economics; International Law; Diplomatic History; Inter-American Affairs; Education; Carnegie Endowment; International Conciliation.

Catholic Association for International Peace, 1312 Massachusetts Avenue, N.W., Washington 5, D. C.
Publication: *Newsletter,* monthly.

Catholic International Organizations, a directory in pamphlet form giving the names and addresses of Catholic International Organizations. Published by Sword of the Spirit, 128 Sloane Street, London SW 1, England.

CELAM, Consejo Episcopal Latinoamericano (Episcopal Council of Latin America), Apartado Aereo 5278, Bogota, Colombia.
Publication: *Boletin Informativo.*

Institute of Mission Studies, Fordham University, New York 58, New York.
Proceedings of the Fordham Conferences of Mission Specialists: *Local Leadership in Mission Lands,* 1954 Conference, 151 pp., paper, $2.00.

International Cooperation Administration, Office of Public Reports, 806 Connecticut Avenue, N.W., Washington 25, D. C.

Nadeau Looms, Inc., 725 Branch Avenue, Providence, Rhode Island.
Manufactures lightweight hand-looms.

National Catholic Welfare Conference, Publications Department, 1312 Massachusetts Avenue, Washington 5, D. C.

Price lists contain titles of encyclicals and addresses of Pope, Bishops' statements, titles on education and related topics, on the social order, on peace, etc.

NCWC—Office of UN Affairs, 138 East 36th Street, New York, New York.

An office of the National Catholic Welfare Conference.

Publication: *Newsnotes,* monthly.

National Planning Association, 1606 New Hampshire Avenue, N.W., Washington 9, D. C.

Encourages joint economic planning and cooperation by leaders from agriculture, business, labor and the professions. An independent, non-political organization interested in national and international problems.

Publication: *Looking Ahead,* a monthly. Also, books and pamphlets.

Pan American Union, Washington 6, D. C.

The General Secretariat of the Office of American States, Pan American Union, promotes juridical, economic, social and cultural relations between the twenty-one American states.

Catalogue of publications free on request. The catalogue lists publications under the following subject headings, among others: Agriculture; Conservation; Cooperatives; Forestry; Bibliographies; Economics; Commerce; Industry; Education; Housing; Planning. Publications are printed in English, Spanish, Portuguese and French.

Periodical: *Americas.*

World Affairs Center for the United States, United Nations Plaza at 47th Street, New York 17, New York.

A service center for civic and other private organizations, educational institutions, and communities throughout the United States. Its purpose is to encourage and assist them in the development of programs for citizen understanding and activity in world affairs.

Publication: *Intercom,* an instrument for the exchange of information about what people are doing to learn, teach, consider or influence what is going on in the world. Monthly, except January, July, August. Annual subscription for non-profit organizations and their members, $5.00.

TOPICAL INDEX

Collier, Mary, quote, 87–88, 89
Collins, William J., ix
Colombia, company town, 177; housing in, 170–171; Popular Education Movement, 1; urban community in, 179
Color, 64
Colorado Plateau, 79
Comber, John W., ix
Commissioners, 142
Communes, in Red China, 143–144
Communication, channels of, 44, 60–61, 67–68; social-psychological aspect, 68; techniques of, 67–68; verbal, 98
Communications, 123, 144, 156
Communism, appeal of, 11; in Bolivia, 140; in Indonesia, 24–25, 150, 249, 253; in Italy, 139; in Java, 248; in Kerala, India, 21; and landlordism, 144–145; papal encyclical on, 6; technique, 12; world revolution, 236
Communist Europe, 143
Communists, missionary's duty to, 32. See Communism
Community, 34, 154; accomplishment of a, 196–197; agricultural, 79; center, 50; in communes, 144; concern for, 225; and cooperatives, 207; cultural values, 68; establishment of, in mission, 34–35; formation of a, 64; importance of, 181; and mission aid, 31–32; observation of a, 70; organization, 62; outside influences, 66–67; planning, viii, 15, 154 sqq.; religio-social activities, 15; in socio-economic movement, 249; and socio-economic program, 9; young people in a, 71–72; work for a, 191; world, 253. See also Christian community; City; Town; Village; Rural community; Urban community; Community development; Community small industries
Community Action, 38

Community development, viii, 19, 86, 124, 166; in Asia, 133; bibliography, 263–264; Church and, 35; criteria for, 44–45; definition, 39; enemies of Church in, 37; essence of, 46; first project, 49; health in, 161; progressive steps in, 48; scope, 37–39; techniques, 15, 34–55
Community Education, 38
Community Education Department, Indonesia, 30
Community Projects Department, India, 47
Community small industries, viii, 16, 137, 215–232; bibliography, 284–285; choice of, 222, 224–228; equipment, 230; goals, 217–218; importance, 22; pattern of, 216–218
Communization, 150
Compensation, for land, 140, 141
Comte, Auguste, 10
Confidence, 21, 45
Conflict, 70
Congo, Christian life conference, 110; socio-economic program, 188–191; urban migration in, 106, 187
Congo Catholic Cinema Center, 188–189
Congolese, 188, 191
Congressional Committee, 11
Consejo Episcopal Latinoamericano (CELAM), 300
Considine, John J., ix; quote, 74–75, 158
Consolidation, of land, 138, 139, 141
Constitutions, human betterment in, 3
Consumer demands, 63
Contracts, union, 246, 252
Control, of behavior, 62, 65
Conventional understandings, 59
Convert making, 193
Converts, 13
Conviction, 40–41